D1531292

Advanced Woodwork and Furniture Making

ADVANCED WOODWORK and FURNITURE MAKING

By JOHN L. FEIRER

Head, Industrial Education Department
Western Michigan University
Kalamazoo, Michigan

Chas. A. Bennett Co., Inc. PUBLISHERS
PEORIA, ILLINOIS

PREFACE

ADVANCED WOODWORK AND FURNITURE MAKING was written for those who are interested in making high-quality furniture and who have access to power tools. This book assumes that the reader has a mastery of hand tools and that he has already discovered the joy of making beautiful things of wood.

During the last 25 years there have been two significant changes in the area of woodworking that are of prime importance to the school and home craftsman. First, power tool manufacturers have designed and developed a line of small- and medium-sized tools especially suited to these craftsmen. With these machines the amateur can produce professional-appearing work in a relatively short time. The second big change has been in furniture styles. Now, every wood craftsman wants to and can make furniture as well as the small trinkets which were commonly made by hand methods before. As a result, there has been a constant demand for well-designed furniture pieces that can be built by the amateur craftsman. Modern or contemporary furniture was developed largely because of our interest in mass producing products on machine tools and is therefore the kind of furniture that is ideal for the amateur to make, since he can easily reproduce processes of industry on his small machines.

The book is organized into *six main sections:*

SECTION I tells how to select, design, and plan the furniture that is to be built and includes information on *design, types of furniture construction, lumber and plywood,* and *how to make and read a drawing.*

SECTION II tells how to get started in machine woodworking

and includes information on *measuring, transferring a design,* and *getting out and gluing up stock.*

SECTION III covers all of the special problems in furniture making such as *constructing all kinds of joints, hanging a door, panel construction,* and many others.

SECTION IV is devoted to the application of a good *finish* to furniture and wood.

SECTION V describes all of the *common power tools.* Each is dealt with thoroughly but only the more important and more common operations are included. SAFETY *is stressed throughout the book.*

SECTION VI contains a suggested list of *furniture pieces.* There are many ideas with which to work and suggested sources for others. In many cases the craftsman using this kind of book *will have a design or idea of his own in mind.*

The planning and development of this book required the co-operation of many individuals. Each company that helped with the illustrations is recognized.

Section VII describes the major furniture styles and gives a short history of each. It provides consumer information that is valuable to all.

Making furniture with power tools is a fascinating experience. The work progresses quite rapidly and can be done with a great deal less effort than by hand methods. You will find that it is not absolutely necessary to have all the different machines. It is essential, though, to have a circular saw, jointer, drill press with attachments, and a sander of some type. For making Early American furniture it is necessary to have, in addition, a band saw or jig saw and perhaps a wood lathe. *It is extremely important to keep all power tools in top working order and all cutting edges sharp.*

CONTENTS

8 CONTENTS

Section IV. WOODFINISHING

Section V. WOODWORKING MACHINES

Section VI. PROJECTS

Section VII. FURNITURE STYLES AND PERIODS

Section I
Selecting, Designing, and Planning

GOOD DESIGN in furniture is many things: A. Exposed joints join top and sides, making each joint a part of the design. B. Fine wood such as these solid teak drawer fronts. C. Excellent drawer construction with the drawer guides recessed into the sides. D. Appropriate hardware shown by the hand grips of carved wood, the only ornamentation on the chest. COURTESY OF JOHN STUART, INC.

BUILDING GOOD FURNITURE

The secret of success in building good furniture is to follow such steps as the ones outlined below. All instructions necessary to completion of each step will be found in this book. While not all pieces of furniture are constructed in the same manner, you can achieve good results by following these steps:

1. Select a good design that fits your needs. It is always best to choose something that is really useful. Remember your ability, however, and don't start making a chest of

1-1. A STEP TABLE that represents usefulness as well as beauty. The top measures 18" x 30" and the over-all height is 24". COURTESY OF THE WIDDICOMB FURNITURE COMPANY.

BUILT-IN CABINETS made of mahogany plywood. An ambitious project for the amateur builder. Note design pattern of doors. Built by the author in his home.

drawers, for instance, if you're in the lamp or tray (beginner's) "stage." Fig. 1–1.

2. Select the right kind of lumber and plywood. Decide on the kind of furniture wood or plywood that will best suit the project. Remember, however, that *working qualities of furniture woods and plywoods differ greatly*. It is easier to work (cut, shape, sand, etc.) mahogany than oak or birch, for example. If you don't have a planer available, you should buy surfaced lumber (S2S). Fig. 1–2.

3. Make an accurate bill of materials. Have a drawing or design and from this make a list of all of the materials (lumber and plywood) you will need as well as the supplies (dowel rod, screws, glue, finishing material, and hardware).

1–2. AN EXAMPLE OF GOOD DESIGN in a table and magazine rack. Notice the grain pattern in the walnut top. COURTESY OF JENS RISOM DESIGN, INC.

13

RADIO-PHONO-SPEAKER HI-FI CABINET of simple, clean-cut design. The cabinet is 36″ x 21″ x 31½″. COURTESY OF JENS RISOM DESIGN, INC.

4. Have the correct equipment. It is difficult to do a job without the right kind of machines and tools. Of course, any step that is done on a machine can also be done by hand. The time it takes is so much greater, however, that sometimes the beginner becomes discouraged, especially if he is building a large furniture piece.

5. Make an accurate layout. Work slowly and carefully as you measure and mark out the pieces to be cut. A common error is cutting the pieces too small. When furniture woods are used, this can be a costly mistake.

14

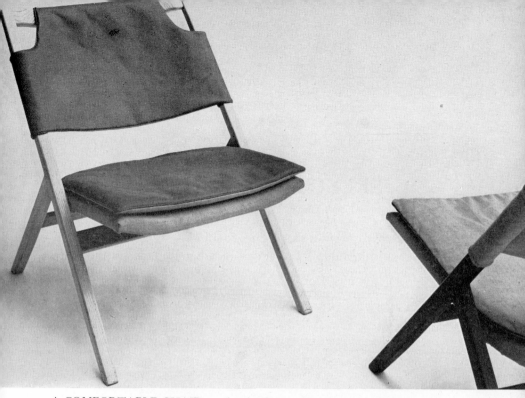

A COMFORTABLE CHAIR can be simple as well as good looking. COURTESY OF ALAN GOULD DESIGNS, INC.

6. Cut the parts to the correct shape. This will include rough cutting to size, squaring up and cutting out the design.

7. Make the joints accurately. A sign of good furniture construction is good, sturdy joints of the right kind. A sloppy dado or a poor-fitting mortise and tenon will make a weak piece.

8. Assemble carefully. Make sure that all parts are completed and carefully sanded. Then glue up the project square and true. A poor job of clamping and gluing weakens an otherwise good piece.

9. Apply the proper kind of finish. A poor finish can ruin a piece that is perfect in every other respect. Be very sure that the finish you select is appropriate and is one that you can apply with relative ease. Today's craftsman has a distinct advantage since there are excellent finishes available that can be applied simply with cloths, others with a brush; and still others that can be applied by spraying.

SELECTING FURNITURE

The first question that comes to mind is "what style of furniture should I build?" Too much of what is made by the beginning craftsman has no style, design, or character. Strangely

2–1. A MODERN DESK with contemporary chair design, combining the best in ageless simplicity. COURTESY OF KNOLL ASSOCIATES, INC.

2–2. THE CHARACTERISTICS OF GOOD MODERN, in a night stand. Top 19″ x 15″, height 25″. COURTESY OF THE WIDDICOMB FURNITURE COMPANY.

enough, it is just as easy to build good, high-quality furniture as it is to make junk.

The craftsman must first decide on the style or period. The most popular furniture is of modern or contemporary design. Fig. 2–1. It is difficult to describe this style because there are many kinds of modern. Good modern, however, is characterized by correct proportion, good wood, excellent workmanship, simplicity, and usefulness. Fig. 2–2. It is often designed to serve

2–3.   A RANCH-TYPE COBBLER'S BENCH. The bench is 49″ long, 22″ wide and 17″ high. COURTESY OF A. BRANDT COMPANY.

more than one purpose. Most modern has simple lines and tends toward rectangular shapes, simple curves, circles and free-form design. Modern design is frequently influenced by other periods and cultures such as the ranch type, or Swedish and Chinese Modern. Fig. 2–3. Modern furniture is most often finished in a light color, either natural or bleached. The most popular woods are mahogany, oak, cherry, birch and redwood. Modern is one of the easiest styles for the beginning craftsman to make.

Another popular style is the Early American or Colonial which is often a refinement or actual reproduction of furniture built and used during the early years of our country. Most of this original furniture was made by hand or with simple machines. Fig. 2–4. The design is simple, useful and practical as well as beautiful, and is characterized by the many turned parts. It can also be made by the beginning craftsman. The most popular woods are maple, cherry, pine, and birch. Fig. 2–5.

2–4. WELL-DESIGNED COLONIAL PIECES. COURTESY OF SPRAGUE & CARLETON, INC.

Style of furniture shown in this book. Another is period furniture of which there are a great many styles. Some of the better known are Chippendale, French Provincial, Sheraton, Hepplewhite, Duncan Phyfe, and Victorian. Most period furniture is quite ornate, involving many curves, carvings, and other surface enrichments. Almost all of these are difficult to make by the simple machine techniques available to the beginning craftsman. Because of this, *only Modern or Contemporary and Early American or Colonial furniture* have been included in this book. The pieces you build, however, if of good design and construction, and if properly selected, should and can blend with existing furniture regardless of style.

19

2–5. TWO EARLY AMERICAN PIECES made of knotty pine. COURTESY OF ATLAS PRESS CO. AND BRANDT FURNITURE CO.

2–6. THE LAMP BASE is 19″ high, 6″ square at the bottom and 1¼″ square at the top. COURTESY OF THE ROMWEBER INDUSTRIES.

Kinds of items to build. The second question that comes to mind is, "What should I build?" Items that can be built may be grouped as follows:

1. ACCESSORIES, including trays, lamps, small shelves, clocks, carved ornaments, shadow boxes. Fig. 2–6.

2. TABLES, including coffee or cocktail, end, game, lamp, snack, dining. Fig. 2–7.

3. STOOLS, benches, and chairs. Fig. 2–8.

4. BOOKCASES. Fig. 2–9.

5. CABINETS, including dish, radio, television, storage, and all-purpose. Fig. 2–10.

6. CHESTS AND DESKS. Fig. 2–11.

There are many others, of course, but these are the ones with which we will be concerned here. The *beginner* will probably

21

2–7. COCKTAIL TABLES. COURTESY OF VISTA FURNITURE COMPANY.

2–8. UPHOLSTERED BENCHES, 24″ x 24″ x 15″. COURTESY OF GRAND RAPIDS
CHAIR COMPANY.

2–9. BOOKCASE, depth 14″, width 36″, height 46″. COURTESY OF CONANT BALL.

want to start by making some accessory. The *craftsman with some experience* will probably tackle a simple table, bookcase, or cabinet. The *more advanced woodworker* may try a chair, chest, or desk. Several suggestions for each of these groups can be found in this book.

Another question often asked is, "Should I design my own furniture?" *When making your first pieces,* it is probably better to follow some existing design, in some cases making small changes or adaptations to fit particular needs. The size may be

2–10. SMALL STORAGE CABINET, 18″ x 18″ x 21″. COURTESY OF THE DREXEL
FURNITURE COMPANY.

changed slightly, for example, provided that the change does not upset the proportion of the piece. For the *more advanced craftsman*, the answer to that question would be to design your own furniture. With close attention to the principles of good design, you can achieve very satisfying and individual results. To help

AVERAGE FURNITURE SIZES

ITEM	HEIGHT	DEPTH-WIDTH	LENGTH
Tables			
Coffee or Cocktail	16″ to 18″	18″ to 24″	36″ to 60″
Card	29″	30″	30″
Game	30″	30″	30″
Writing	30″	24″	36″ to 40″
Kitchen	32″	30″	42″
End	30″	15″	24″
Dining	29″ to 32″	42″	60″
Chairs			
Desk	16½″	15″ to 18″	15″ to 18″
Dining	16″ to 18″	15″ to 18″	15″ to 18″
Cabinets			
Sectional	30″	12″ to 14″	Any
China Storage	54″ to 60″	20″ to 22″	Any
Kitchen	32″ to 36″	12″ to 24″	Any
Chests	32″ to 54″	24″	Any
Bookcases	32″ to 82″	18″	Any
Desks	30″	24″ to 30″	40″ to 60″

2–11. DESK, 24″ x 42″ x 30″. COURTESY OF THE WIDDICOMB FURNITURE COMPANY.

in designing your own furniture, the preceding chart shows the standard sizes of certain pieces.

Sometimes you will see a picture or sketch of a furniture piece you would like to make. With careful planning you can design one that is very similar to it, following this procedure:

1. Make a full-size outline of the over-all size of the

piece. In most cases, the width, length, and height will be available. This outline can be made in the same way as you would start an orthographic projection, cabinet, or isometric drawing.

2. Determine the approximate scale of the picture or sketch. By measuring the full-size outline and then the actual picture, the approximate scale can be determined. For example, if the over-all height of the object is 36 inches, and the height on the picture measures $1\frac{1}{2}$ inches, the scale is about $\frac{1}{2}$ inch to the foot. This scale can then be followed to determine the approximate size of all the major parts. Remember, however, that these dimensions will be only approximate. The craftsman, himself, will need to figure out the exact size in order to insure good proportion in the finished piece.

3. Lay out the sizes of each part on the full-size drawing. Determine the best method of joining the various parts, remembering that there are a great number of different kinds of woodworking joints.

4. Now, "Plan your work, and then **work your plan,"** as described in the following sections of the book.

DESIGNING FURNITURE

It is almost impossible to give specific rules that will insure good design in a piece of furniture. Often, the mere use of rules will fail to produce a well-designed piece. The *taste or feeling* for good design can be acquired by observing quality in all manufactured products and by adhering to certain fundamentals.

The first point to remember is that an article is well designed only if it is made for use. Fig. 3–1. For example, a chair must be comfortable to sit in and a table must be the right size and height for its particular use. There are standards for most of these measurements.

3-1. THIS PIECE WAS DESIGNED for an apartment or hotel room and combines chest, dressing table, desk, storage area, and luggage rack in one piece. Utility has been emphasized as well as beauty. COURTESY OF THE HERMAN MILLER COMPANY.

A second point is that the materials selected must be appropriate. Fig. 3–2. Certain kinds of furniture woods possess ideal lasting qualities of beauty and durability. Other materials are satisfactory only for the internal parts of furniture.

A third point is that the methods of construction must be fundamentally sound. A flimsy construction is in itself poor design. A chair that wobbles or a table that tips is useless. Fig. 3–3.

A fourth point is the outward appearance or visual aspect. Fig. 3–4. Here is the point of greatest difference. Some people prefer modern or contemporary, others are satisfied only with

3–2. A LAMP TABLE made of bleached mahogany. Mahogany and oak are two woods that are easily bleached. Top 24″ x 24″, height 22″. COURTESY OF THE IMPERIAL FURNITURE COMPANY.

Early American, while others still choose traditional furniture. Fig. 3–5. If the pieces are true to their style, they are all attractive and in most cases represent the principles of good design. When a questionable or non-existent style is concocted, however, a poor design usually results.

All good design follows a few basic rules:

1. The parts must be in balance. This has been carried out

NOTE THAT FROM THIS VIEW the shelves seem shorter on one side than on the other, yet they are actually the same length. Even a systematically balanced form is seldom looked at head-on, and never is exactly equal on each side unless you stand in front of it. That is what is meant by judging a design by whether or not it looks "at rest." DREXEL FURNITURE COMPANY.

when the object appears to have equal weight on either side. It need not be *symmetrical* (formal balance) but must give the appearance of *being at rest* which is informal balance.

2. The article must be in good proportion. A *large* chair

3-3. THE STRONG LAP JOINTS on each corner of this coffee table are in themselves decorative and make the table a sturdy piece. COURTESY OF THE CALIFORNIA REDWOOD ASSOCIATION.

with spindly legs or a *dainty* coffee table with bulky ones is in poor proportion. Sometimes only a slight variation in the size of parts will influence proportion.

3. The parts must be in harmony with one another. Many times, different materials are combined or different shapes are put together but the whole must appear in harmonious unity, and invite the use for which it is intended. Thus a "perfect chair" will look as if it is meant to be sat on and enjoyed.

4. Each furniture piece needs a point of emphasis. This may be the over-all appearance of the piece itself, the fine finish, a simple piece of hardware, or some point in its construction.

The most common mistakes made in furniture design in the home and school shop, which result in a homemade appearance, are:

1. A definite style of furniture was not selected. Too often an individual will design a piece that represents no style but is rather a combination of many styles.

2. A basic principle of design is ignored. Too often a part is out of balance or proportion.

3–4. EVERYONE AGREES that this is a beautiful desk and chair, even though differing about the style. Top 24″ x 48″, height 30″. COURTESY OF CONANT BALL.

3-5. HERE, TOO, IS A STRIKING TRADITIONAL PIECE that can be appreciated by all regardless of personal taste. COURTESY OF THE BRANDT CABINET WORKS, INC.

3. A poor selection of materials is made. It is difficult to make quality furniture from cheaper woods. Only good furniture woods should be chosen. It is usually faddish and cheap to combine woods of highly contrasting color or quality. The wood must also be chosen for a particular style of furniture. For example, Early American is made of cherry, birch, maple, or pine.

4. The beginner often overdecorates. Surface decoration must be used sparingly. Most modern pieces have little or no surface decoration but depend upon the natural beauty of the wood. Grooving, beading, fluting, inlaying, and other embellishments must be used sparingly and in their proper places.

5. The finish is often poor. A smooth, even finish is a characteristic of good furniture. One that is applied irregularly or with an uneven color or surface is definitely bad.

In selecting or designing a piece of furniture for yourself, follow these simple rules:

1. Determine your needs (what the function of the furniture will be). Make only what you can use.

2. Make a sketch of the object.

3. Develop the sketch into a finished drawing or model. This will provide an opportunity to study the piece for possible revisions.

4. Construct the object of the proper woods, following good techniques.

5. Judge the article to determine if it fits your needs and is satisfactory in every other respect.

TYPES OF FURNITURE CONSTRUCTION

When you observe many pieces of furniture and accessories, you find that all can be classified into a few basic types. These are as follows:

1. One-member piece. The simplest of all is the one-member accessory such as the turned bowl, a cutting board, or a carved ornament. Fig. 4–1.

2. Duplicate part. This type has two or more identical parts which can be cut and shaped simultaneously, or one part can be

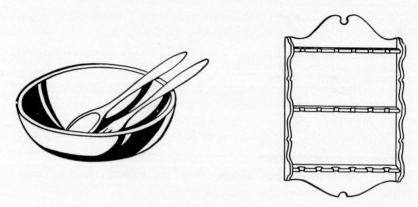

4-1. SALAD BOWL. A one-member project. 4-2. SPOON RACK with
duplicate parts.

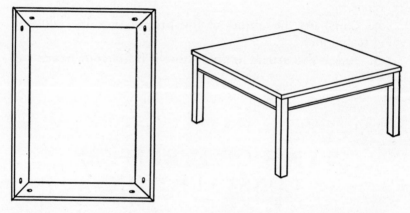

4-3. FRAME, and 4-4. COFFEE TABLE showing leg and rail construction.

made first and then duplicated. Fig. 4–2. A tray with identical
sides or ends or a simple whatnot shelf are common examples.

3. Frame. The frame is an assembly of four parts used for
picture frames, mirrors, bulletin boards, and in many parts of
furniture. It is joined together at the corner with miter or lap
joints. Fig. 4–3.

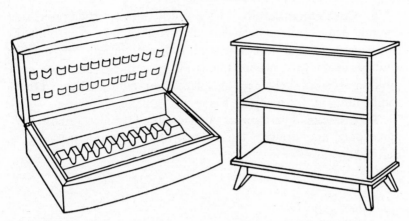

4-5. SILVER CHEST. A simple box construction. 4-6. BOOKCASE. A case construction.

4-7. END TABLE WITH DRAWER AND STORAGE CABINET. An example of carcass construction.

4. Skeleton or leg and rail. Most chairs and tables are of this kind of construction. It usually consists of four legs and four or more rails. Fig. 4-4. The rails are joined to the legs with a dowel butt joint or mortise-and-tenon joint.

5. Box. The box is made up of four sides with a bottom and a top. The corners are joined with a simple butt, rabbet, or miter joint. The space inside a box may be divided with partitions. A drawer is a simple box. Fig. 4-5.

6. Case construction. This is simply a box turned on its side or end. Almost all bookcases, radio cabinets, and most built-ins are of case construction. The back is usually installed by cutting a rabbet around the inside. The front sometimes is trimmed with molding. If solid shelves are installed, dado joints are made. Doors can be hung in the openings. Fig. 4–6.

7. Carcass. This consists of an enclosed cabinet, usually having a door and drawer. Parts are often of panel construction. Fig. 4–7.

SELECTING LUMBER AND PLYWOOD

You should be acquainted with the important kinds of woods and with the terminology common to them.

Parts of a tree. Fig. 5–1 shows the parts of a tree. The center is called the pith. Around this are annular rings which form the grain of the lumber. The dark rings show the *summer growth*, when the tree grows slowly; the light rings show the *spring growth*, when the tree grows rapidly. The center part of the tree around the pith is called the *heartwood*, which is darker in color, while the outer area is called the *sapwood*, which is lighter in color. The rays running at tangents from the center or pith are called *medullar rays*. These are pronounced in some woods—oak for instance—while in others they are less noticeable. The outside of the tree, of course, is the *bark*.

The structure of the tree itself is composed of long, narrow tubes or cells which are lined with fine, spiral strands of cellulose. The tubes themselves are held together with a substance called *lignin*. Fig. 5–2. In some woods these tubes are relatively large in size, making an open-grain wood, while in other, closed-grain

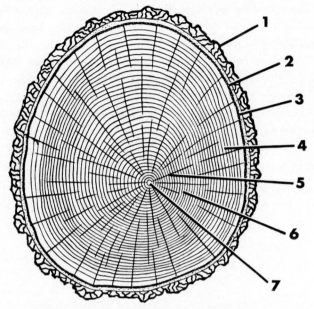

5-1. PARTS OF A TREE: (1) bark; (2) phloem; (3) cambium; (4) sapwood; (5) heartwood; (6) wood ray; (7) pith.

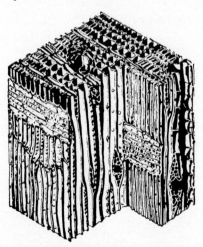

5-2. AN ENLARGED VIEW showing tube structure of wood.

woods the tubes are very small. It is plain to see why it is easier
to work (cut, shape, form, etc.) *with* the grain than across it.

Classification of lumber. All lumber is classified by the tree
leaf. The everbearing or coniferous—such as fir, pine, cedar and
cypress—are called *softwoods*, while those that shed their leaves
annually—such as oak, walnut, maple, birch, and cherry—are
called *hardwoods*. In working qualities, however, many of the
so-called softwoods are harder than some of the hardwoods.
There are several hundred kinds of wood, only a few of which
are used in furniture making. Fig. 5–3 shows these common kinds

WOODS FOR FURNITURE CONSTRUCTION

KIND	COLOR	WORKING QUALITIES	WEIGHT	STRENGTH	LASTING QUALITIES (OUTSIDE USE)
Hardwoods					
Basswood	Lt. Cream	Easy	Light	Weak	Poor
Birch	Lt. Brown	Hard	Heavy	Strong	Fair
Cherry	Dk. Red	Hard	Medium	Strong	Fair
Gum (Red)	Red-Brown	Medium	Medium	Medium	Medium
* Mahogany (Honduras)	Gold-Brown	Easy	Medium	Medium	Good
* Mahogany (Philippine)	Med. Red	Easy	Medium	Medium	Good
Maple, hard	Red-Cream	Hard	Heavy	Strong	Poor
Maple, soft	Red-Brown	Hard	Medium	Strong	Poor
* Oak, red	Flesh-Brown	Hard	Heavy	Strong	Fair
* Oak, white	Grey-Brown	Hard	Heavy	Strong	Fair
Poplar	Yellow	Easy	Medium	Weak	Fair
* Walnut	Dk. Brown	Medium	Heavy	Strong	Good
Softwoods					
Cedar	Red	Medium	Medium	Medium	Good
Fir, Douglas	Orange-Brown	Medium	Medium	Medium	Medium
Pine, Ponderosa	Orange to Red-Brown	Easy	Light	Weak	Poor
Redwood	Dk. Red-Brown	Easy	Light	Medium	Good

Woods marked with (*) are open grain woods and require a paste filler.

5–3.

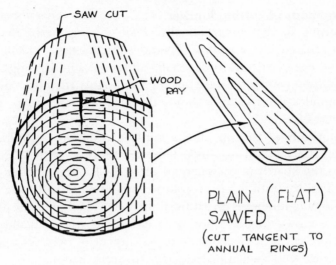

5-4. PLAIN (flat) sawed.

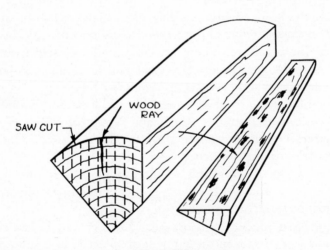

5-5. QUARTER sawed.

of woods, including color, classification, hardness, strength, and other qualities.

Methods of cutting lumber. There are two general methods of cutting lumber longitudinally. *Plain sawing* means that the log boards are cut in groups of various thicknesses. In plain sawing the log is cut into boards tangent to the annular rings. Fig. 5–4. *Quarter sawing* means cutting the boards at right angles to the annular rings, which shows the medullar rays to best advantage. Fig. 5–5.

Methods of drying. There are two common methods. *Air drying* is a method in which lumber is stacked with space between the boards in the open air or in sheds. This lumber is allowed to dry until it has a moisture content of 12 to 15 per cent. *Kiln drying* lumber is an artificial method. The lumber is placed in an enclosed kiln and hot air is circulated around it until the moisture content is about 6 to 12 per cent. Always specify kiln-dried wood when ordering for furniture making.

Grades of lumber. The so-called softwoods are graded into three groups: yard, factory or shop and structural lumber. Yard lumber, the kind usually available from lumberyards, is divided into two classes, *select* and *common*. Only select would be satisfactory for furniture. There are four grades of select, ranging from *A* to *D*. *A* is practically clear and *D* contains knots and other defects. Factory or shop (common) lumber is intended for manufacturing, such as in making windows and doors. This is available in two grades, *No. 1* and *No. 2*, of which No. 1 is the better. The third group is *structural lumber*, with which the woodworker is not concerned.

Hardwoods are available in three grades, *firsts and seconds* (FAS), *select*, and *No. 1 common*. Generally, firsts and seconds are used for furniture construction.

Standard lumber thicknesses. Lumber can be purchased rough as it comes from the sawmill or surfaced two sides (S2S) or surfaced four sides (S4S). The surfaced or dressed lumber has been run through a planer or surfacer. Dressed lumber is smaller than the quoted size. Fig. 5–6. For example, 1″ (S2S) walnut would measure only $1\frac{3}{16}$″ in thickness.

STANDARD SIZES OF SOFTWOODS		STANDARD THICKNESS OF HARDWOODS	
Stock Size	Actual Size	Rough	S2S
1" x 2"	$\frac{3}{4}$" x $1\frac{5}{8}$"	$\frac{3}{8}$"	$\frac{3}{16}$"
1" x 3"	$\frac{3}{4}$" x $2\frac{5}{8}$"	$\frac{1}{2}$"	$\frac{5}{16}$"
1" x 4"	$\frac{3}{4}$" x $3\frac{5}{8}$"	$\frac{5}{8}$"	$\frac{7}{16}$"
1" x 8"	$\frac{3}{4}$" x $7\frac{1}{2}$"	$\frac{3}{4}$"	$\frac{9}{16}$"
1" x 10"	$\frac{3}{4}$" x $9\frac{1}{2}$"	1"	$1\frac{3}{16}$"
2" x 2"	$1\frac{5}{8}$" x $1\frac{5}{8}$"	$1\frac{1}{4}$"	$1\frac{1}{16}$"
2" x 4"	$1\frac{5}{8}$" x $3\frac{5}{8}$"		
2" x 6"	$1\frac{5}{8}$" x $5\frac{5}{8}$"		
2" x 10"	$1\frac{5}{8}$" x $9\frac{1}{2}$"		
4" x 4"	$3\frac{5}{8}$" x $3\frac{5}{8}$"		

5–6.

Lumber defects. There are several lumber defects that must be avoided in the selection of lumber:

1. *Check* is a slight separation lengthwise in a board. This is often found at the end of the board and therefore must be trimmed off before cutting stock to length.

2. *Decay* is a rotted area in the wood which causes a soft spot.

3. *Knots* are places at which the branch of a tree has caused a fibrous, woody mass to form. Sometimes these knots are solid and are in demand for such things as knotty pine paneling, but most often they are a defect that must be removed from furniture lumber.

4. A *split* is a large break in a board.

5. *Warp* in a board is a curve across grain which occurs during the drying-out process.

6. *Wind* is a longitudinal twist in a board.

Measurement of lumber. Lumber is purchased by the *board foot*. This is a piece 1 inch thick, 12 inches wide, and 12 inches long. Lumber less than 1 inch thick is figured as 1-inch thickness when sold. In figuring the board feet in lumber, then, thickness x width in inches, x length in feet over 12, is the for-

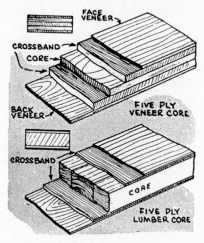

5-7. TWO TYPES OF PLY-WOOD. Lumber-core plywood is the best for fine furniture.

mula used. Some lumber less than 4 inches wide, especially moldings, is sold by the linear foot or running foot. In ordering lumber, the number of pieces, kind of lumber, size, quality, method of drying, and lumber surface should be specified. For example, one piece, mahogany, $13/16''$ x 8'' x 6', FAS, KD, S2S, means that you want a piece of mahogany of that specified size of *firsts and seconds* quality, *kiln dried*, and *surfaced two sides*. Notice that the thickness is specified as $13/16''$, which is standard 1-inch hardwood S2S.

If you specify a piece of pine 1'' x 6'' x 8', B Select or better, AD, Rgh, it means that you want a piece of pine of that *specified size* of *high quality, air dried* and *rough* as it comes from the saw mill.

Plywood. Plywood is made of layers or crossbands of wood glued together under great pressure. The two principal methods of plywood construction are *veneer construction* and *lumber-core construction*. Fig. 5–7. Plywood is referred to as 3, 5, 7 or 9 ply, which refers to the number of layers. The face veneer is usually about $1/32$ inch thick. There are three principal methods of cutting the veneer: *rotary cutting, flat slicing,* and *quarter slicing.* Fig. 5–8.

Plywood is made in thicknesses of $1/8''$, $1/4''$, $5/16''$, $3/8''$, $1/2''$, $3/4''$ and 1'', in widths of 24 to 48 inches and lengths of 36 to 96 inches. The most common size is 4' (48'') x 8' (96'').

There are five grades of *hardwood plywood. Custom grade* is a very special selection of woods and is used for interior paneling and fine furniture. *Good grade* (1) has a matched grain for pleasing effect and is designed to take a natural finish. *Sound grade* (2) is designed for a smooth paint surface. *Utility grade* (3) is a less desirable grade for painting. *Backing grade* (4) is used for the backs of cabinets, crates, etc. Hardwood plywood is made with three types of glue. *Type I* is for boat building and exterior use. *Type II* is a weather-resistant bond, and *Type III* is for interior use only. Hardwood plywoods can be purchased with the same grade of veneer on both sides or with a lesser grade on one side. For example, G1S is good one side and G2S is good two sides.

Softwood plywoods such as fir plywood are made waterproof for exterior use or not waterproof for indoor use. The grades of the face veneers are: A—smooth surface; B—solid surface with minor defects; C—major defects, or repaired, for underlayment only; and D—with large knotholes. For most project construction A–A grade and/or A–B grade should be used. For example, Ext. A–A should be chosen for a boat.

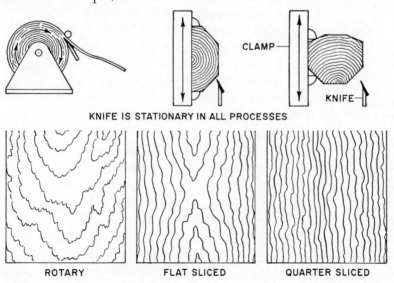

KNIFE IS STATIONARY IN ALL PROCESSES

ROTARY   FLAT SLICED   QUARTER SLICED

5–8.

READING A DRAWING

Drawings for furniture and accessories are available from many sources. Examples of a few of these drawings are shown in this book. Others can be secured from magazines, project books, and commercial companies. See Appendix, "Furniture Plans." In some cases, a full-size, pattern drawing is available in which the parts are drawn to full size and dimensioned so that the pattern can be laid directly on the wood. Most furniture drawings, however, are made to scale. Use the dimensions indicated on the drawing to make up the bill of materials, the stock cutting list, and the layout.

If the drawing contains irregularly shaped parts, it is frequently shown cross-sectioned in order that these parts can be enlarged to full size and the pattern thus duplicated.

Kinds of drawings. There are three kinds of drawings commonly used in furniture construction: orthographic projection, isometric and cabinet. In *orthographic projection*, two or more views are shown, usually three, which are most frequently the front, top, and right side or end view of a project. This kind of drawing shows the true shape of all parts. Fig. 6–1. An *isometric* drawing is one in which the sides are drawn at an angle of 30 degrees to the horizontal and all views are shown as one drawing. Fig. 6–2. A *cabinet* drawing is one in which the front view is exactly like that of the orthographic projection but the sides are drawn at an angle of 45 degrees. These sides are foreshortened to *half their true length*, giving the object the proportions it would have in a photograph. Fig. 6–3.

When the isometric or cabinet drawing is used, additional details are usually needed to show construction techniques. These two kinds of drawings are most often used for modern furniture

6–1a.　MODERN shadow box.

pieces, so that a "picture" of the piece can be combined with dimensioning.

How to read a drawing. In reading a drawing, you will derive a certain meaning from each line. Fig. 6–4. These are:

1. *Solid line.* Body or outline of the object.

2. *Invisible line.* Indicates a part that cannot be seen from the surface.

3. *Center line.* Divides the drawing into equal or symmetrical parts.

4. *Extension line.* Extends out from the solid line to provide lines between which dimensions can be shown.

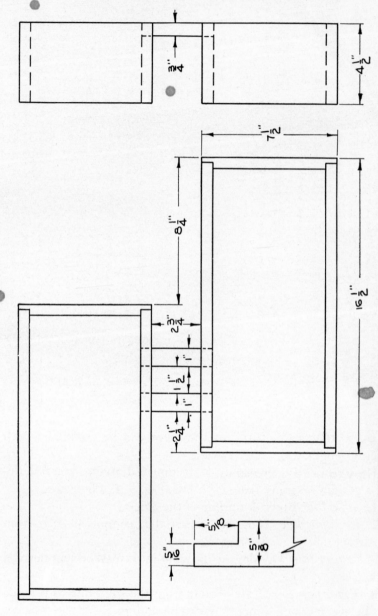

6-1b. AN ORTHOGRAPHIC PROJECTION drawing of a modern shadow box, shown on page 45.

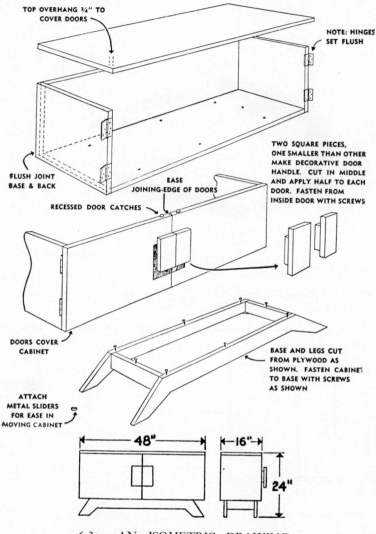

TOP OVERHANG ¾" TO
COVER DOORS

NOTE: HINGES
SET FLUSH

FLUSH JOINT
BASE & BACK

EASE
JOINING-EDGE OF DOORS

TWO SQUARE PIECES,
ONE SMALLER THAN OTHER
MAKE DECORATIVE DOOR
HANDLE. CUT IN MIDDLE
AND APPLY HALF TO EACH
DOOR. FASTEN FROM
INSIDE DOOR WITH SCREWS

RECESSED DOOR CATCHES

DOORS COVER
CABINET

BASE AND LEGS CUT
FROM PLYWOOD AS
SHOWN. FASTEN CABINET
TO BASE WITH SCREWS
AS SHOWN

ATTACH
METAL SLIDERS
FOR EASE IN
MOVING CABINET

48"   16"   24"

6–2a.   AN ISOMETRIC DRAWING
with a simple orthographic projection
drawing of a storage cabinet. COURTESY OF
CANADIAN FOREST PRODUCTS LIMITED.

6–2b. PICTURE drawing of finished storage cabinet.
See page 47.

5. *Dimension lines.* Have arrowheads at one or both ends
and line is broken in the center. These lines run between the
extension lines.

It is extremely important in reading a drawing to observe

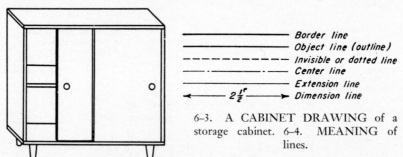

6–3. A CABINET DRAWING of a
storage cabinet. 6–4. MEANING of
lines.

the dimensions carefully. Never measure the drawing directly.
Every part on the drawing should be dimensioned to show its
thickness, width, and length. Frequently, however, the length
will not include the stock needed to make the joints. For example, when a rail has been dimensioned, the length is frequently
shown from leg to leg. Add an amount to provide for the joints.

MAKING A BILL OF MATERIALS

When you have selected the furniture design and a drawing or sketch is at hand, make a *bill of materials*. This is a complete list of all the lumber, plywood, hardware, supplies, and finishing materials you will need. It is a good idea to use a simple form which has columns for (1) the number of pieces; (2) the size, including thickness, width and length; (3) the name of each part; and (4) the kind of material. (Often this bill of materials is given with the drawing.) In making this list, start at the top or bottom of the project and list each separate item. Fig. 7–1. *For*

BILL OF MATERIALS:

No. of pieces	Size			Name of part	Material
	T	W	L		

7–1. A BILL OF MATERIALS form.

example, in making a simple table, you will need one top, four rails, four legs, four corner blocks, and other supplies and finishing materials.

When this is completed, make a *stock cutting list*. This is the same list of items in the bill of materials, with amounts added

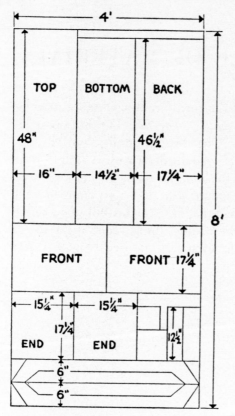

7-2. A LAYOUT for cutting the parts for the storage cabinet shown in Fig. 6-2.

to the thickness, width and length for the rough cutting size of each piece. Usually, $\frac{1}{16}''$ to $\frac{1}{8}''$ is added to the thickness, about $\frac{1}{4}''$ to the width, and about $\frac{1}{2}''$ to the length. In making parts that require joints, additional material must be added to the length. The items, then, should be grouped with all pieces of the same thickness and kind of material together. From this you can make a layout to determine how much stock of each thickness to buy. Fig. 7-2.

In designing a project it is well to keep in mind the standard sizes of lumber and plywood. For example, in making chests, cabinets, or built-ins from standard 4' x 8' plywood, the width of shelves or sides should be $11\frac{3}{4}''$, $15\frac{7}{8}''$, or $23\frac{7}{8}''$ for the most economical cutting.

Section II

First Steps in Furniture Construction

PORTABLE ELECTRIC AND HAND TOOLS

Portable Electric Tools

The five most common portable electric tools are the cutoff (power hand, or circular) saw, jig (or saber) saw, drill, router, and sander (belt and finishing). Routers and sanders are described in other sections of this book.

1. The *cutoff (power hand, or circular) saw* is used primarily for straight-line cutting on heavier lumber and plywood. It will cut ten times faster than the hand saw. It is the ideal choice for carpentry and building construction since it can do cutting after assembly. The size is determined by blade diameter. Blades range from 6″ to 10″. The good size is a one-half horsepower motor with an 8½″ blade. Because the saw cuts from the bottom of the material, it leaves a smoother cut at the bottom than at the top. Plywood should be cut with the good side down. The blade is on the right side of the motor which makes it convenient for the right-handed person.

Parts

The saw consists of a motor, handle, baseplate, or shoe, a fixed and a movable guard, a blade and a switch. Fig. 8–1. Blades used are the same type as for the circular saw. (See pages 162 to 165.) Just be sure that the saw blade has the correct size arbor hole and the correct diameter.

Safety

1. Make sure the teeth of the blade are sharp and set correctly.

2. Never make an adjustment on a saw when it is running.

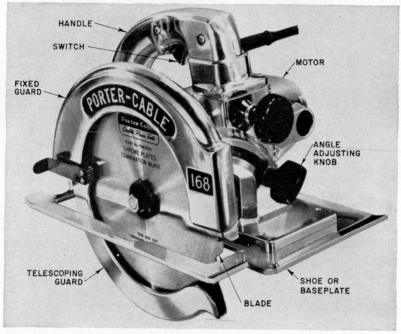

8-1. PARTS of a cut-off, or hand power, saw.

3. If a saw stalls in heavy material, never turn off the switch. Back out the saw until the blade runs freely again.

4. Always keep the guard in place and the blade adjusted for the correct depth of cut.

STRAIGHT CUTS

1. Mark the cut-off line on the right end of the board whenever possible. This will give better support as the cut is made. Place the work over the saw horses or support it securely in some other way so that the cut-off line is clear.

2. Loosen the nut or clamp to adjust the depth of cut. Only about ⅛" of the blade should show below the stock. Fig. 8–2. Place the baseplate, or shoe, on the work with the blade in line with the layout line. Turn on the power and allow it to come up

8–2. ADJUSTING THE SAW for the correct depth of cut. 8–3. STRAIGHT CUTTING. Notice how the guard covers the exposed blade.

to full speed. Guide the saw firmly but without too much pressure across the board, following the layout line. Fig. 8–3. A guide such as is shown in Fig. 8–4 will make crosscutting much more accurate. A long ripping cut can be made freehand following the layout line. It is much better, however, to use a ripping fence as shown in Fig. 8–5.

MITER CUTS

Angle or miter cuts can be made freehand except that it is more difficult to start the cut on the layout line. A protractor attachment is ideal to use for making miter cuts. This device is marked in degrees and can be set to cut any angle by moving the projecting arm to the correct degree. To use this attachment,

8–4. USING A PROTRACTOR GUIDE for cutting. This can be adjusted to any angle to make miter cuts. 8–5. RIPPING WITH A FENCE. When ripping a long board, either walk slowly with the saw or stop the saw and pull it back in the kerf a little way, taking a new position to finish the cutting.

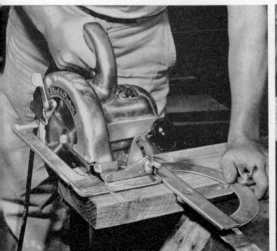
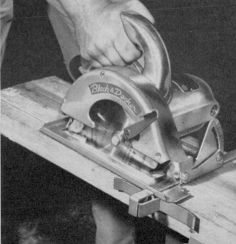

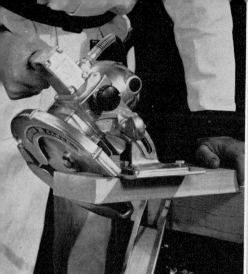

8–6. MAKING A BEVEL CUT.

8–7. A JIG, OR SABER, SAW.

Heavy cuts 2" x 4" at 45°	6 teeth per inch
General cutting	7, 10
Smooth cuts	12
Plywood	12
Hardboard	12
Cardboard	Knife
Leather	Knife

8–8. SELECTING THE CORRECT BLADE

the baseplate, or saw shoe, is lined up with the protractor straightedge. Then saw the same as for any cut.

BEVEL CUTS

On most saws the baseplate, or shoe, can be adjusted between 45 and 90 degrees. Loosen the wing nut or handle and tilt the shoe to the desired angle. Then retighten the wing nut or handle. Adjust the saw for the correct depth of cut. Make the bevel cut freehand or use a jig to guide the saw. Fig. 8–6.

2. The *jig* (*saber, sabre, or bayonet*) *saw* is the best choice for an on-the-job cutting tool for straight or irregular cutting. This tool can do the same cutting as a floor-type jig or band saw with the added convenience of a hand tool. A larger jig saw can cut through material 2" thick. It also can cut through a 2" x 4" piece in less than 15 seconds. It will cut metal, wood,

plastics and many other materials. Most hand jig saws use orbite action (cutting the material on the up stroke and moving away from it on the down stroke). Because of this, cutting speed is greatly increased and the saw cuts with a cleaner edge.

PARTS

The design of this tool varies with the manufacturer. However, all of them consist of a motor, a handle, a mechanism to change rotary action into up-and-down action, and a baseplate, or shoe. Fig. 8–7. The saw blades are designed to do different types of cutting. Fig. 8–8. At least two teeth must be on the cutting surface at all times. To install the blade, loosen the set screws and/or clamp and slip the blade into the slot under the chuck cover until you are sure it is tightly seated. Then tighten the set screw or clamp.

STRAIGHT AND IRREGULAR CUTTING

Mount the work so it is held rigid. Fig. 8–9. Make a layout line that can be followed. Set the shoe of the tool on the work. Start the motor and allow it to come up to full speed. Then move the saw along slowly. Fig. 8–10. Don't force the cutting. Use only enough pressure to keep the saw cutting at all times. The tool is always held in the one hand. The other hand can hold the work or steady the saw. For more accurate straight cutting, a ripping fence can be installed. Fig. 8–11. The ripping fence can also be used for cutting circles. A nail or peg must be driven into the center of the circle.

8–9. CUTTING A CURVE. Notice how the work is clamped to the table.
8–10. STRAIGHT CUTTING.

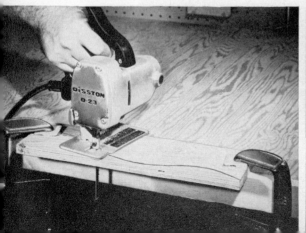
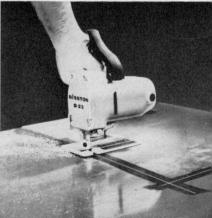

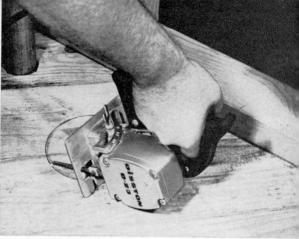

8–11. USING A FENCE to do ripping. 8–12. STARTING AN INTERNAL CUT. When possible, it is better to drill a small hole in the waste stock.

PLUNGE OR INTERNAL CUTTING

The jig saw can be used to cut out an internal area without first drilling a hole. This is called plunge cutting. Mark out the area to be cut with a pencil. Choose a convenient starting place inside the waste stock. Tip the tool forward with the shoe resting on the surface of the material and the top of the blade clear of the work surface. Fig. 8–12. Turn on the power. When the blade reaches full speed, slowly lower the back of the machine until the blade cuts through the material to the full depth. Then cut out the opening.

BEVEL CUTTING

The shoe of some saws can be adjusted from 0 to 45 degrees for bevel cutting. Fig. 8–13. The bevel cutting can be done free-hand, as shown in Fig. 8–14, or with a guide.

8–13. ADJUSTING the shoe, or baseplate, for bevel cutting. 8–14. CUTTING a bevel with the jig saw.

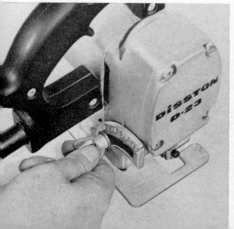

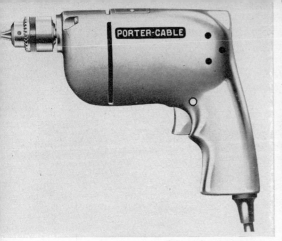

8–15. AN ELECTRIC DRILL. 8–16. USING AN ELECTRIC DRILL to
bore a hole.

3. The *electric hand drill* is the perfect tool for drilling and
boring holes. The drill consists of a housing with a handle, a
motor, and a chuck. Most drills have a key-type chuck. Fig.
8–15. The most common sizes have a ¼- or ½-inch chuck.
Many of the common cutting tools shown in Fig. 26–6, page
261, are made with quarter-inch shanks or stems so that they
will fit the quarter-inch drill. Fig. 8–17.

DRILLING WOOD

Mark the location of the hole and make a small dent with a
nail or scratch awl. This will help the drill to start correctly.
Open the chuck jaws with a chuck key and install the drill or
bit and then tighten it. Make sure that the tool is in straight.
Clamp the work to be drilled or hold it firmly against a bench
or table top. Fig. 8–35. Always start with the power off. Place
the point of the drill on the location of the hole. Turn on
the switch and slowly guide the tool into the work. If necessary,
use your left hand to support the tool. Any movement of the
tool will break a small drill. When using a boring tool, it is a
good idea to fasten a piece of scrap stock to the back of the
stock so that it does not break out.

8–17. A SPEED BIT with a ¼″ shank for a small electric drill.

8–18. HAND SAW.

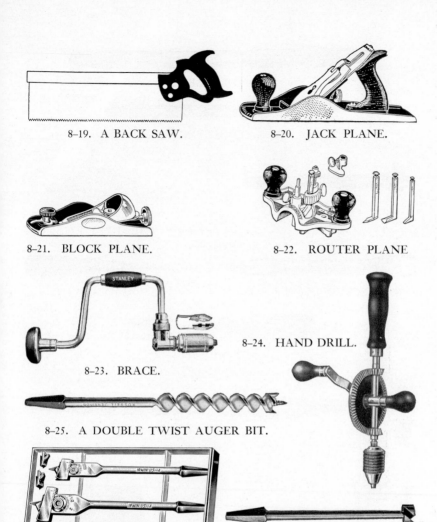

8–19. A BACK SAW.

8–20. JACK PLANE.

8–21. BLOCK PLANE.

8–22. ROUTER PLANE

8–23. BRACE.

8–24. HAND DRILL.

8–25. A DOUBLE TWIST AUGER BIT.

8–27. EXPANSION BIT.

8–26. FOERSTNER BIT.

Hand Tools

The common hand tools exclusive of measuring tools and clamps needed for making furniture are shown in Figs. 8–18 to 8–38. (Complete instructions on the use of hand tools can be found in the books *I. A. Bench Woodwork* and *Industrial Arts Woodworking* by the same author.)

8-28. DRILL BIT.

8-29. TWIST DRILL.

8-30. COUNTERSINK

8-31. DEPTH GAUGE.

8-32. SCREW-DRIVER BIT.   8-33. SCREW DRIVER.

8-34. CHISEL.

8-35. CLAW HAMMER   8-36. NAIL SET.

8-37. WOODEN MALLET.   8-38. HAND SCRAPER.

MEASURING AND MARKING
OUT STOCK

Good furniture construction depends upon accurate measurement and layout. A most common error is to cut a board too small, thereby ruining a good piece of wood.

Measuring tools

RULES

1. The *bench rule* is a wooden rule 1 foot long with a brass cap on either end. It is divided into 16ths of an inch. Fig. 9–1.

2. The *3-foot rule* or yardstick is similar to the bench rule except that it is 3 feet long. It is particularly useful in furniture making. Fig. 9–2.

9–1. BENCH RULE.

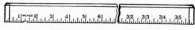
9–2. THREE-FOOT RULE.

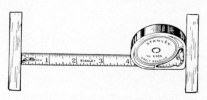
9–3. FLEXIBLE STEEL TAPE.

3. The *folding* or *zigzag rule* is made in 6- or 9-foot lengths which can be folded into a $6\frac{1}{2}$-inch unit.

4. The *flexible steel tape* or *push-pull rule* is excellent for

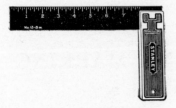

9–4. TRY SQUARE.

9–5. A 45-DEGREE TRY
SQUARE.

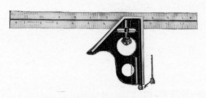

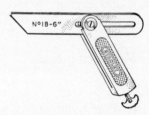

9–6. COMBINATION SQUARE.

9–7. SLIDING T BEVEL.

9–8. CARPENTER'S OR FRAMING SQUARE.

measuring inside, outside and curved surfaces. There is a hook on the end to help in making long measurements. Fig. 9–3.

SQUARES

1. The *try square* is made with a 6- or 8-inch blade with a metal or wood handle. Fig. 9–4. It is used to mark a line across a board, to check the squareness of two surfaces, and to make

short measurements. On some types, the handle near the blade is cut at 45 degrees. Fig. 9–5. This is convenient for accurately laying out miter cuts as well as right-angle cuts.

2. The *combination square* is an all-metal tool with a blade that slides along a handle. Fig. 9–6. One side of the blade makes a 90-degree angle with the blade and the other side makes a 45-degree angle. There is also a small level in the handle.

3. The *sliding T bevel* has a blade that can be adjusted to any angle to the handle. The angle can be set on the carpenter's square or with a protractor. Fig. 9–7.

4. The *carpenter's* or *framing square* has one long and one short blade. It is used for making layouts on larger pieces of stock and for checking an assembly. Fig. 9–8.

MARKING TOOLS

1. A *sharp pencil* is very satisfactory for most marking.

2. A *sloyd knife* can be used wherever a line is to be sawed or cut. Fig. 9–9.

3. A *marking gauge* is used for marking the thickness or width of stock. It has an adjustable head that can be moved to any position along the beam. Fig. 9–10.

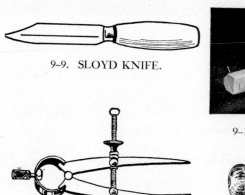

9–9. SLOYD KNIFE.

9–10. MARKING GAUGE.

9–11. DIVIDERS.

9–12. SCRATCH AWL.

9–13. MEASURING the thickness of stock.

4. The *dividers* is for laying out circles or parts of circles and to lay out equally spaced distances along a line. Fig. 9–11.

5. The *scratch awl* is used to mark the location of holes and to help to start screws in softwood. Fig. 9–12.

Suggestions for measuring and marking out

1. *Hold the rule on edge for all marking* in order to secure more accurate layout.

2. *To measure the thickness or width of stock,* place one end

of the rule over one edge of the stock and slide your thumb along until the measurement is indicated. Fig. 9–13. When measuring the width of stock be sure to hold the rule square with the edge.

3. *To lay out length before cutting,* hold one end of the rule over the end of the board with the rule parallel to one edge and mark the length. Then hold the try square or framing square firmly against the edge and guide the pencil or knife to square a line across the board. Fig. 9–14.

4. Whenever possible *mark all pieces at the same time.* Hold the pieces on edge and mark the positions along one edge. Draw lines across the edges; then each piece can be marked across the face surface separately. Fig. 13–2.

5. A *marking gauge,* as said, is used to mark thickness or width of stock. Fig. 9–15. Set the tool by placing the end of a

9–14. HOLDING ONE LEG of a framing square against the edge of stock and marking the line across to locate the position for a dado.

rule against the head. Slide the head along until the exact measurement to the point is reached. When using the marking gauge, hold the head firmly against the surface or edge of the board. Twist the tool slightly as it is pushed or pulled along.

6. *Set the dividers* by holding one point on the inch mark and opening the dividers until the correct radius is indicated. Hold one point over the center of the circle or arc and scribe the line by turning the tool in a clockwise direction. To avoid marring the surface of the wood, it is a good idea to put a small eraser over the point that acts as center. Fig. 9–16.

9–15. USING A MARKING GAUGE.

9–16. USING A DIVIDERS to lay out stock for face plate turning.

ENLARGING A PATTERN AND
TRANSFERRING A DESIGN

Many project designs are available in full-size patterns that can be transferred directly to the lumber. More often, though, in books and magazines, the irregular shapes are drawn in some smaller size and you must enlarge them. This can be done very simply as follows:

1. Check the drawing to see how much it must be enlarged. Most irregular shapes are covered with squared lines and the size

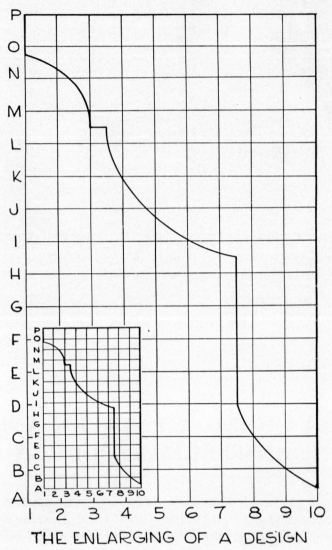

THE ENLARGING OF A DESIGN

10-1. ENLARGING A PATTERN for a double-bracket shelf.

of square indicates the size for a full-size pattern. Usually the drawing will show ½-inch or 1-inch squares.

2. Secure a piece of paper large enough for a full-size pattern and lay out squares of the required size. This can be done on a piece of wrapping paper.

3. Start at the lower lefthand corner of the original drawing to letter each horizontal line a, b, c, etc., from bottom to top. Number each vertical line from left to right 1, 2, 3, etc. Fig. 10–1.

4. Letter and number the lines on the full-size pattern in the same manner. Now locate a point on the original drawing and transfer it to the full-size pattern. Continue to do this until enough points have been located to draw in the lines for the full-size pattern. Usually a French curve is used to draw in the curves. Another method is to bend a piece of wire solder to follow the points and then draw in the lines by tracing along the wire.

5. The pattern can then be transferred to the stock by one of the following methods:

   a. Place the pattern over the stock with carbon paper underneath it and trace a design.

   b. Cut out the pattern. Place it over the stock and trace around it.

   c. If many parts of the same design are to be made, it may be a help to make a plywood template or pattern.

GETTING OUT STOCK AND SQUARING IT UP

The first step in the actual building of a piece of furniture is *cutting the stock to rough* (stock-cutting) size. In getting out the stock, always cut the pieces of like thickness before going on to the next. Regardless of whether the stock is Rgh. (rough) or surfaced (S2S or S4S), first examine the end of the board to see

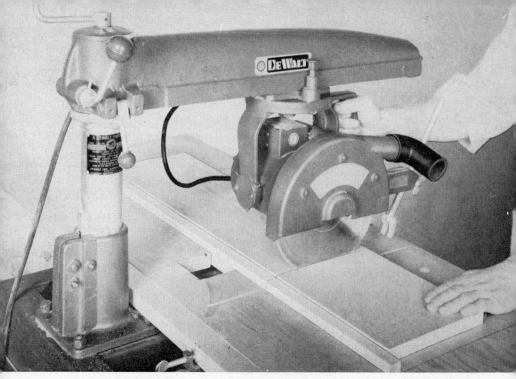

11–1. CUTTING STOCK TO LENGTH with a radial arm saw. Allow about ½″ for squaring. See pages 155–157 for instructions on the use of this machine.

if it is split, checked, or otherwise imperfect. If necessary, trim off a small amount to remove any imperfection and to square off the end. Now examine both surfaces of the board for any serious imperfections such as a knot, split, check, or dry rot. With proper layout, only small areas need to be wasted, even if there is an imperfection.

Rough cut the pieces to length, allowing enough material for squaring up. This can be done on a *radial, cutoff,* or *circular saw*. Fig. 11–1. Now check each piece of stock to determine which appears to be the best side. Arrange the lumber so the best side will appear on the exterior of the furniture piece. Frequently, the first side that is surfaced will be the poorer side, but this will always be called the *face surface*. The first edge to be surfaced will be called the *face edge*. These must be the most accurate, so, when laying out joints, always mark from the face surface and face edge.

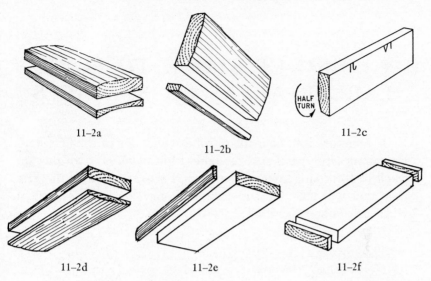

11–2a

11–2b

11–2c

11–2d   11–2e   11–2f

The common procedure for squaring up rough stock (six steps) is:

1. *True up one face.* Plane the face surface on the jointer to smooth the stock and remove any warp or wind. Fig. 11–2a.

2. *True up one edge.* Joint the first edge by holding the face surface against the fence of the jointer. Fig. 11–2b. Mark the face surface and edge. Fig. 11–2c.

3. *Plane to thickness.* Use a thickness planer if one is available. If not, mark the thickness and plane the second surface on the jointer. Fig. 11–2d.

4. *Cut and plane to finished width.* Adjust the circular saw to about $\frac{1}{16}''$ to $\frac{1}{8}''$ over finished width and rip. Then plane to finished width on a jointer. Fig. 11–2e.

5 and 6. *Cut and/or plane to finished length.* Cut one end square on the circular saw. Lay out the correct length and cut to finished length. Remember to allow enough for joints. If the end grain must be exposed, cut one end square and surface it on the jointer. Then cut the other end $\frac{1}{16}''$ too long and surface to exact length on the jointer. Fig. 11–2f.

GLUING UP STOCK TO FORM LARGER AREAS OR SURFACES

If furniture is to be made of solid wood, one of the first steps in making large parts such as table tops and legs is to glue up stock to form large areas or surfaces. Fig. 12–1. This is the first time you will use glue and clamps. Later you will need them when assembling furniture.

12–1. TO MAKE THIS TABLE it was necessary to glue stock that could be squared up to form a piece 33" x 33". COURTESY OF VISTA FURNITURE COMPANY.

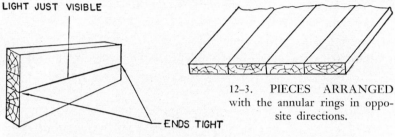

LIGHT JUST VISIBLE

ENDS TIGHT

12–2. SPRING-JOINT construction.

12–3. PIECES ARRANGED with the annular rings in opposite directions.

Gluing up stock edge-to-edge. If the stock is 8″ or more in width, cut it into narrow strips about 4″ to 6″ wide. Plane one surface and two edges of each piece. The jointed edges should be square with the face and should be slightly concave along their length, so that, when the two pieces are held together edge to edge, a small amount of light comes through the center of the joint. This is called a *spring-type joint*. Fig. 12–2. Arrange the pieces, keeping in mind the following:

1. Make sure the grain runs in the same direction on all pieces.

2. Match the color and grain so there is not a light piece right next to a darker one.

3. Arrange adjoining pieces with the annular rings on the ends facing in opposite directions. This will help to prevent the surfaces from warping after they are glued up. Fig. 12–3.

4. Check the assembly to make sure the pieces fit properly by placing one board in a vise with the joint edge up and stacking the other ones on this. Observe the following:

  a. Touch the upper boards to make sure they don't rock.

  b. Look along the edge of each board to see that the ends are tight and that a small amount of light shows through the center.

  c. Hold a straightedge against the face surface to see that the boards form a flat surface.

d. Push lightly on the ends of the boards to see that they are tight.

After doing this, mark each adjoining surface with a matching number so that you can easily identify the pieces when gluing up. If added strength is needed, insert dowels or a spline in each joint.

If an extremely wide board is needed and the planer is too narrow, it may be wise to glue up the piece in two sections. Surface both sections to within $\frac{1}{16}''$ finished size before completing the gluing. *Proceed with the gluing* as follows:

1. Make sure that you have enough clamps of the right size and kind. There should be a bar clamp at least every 15 inches. On wide assemblies, cut some cleats or battens that are long enough to go crosswise at either end to hold the assembly flat. Fig. 12–4. It is a good idea to hold the bar clamps in a simple jig when gluing up. Open the clamps slightly wider than the stock to be glued up.

12–4. FASTENING CLEATS to glued-up stock to keep the surface true.

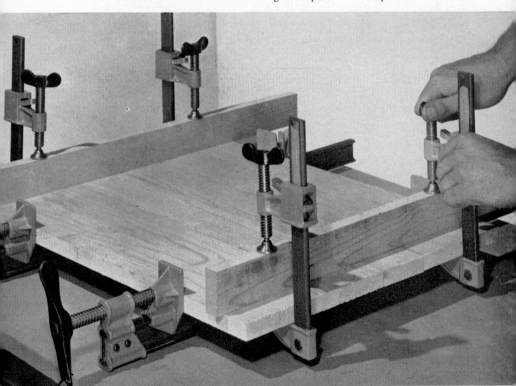

12-5. GLUING UP A WIDE ASSEMBLY. Notice that the clamps are placed alternately.

2. Mix the glue and have everything ready.

3. Hold the two matching edges together or clamp them in a vise. If dowels or splines are being used, dip half in the glue and drive into one edge. Cover both edges and exposed dowel or spline evenly with a thin coating of glue. *Do not apply too much.* Work quickly and accurately.

4. Slip these pieces together and then proceed with the other edges in a similar manner. If necessary, use a rubber or wooden mallet to bring the pieces into place.

5. Tighten all the bar clamps slowly and evenly, a little at a time. Fig. 12-5. When several bar clamps are used, put them on alternately from opposite sides.

6. Place the wooden cleat or batten across either end with a piece of paper underneath and clamp in place with a C clamp or hand screw. Wipe off any excess glue immediately.

7. Allow to dry the specified time. Always scrape off any exposed glue before machining the piece further.

Gluing up stock face-to-face. When gluing up stock for legs or similar parts, plane the *face surfaces* of the two pieces that are to be glued together. If more than two pieces are needed, the inside stock should be squared up so that both face surfaces are true and the stock is of equal thickness throughout. Apply glue evenly to both surfaces and clamp together with hand screws or C clamps. Fig. 12–6.

If C clamps are used place wooden cleats or battens across the stock to equalize the pressure.

12–6. STOCK GLUED FACE TO FACE, using C clamps.

CLAMPS AND THEIR USES

Kind	Size	Use
C or Carriage (Fig. 12–7)	Available from 2″ to 20″. 6″ to 10″ size best for general use.	For clamping irregular-shaped parts together. For clamping jigs or fences to machines. For clamping metal parts together.

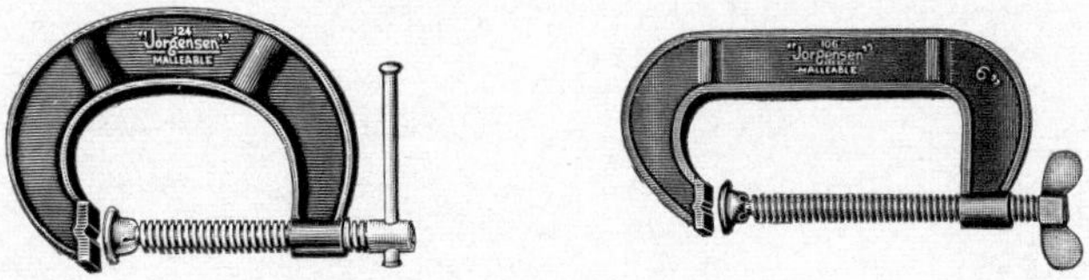

12-7. C CLAMPS.

Hand Screw (Fig. 12–8)	Length of clamp from 6″ to 20″. Opening from 4″ to 20″. The 8″ and 12″ size best for general use.	For clamping face to face. For clamping tops to bases. For clamping uneven or tapered surfaces together. Can be used on finished surfaces without protective pieces.

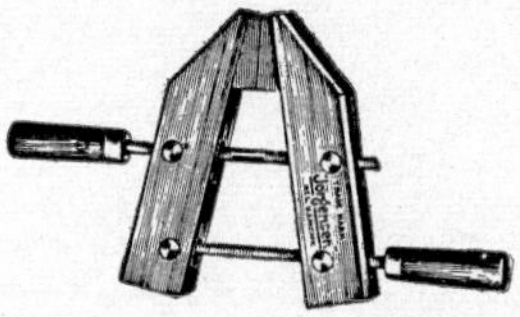

12-8. HAND SCREW.

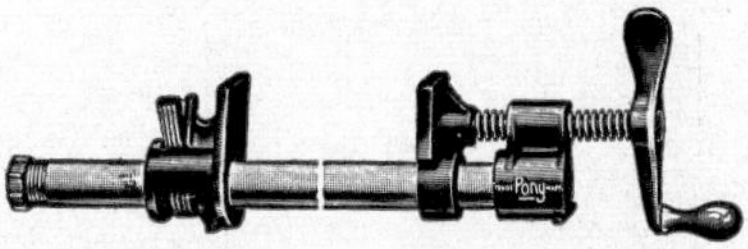

12–9a

Single or Double Bar (Fig. 12–9 a b c)	Length from 2′ to 8′. 4′ or 5′ size best for general use.	For clamping wide assemblies together.

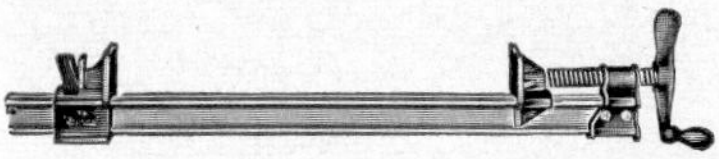

b 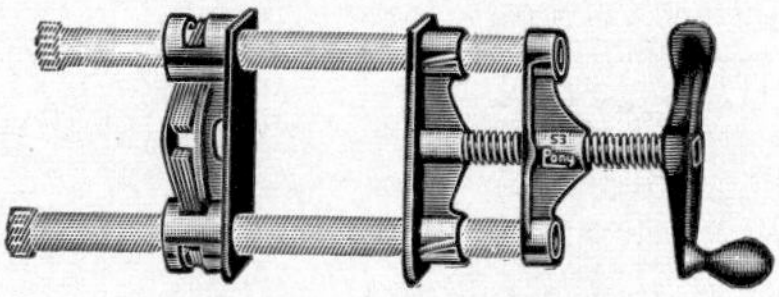   c

12-9. (a) Single-bar pipe type clamp. (b) Single-bar "I" type clamp. (c) Double bar pipe type clamp.

Hints for clamping

Always select the correct size and number of clamps needed.

Always open the clamps slightly wider than necessary before beginning the assembly work.

Always place protective pieces of scrap wood on the finished surface of stock when using C or bar clamps.

When using several, fasten clamps on alternate sides of the stock to equalize the pressure.

GLUES AND GLUING

Type	Uses	Advantages	Disadvantages
Animal: Available as a liquid or powder or stick.	For good furniture construction and all kinds of cabinet work	Strong, makes light-colored joints, is mold resistant, does not require bleaching.	Not waterproof. Stick or powder requires heating in glue pot which takes a great deal of time.
Casein: Made from milk curd. Available in powder form which is mixed with water.	Excellent for all inside and outside gluing, especially for oily woods.	Easy to mix and apply. Can be used in cool weather. Almost waterproof.	Some kinds require bleaching. Will deteriorate with age. Can't be stored too long.
Plastic resin: Made from chemicals. Available in powder form.	Good for all furniture work including outdoor furniture and boat-building.	Moldproof, easy to mix, does not require bleaching, is waterproof.	Requires excellent fitting joints. Powder must be kept cool and dry. Must be used in dry weather.
White liquid resin: Made from chemicals in white liquid form. Use in squeeze bottle.	Good for indoor furniture and cabinet work. A fine general purpose glue that is easy to use.	Always ready to use. Nonstaining, economical, clean and white. It is quick-setting.	Not sufficiently resistant to moisture for outdoor furniture. Not so strong and lasting as liquid-hide glue for fine furniture.
Resorcinol: Made from chemicals. Comes in two-part can: liquid and powder catalyst or hardener. Mix as needed.	Good for outdoor furniture, boats and sports equipment.	Completely waterproof. Good for oily woods. Can be used with poor-fitting joints. Fills gaps.	Dark color. Must be used in temperatures about 70 degrees.
Fish glue: Available in liquid form.	For small repairs or models and toy making.	Easy to apply and use.	Not waterproof and quite expensive.

Hints for gluing

The surfaces must be clean and dry.

The joints should be properly made. Fig. 12–10.

The correct kind of glue should be selected.

The correct mixture should be followed. Follow manufacturer's directions on each can. Never vary the amounts.

Mix only enough glue for one job. Most glues deteriorate with age.

Make sure the temperature is correct. Some glues must be used only at 70 degrees or above. Others can be used at any temperature.

Mark the pieces to be glued with corresponding numbers.

Have the proper clamps ready and set.

Apply glue with stick, brush, or squeeze bottle. Fig. 12–11 and 12–12.

When gluing end-grain stock, apply a thin coat, let it become tacky, and then apply a second coat before joining the parts.

Clamp all parts properly. Do not apply so much pressure that all the glue squeezes out. This may create a glue-starved joint that is very weak. Fig. 12–13.

Remove excess glue before it dries.

Allow the assembly to dry thoroughly as recommended by the manufacturer.

When dry, remove bits of glue with a small chisel or knife. *Never try to remove this by planing or surfacing*.

If glue stains are present around the joint, bleach with oxalic acid before applying finish.

12–10. MAKE SURE you have a good fit before gluing the joint. 12–11. APPLYING liquid-hide glue with a stick.

12–12. LIQUID-RESIN GLUE in a squeeze bottle. 12–13. CLAMP THE JOINTS tightly. Place blocks of wood under the jaws of the clamps to protect the project.

MAKING JOINTS

Many different kinds of joints are used in the construction of furniture. There are over 100 different varieties but most of them are adaptations of eight basic ones which will be discussed in this section. There are four steps in the construction of all joints and, while the procedure for each varies, these four steps should be followed carefully and in order.

STEP 1. MAKING THE LAYOUT

1. Make sure that you have accurate instruments—rule, try square, marking gauge, etc.—and a sharp pencil or knife. It is extremely important that the layout be accurate. A knife can be used whenever a line is to be cut. A sharp pencil can be used for all layouts but especially when only part of the area is cut away.

2. Select the wood for the joint carefully and make sure that the grain runs in the right direction. Certain kinds of joints can be made only across grain, since they would break out otherwise.

3. Make all your measurements from a common starting point, edge, or surface. Start from one end of the piece. Always measure from this point for each joint, never from the next mark.

4. Always use the *superimposing method* of laying out the joint. That is, mark one location of the joint and then hold the second part over it to mark the width and/or length. Fig. 13–1.

5. Lay out all identical joints at the same time. Sometimes this can be done by clamping the pieces of stock together and marking across all of them. Fig. 13–2.

80

13-1. MARKING THE WIDTH of a rabbet by superimposing one piece over another.

6. Always identify the two members of each joint with a pencil mark (*1-1, 2-2,* etc.) so they can be quickly identified during assembly.

STEP 2. CUTTING THE JOINT

1. Use the right machine for making each cut. Most cuts are made on the circular saw with or without a dado head. Others are cut on the shaper, on a drill press with a mortising attachment, on a router, on a jointer, and even on the band saw or jig saw. Often there is more than one way of making the cut.

2. Always make the cuts in the waste stock just inside or outside the layout line. A tenon, for example, should be cut outside the line and a dado inside the line.

3. When necessary, trim out the joint with a router plane or chisel.

STEP 3. FITTING THE JOINT

1. A well-fit joint is one that can be assembled with hand pressure but is not so loose that it falls apart by itself.

13–2. MARKING LAYOUT LINES on several pieces at the same time.

2. If a joint must be trimmed, always remove the stock from the piece fitting into the second member. Trim the tenon, for example, not the mortise.

STEP 4. ASSEMBLING THE JOINT

1. Always choose the proper kind of clamping devices.
2. Cut enough scrap blocks to go between the clamps and the project to protect it when using C or bar clamps.
3. Make a trial assembly to make sure that each joint fits properly.
4. Determine the correct method of fastening: glue, nails,

screws, dowels, splines, keys, corrugated fasteners, or a combination of two or more.

5. Mix just enough glue for the one job. Apply the glue carefully with a stick or brush. *Do not apply too much*. If the wood is to be bleached, use a glue that will not stain. If pounding must be done, use a rubber mallet.

6. Check to see that the project is square and aligned before it is dry. This often requires a little pounding or shifting of clamps. Make several measurements with a try square and rule.

7. On complicated projects, glue up sub-assemblies and then the final project. On many tables, for instance, it is well to glue up the ends, allow them to dry, and then glue up the entire project.

Methods of strengthening joints

DOWELS

Many types of joints—especially the edge, butt, miter, and mortise and tenon—are strengthened by installing dowels. Dowel rod is made of birch or maple and can be purchased in diameters from ⅛" to 3", in 3-foot lengths, with either a plain or grooved surface. The grooved surface allows the glue to run more freely into the joint. Install dowels as follows:

1. Locate accurately the position of the dowel holes in the two adjoining surfaces. To do this, mark the location of the dowels on the surface of the two adjoining pieces. Fig. 13–3. Then with a try square mark a line across the edges and/or end.

2. With a marking gauge set at half the thickness of the stock, mark a line along the edge or end that will intersect the other line to locate the center of the hole. This step is unnecessary when using a doweling jig or a fence on a drill press.

3. In selecting the size dowel rod to use, a general rule to follow is that the diameter should be not more than half the thickness of the stock. The depth of the hole will vary with the

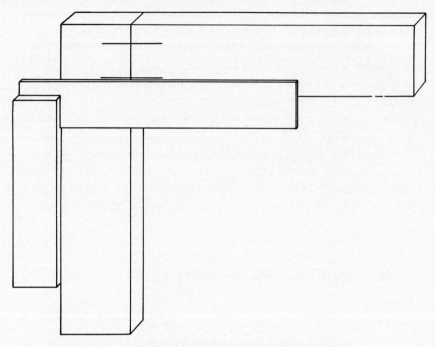

13–3a. MARKING THE LOCATION for dowels.

kind of joint. The length of the dowel rod should always be cut about ¼″ shorter than the total of the two holes. The ends of the dowel pins should be cut with a bevel. Use a dowel pointer or sand the bevel. Fig. 13–4.

4. The holes can be bored with an auger bit and brace, but this requires careful sighting and extremely accurate work. A doweling jig is a device that can be used for locating the position of the holes and guiding the auger bit accurately for boring. Fig. 13–5. This jig has several guide rods for different diameter bits. This guide rod can be adjusted to center on any thickness of stock. The jig is then clamped over the stock and aligned with the cross line. Fig. 13–6. Always remember to place the jig on the stock with the solid side against the face surface. A stop is

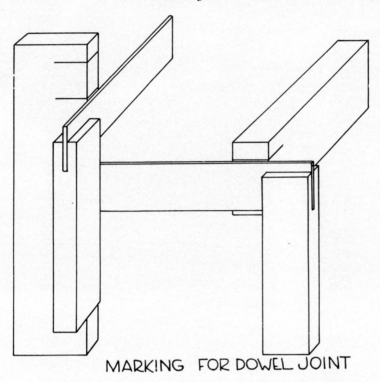

MARKING FOR DOWEL JOINT

13-3b. MARKING THE LOCATION for dowels by squaring lines across the edges.

13-4. DOWEL pointer. This tool is used in a brace to bevel the ends of dowel.

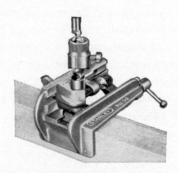

13-5. DOWELING jig.

13–6. USING a doweling jig.

clamped to the auger bit to control the depth of the hole. Dowel holes can also be made on a drill press as shown in Figs. 26–11, 26–16, and 26–17.

SPLINES

A spline is a thin strip of wood inserted in a groove cut in the two adjoining surfaces of a joint. It is used extensively on edge and miter joints. The groove is cut on a circular saw or shaper to a specific width and depth. A thin piece of stock is then cut to fit into this groove. Figs. 22–28, 22–30, and 22–38. This stock should be cut so the grain runs at right angles to the grain of the joint.

KEY OR FEATHER

A key or feather is a small piece of wood inserted in one or both members of a joint to hold it firmly together. This is commonly used for miter and mortise-and-tenon joints. Fig. 22–32 shows the method for cutting a groove for a key in a miter joint. The key in the mortise-and-tenon joint is commonly used in Mission and Early American furniture and in some kinds of modern ranch-type furniture.

Kinds of joints

EDGE JOINTS

The first basic joint is the edge joint. Fig. 13–7. Adaptations of this are the *dowel, spline, tongue-and-groove,* and *rabbet-edge* joints. The edge joint is constructed whenever it is necessary to make up larger surfaces such as tops for tables, desks, and other large parts. Added strength can be secured by installing several dowels or a spline along the adjoining edge. A tongue can be cut on one adjoining edge and a groove on the other on the shaper. This kind of joint is often used when paneling a surface. Cutting a rabbet on either adjoining edge provides greater gluing area and strengthens the joint.

BUTT JOINTS

A butt joint is found in simple box construction, bookcases, cabinets, inexpenseive door and frame construction, to name but a few. In a butt joint, the square end of one member fits against the flat surface, edge, or end of the second member. Fig. 13–8. A simple butt joint can be made on edge or flat. The corner of a butt joint can be strengthened by installing glue blocks or dowels. The *end butt with dowels* is a joint in which two ends are joined together to lengthen a board. The *middle-rail butt with dowels* is used to install shelves and partitions in box and case work. The *frame butt with dowels* is used for making a frame. The *rail-to-leg butt with dowels* is often found in inexpensive furniture to replace mortise-and-tenon joints.

To make a butt joint, cut the end accurately to fit against an edge or surface. Dowels are installed as described previously.

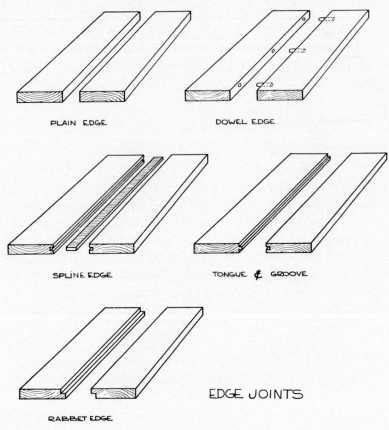

PLAIN EDGE

DOWEL EDGE

SPLINE EDGE

TONGUE & GROOVE

RABBET EDGE

EDGE JOINTS

13-7. EDGE JOINTS.

RABBET JOINTS

The rabbet joint is one in which a rabbet is cut in the end or edge of one board and a second member fit into it. Fig. 13-9. The rabbet is found in simple corner construction for cabinets, bookcases, and drawers. It is also used to install a top or bottom to a box or case. The rabbet can be made on edge or flat. A *back-panel rabbet joint* is commonly used to install a panel in the back

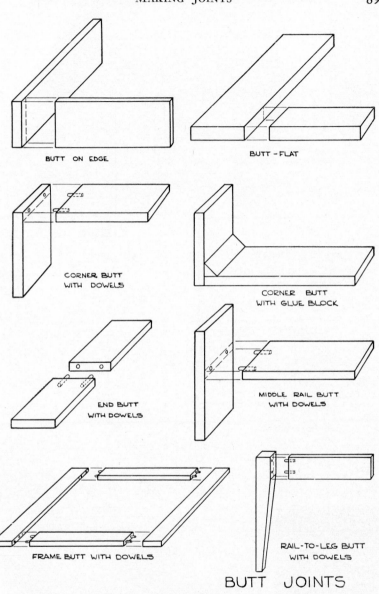

BUTT ON EDGE

BUTT – FLAT

CORNER BUTT
WITH DOWELS

CORNER BUTT
WITH GLUE BLOCK

END BUTT
WITH DOWELS

MIDDLE RAIL BUTT
WITH DOWELS

FRAME BUTT WITH DOWELS

RAIL-TO-LEG BUTT
WITH DOWELS

BUTT JOINTS

13–8. BUTT JOINTS.

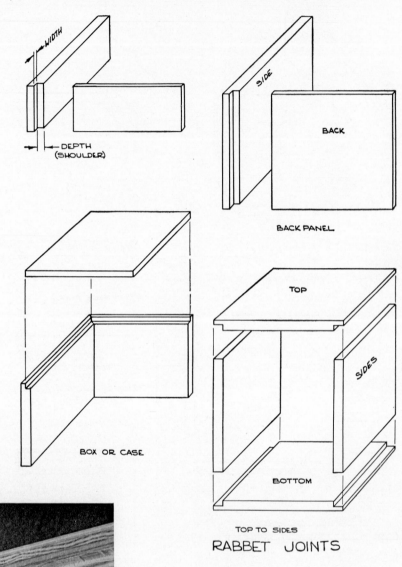

WIDTH

DEPTH
(SHOULDER)

SIDE

BACK

BACK PANEL

BOX OR CASE

TOP

SIDES

BOTTOM

TOP TO SIDES

RABBET JOINTS

13-9. RABBET JOINTS. The photo shows
the use of the rabbet joint in the back panel
of case construction.

of case construction. A rabbet is cut around the back, on all four sides, and a panel installed.

To lay out a rabbet joint, hold one edge of the second member over the end or side of the first and mark the width of the rabbet. Then draw a line down the sides or end and measure one half to two thirds the thickness of the first member as the depth of the rabbet. The cuts can be made on the circular saw, jointer, or shaper.

Dado joints

Dado joints are used primarily to install shelves, partitions, or steps in bookcases, chests, cabinets, and the like. A dado joint is one in which a dado is cut in one member and a second member fit into it. Fig. 13–10. A *plain dado* is one which has a rectangular groove cut across grain. A *dovetail dado* is one in which a dovetail is cut across grain and notches cut in the end of the second piece to fit into this dovetail. A *blind dado* or *gain* is one in which a dado is cut only partway across the first member and a corner cut out of the second member to fit into it. This is found frequently in better furniture construction when the joint should not be visible from the front edge. A *corner dado* has a rectangular groove cut cornerwise across one member and a corner cut off the second member to fit into the first. This is constructed frequently for installing a lower shelf in many different types of tables.

Make a *plain dado* as follows:

1. Mark a line across the stock to indicate one side of the dado.

2. Hold the second member over it and mark the width of the dado. Draw a line across either edge and mark the depth of the dado. This is usually half the thickness of the stock.

3. Cut the dado on a circular saw with or without a dado head, on a shaper or with a router attachment. Remember always to cut the dado in the waste stock. The dovetail dado must be cut

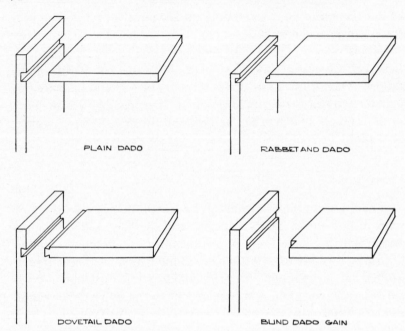

PLAIN DADO

RABBET AND DADO

DOVETAIL DADO

BLIND DADO GAIN

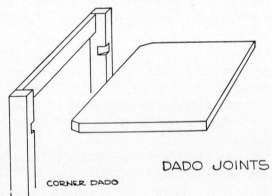

DADO JOINTS

CORNER DADO

13-10. DADO JOINTS. A dado joint can be made easily with a power saw. It is the ideal joint for shelves. The photo shows a plain dado used in shelf construction.

with a router or router attachment. When a dado is cut with a single saw blade, several passes should be made through the waste stock and then the excess trimmed out with a router plane or chisel. When many dados are cut at one time, it is simpler to fit the saw with a dado head to make the correct width of dado.

Make a *blind dado* as follows:

1. Lay out in the same general manner as a simple dado, indicating the length of the blind dado from the back edge.

2. Bore a round hole at the end of the cut or, better still, cut a square hole with a mortising attachment.

3. Cut up to the hole with a dado head. Fig. 22–45. If a round hole has been bored, the corner must be trimmed out by hand.

4. Cut a notch in the second member to fit into the blind dado.

The *rabbet-and-dado joint* is a combination of these two. A dado is cut in one member and a rabbet cut on the end of the second. The dado is cut equal to half the thickness of the stock and to a depth equal to one half to two thirds the thickness. This joint is frequently used for joining the back to the sides of drawers, or for bookcases and cabinets, since, by its very construction, it holds the two pieces square.

MITER JOINTS

A miter joint is one in which the corners of the two members are cut at 45 degrees. Fig. 13–11. It is found in modern furniture construction in the corners of cabinets, frames, boxes, moldings, and other things. The simple miter can be cut flat by adjusting the miter gauge to 45 degrees or can be cut on edge by setting the miter gauge at 90 degrees and tilting the blade to 45 degrees. The simple miter is not very strong and requires strengthening by dowels, splines, or keys. A spline can be cut along the ends for either a flat miter or a miter on edge. One or more dowels can be installed across the corner. The holes for these can be drilled as shown in Figs. 26–11, 26–16, and 26–17. A key miter is an-

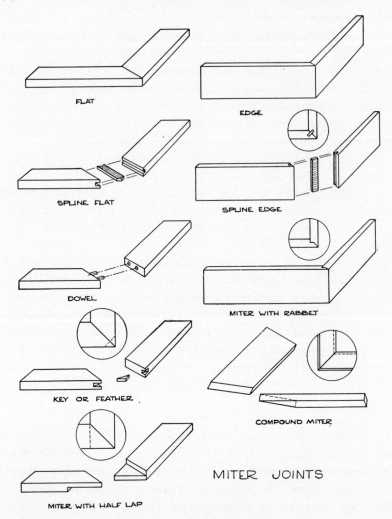

FLAT

EDGE

SPLINE FLAT

SPLINE EDGE

DOWEL

MITER WITH RABBET

KEY OR FEATHER

COMPOUND MITER

MITER JOINTS

MITER WITH HALF LAP

13–11. MITER JOINTS.

other method of strengthening the corner. Fig. 22–32 shows how to cut the key opening. A *miter with half lap* is an adaptation of the miter and lap joint which gives added strength to a corner. A *miter with rabbet* is one that combines the features of the rab-

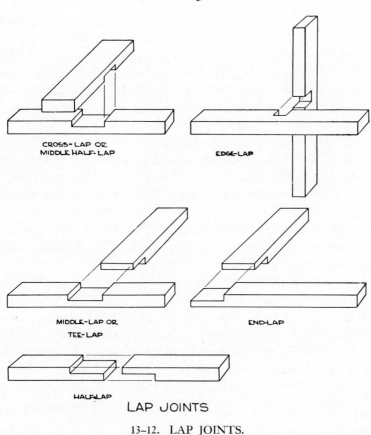

CROSS-LAP OR
MIDDLE HALF-LAP

EDGE-LAP

MIDDLE-LAP OR
TEE-LAP

END-LAP

HALF-LAP

LAP JOINTS

13–12. LAP JOINTS.

bet joint with the miter joint. A compound miter, or hopper, joint is used to make such projects as picture frames and shadow boxes. To cut a compound miter with the sides at a slope (work angle) of 45 degrees, set the miter gauge to an angle of 54¾ degrees and tilt the blade to an angle of 30 degrees. For other slopes see Appendix B. See page 416.

LAP JOINTS

The lap joint is found in simple furniture legs, frames, tables, and chairs, as well as many other pieces. Fig. 13–12. The basic one is the *cross-lap* or *middle-half-lap*. Adaptations of this are the *edge-lap*, *middle-* or *tee-lap*, *end-lap*, and *half-lap*. The cross lap is one in which two pieces cross with the surfaces flush. They may cross at 90 degrees or any other necessary angle. On modern furniture legs, for example, they frequently cross at 45 degrees.

Make a *cross-lap joint* as follows:

1. Mark a line across one surface of one member to indicate one side of the dado. Place the second member over it and mark the width.

2. Invert the pieces and mark the width on the second member.

3. Draw lines down the edges of both pieces and mark the depth of the dado, which should be one half the thickness of the pieces.

4. Make the cut in the same way as a dado, which it actually is.

The edge-lap joint is identical except that the members cross on edge. The middle-lap or tee is made with one member exactly like the cross-lap and the second member cut as a rabbet. The end-lap joint, which is used in frame construction, is made by laying out and cutting both pieces as rabbets. The half-lap is cut in the same way except that the pieces are joined end to end.

MORTISE-AND-TENON JOINTS

The mortise-and-tenon joint is one of the best, primarily used in leg and rail construction for tables, chairs, and benches, as well as for installing stretchers and making frames. Fig. 13–13.

There are many kinds of mortise-and-tenon joints. The *blind mortise-and-tenon*, which is found in leg-and-rail construction, has a mortise cut in the leg and a tenon in the rail. The *bare-faced mortise-and-tenon* is similar to a blind except that all the stock for making the tenon is removed from one surface and one edge and the surfaces of the rail and leg are flush. This is most common in modern furniture. A *stub mortise-and-tenon* is simply a short

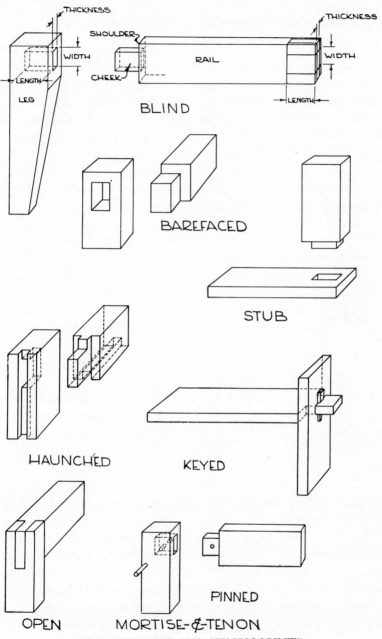

THICKNESS

SHOULDER

THICKNESS

WIDTH

RAIL

WIDTH

LENGTH

CHEEK

LENGTH

LEG

BLIND

BAREFACED

STUB

HAUNCHED

KEYED

OPEN

PINNED

MORTISE-&-TENON

13–13. MORTISE-AND-TENON JOINTS.

97

tenon that fits into a second member. This is often used in install-ing a stretcher. The *haunched mortise-and-tenon* is used prima-rily in panel construction. A groove is cut in one member and a mortise cut deeper in the same member the same width as the groove. A tenon with the corner notched out is cut in the end of the second member to fit this. The *keyed mortise-and-tenon* is found in Early American, Mission, and ranch-type furniture. An *open mortise-and-tenon joint* is used often in simple frame con-struction such as storm windows and screens. A *pinned mortise-and-tenon* is one in which a dowel rod is installed through the mortise and tenon to strengthen it.

It is usually necessary to make eight mortise-and-tenon joints to join the four legs and rails. Hold the legs and rails up as they will be in the finished article, with the face side and edge of the legs in and the face side of the rails in. Mark each adjoining rail and leg *1–1, 2–2*, etc., so they can be easily identified. Place those numbers so that they will not be removed when cutting the joints.

Laying out and cutting the tenon:

1. Measure the length of the tenon from the end of stock and draw a line completely around the stock, using a try square. Do this on either end on all rails and then check the length of the rails from shoulder to shoulder to make sure they are exactly the same.

2. Lay out a line across both edges and ends to indicate the amount of stock to be removed on either side of the tenon. Hold a marking gauge against the face surface to make these measure-ments. If not otherwise specified, the tenon should be about half the thickness of the stock. In all cases, however, it should be some standard thickness such as ¼″, ⅜″, ½″, etc., so that it will fit into a standard mortise opening. In making a bare-faced mortise-and-tenon, remove all of the stock from one side.

3. Determine the amount of stock to be removed from either edge to form the width of the tenon. This is usually ¼″ to ⅜″.

With a marking gauge held against the face edge, mark a line across each surface and end to indicate the amount of stock to be removed.

4. Cut the tenon on a circular saw, making the shoulder cut first and then the cheek cut. In some cases, the cheek cut can be made on the jointer.

Laying out and cutting the mortise:

When a mortising attachment or a mortising machine is used, it is necessary to lay out only one mortise in each location, because then the machine is set and will take care of the others automatically.

1. Mark a line in from the face edge of the leg to indicate one side of the mortise. Mark a second line to indicate the thickness of the mortise. The thickness of the mortise is the same as the thickness of the tenon. The distance to the mortise from the outside of the leg should equal the amount of stock removed from one side of the tenon plus the amount the rail is to set back from the leg. When the leg and rail are to be flush, the mortise is set in a distance equal to only the amount of stock removed from the outside surface of the rail.

2. From the end of the leg mark two lines to indicate the width of the tenon.

3. Select a mortise bit of the correct size and cut the mortise as described in section on MORTISERS AND MORTISING ATTACHMENTS. Pages 291–297. The mortise can be cut by hand by boring a series of holes in the waste stock and trimming out the joint with a chisel.

Making other kinds of mortise-and-tenon joints:

1. The open mortise-and-tenon joint is made very simply because both the mortise and the tenon can be cut on the circular saw. One member of the open mortise is simply a deep dado.

2. The keyed mortise-and-tenon joint is made by cutting a square opening completely through the first piece. A notch is cut

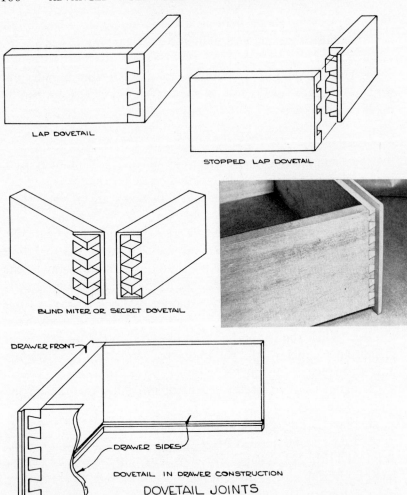

LAP DOVETAIL

STOPPED LAP DOVETAIL

BLIND MITER OR SECRET DOVETAIL

DRAWER FRONT

DRAWER SIDES

DOVETAIL IN DRAWER CONSTRUCTION

DOVETAIL JOINTS

13-14. DOVETAIL JOINTS. The dovetail joint is the best one for joining the front of a drawer to the sides. The photo shows the use of the dovetail on a lip drawer.

out of either side of the rail or stretcher so that the tenon slips completely through the mortise, with part of the tenon extending beyond. A square hole is cut in the tenon, through which a key or pin is fastened.

Dovetail joints

The dovetail joint is found in the finest quality drawer and box construction. Fig. 13–14. The common types are the lap, stopped-lap, and blind miter or secret dovetail. These are so difficult to make by hand, however, that most hand craftsmen never do it. With a portable router and a dovetailing attachment, the dovetail joint can be made very quickly as described in the section on ROUTERS. Pages 296–302.

FURNITURE DETAILS

Doing panel construction. Panelled frames are found in doors, desks, and other case construction in which large areas must be enclosed. Fig. 14–1. The advantage of panel construction is that the complete unit does not warp as badly as a solid piece of similar size. Figs. 14–2 and 14–3.

The vertical members of the frame are called *stiles* and the horizontal members are called *rails*. There may be two or more rails, depending on how many panels are to be installed in a single unit. The rails are joined to stiles with either dowels, a stub mortise-and-tenon joint (sometimes called tongue-and-groove), or a haunched mortise-and-tenon joint.

1. Determine the size of the frame. The stiles are cut to the exact size and the rails are cut to provide sufficient material for the tenon.

2. Square up the stock.

3. Select the panel that is to be installed in the frame and decide on the method of installation. Usually a ¼″ or ⅜″ panel is used. Remember that the panel must be cut large enough to cover the opening and to fit into the groove.

4. Lay out and cut a groove on all edges in which the panel is to be fit. The groove is cut as deep as or slightly deeper than it is wide. This can be done on a circular saw or shaper.

14–1. PANEL CONSTRUCTION IN THE DOORS of a water pitcher cupboard. The cupboard is 61″ high, 44″ wide, and 20″ deep. COURTESY OF W. F. WHITNEY COMPANY, INC.

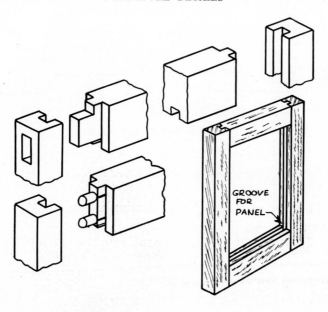

14–2. PANEL CONSTRUCTION.

5. Make the joint for joining the rails to the stiles. In making a stub mortise-and-tenon, the thickness of the tenon is the same as the width of the groove and the length of the tenon is the same as the depth of the groove. In making a haunched mortise-and-tenon joint, the thickness of the mortise should be the same as the width of the groove. The mortise should be started far enough away from the ends of the stiles to prevent breaking out. The width and depth of the mortise should be about two thirds the width of the rail. The length of the tenon should be equal to the depth of the mortise plus the depth of the groove. Cut a notch in the tenon so that the long part of the tenon will fit into the mortise opening and the short part will fit into the groove.

6. Make a trial assembly of the panel in the frame. Then take it apart and wax the edge of the panel. In gluing up the panel,

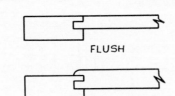

FLUSH

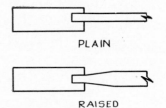

PLAIN

ELEVATED

RAISED

14–3. TYPES of panel surfaces.

apply the glue to the joint itself but *never to the edge of the panel or to the groove.*

7. In some cases, panel construction is made with a rabbet cut around the inside edge of the frame so that this side of the door is flush. In such a case, the panel must be glued or fastened in place.

Treating the edge of plywood. Plywood is a very desirable material for building modern furniture. Fig. 14–4. Its chief dis-

14–4a. HERE'S ANOTHER METHOD of edge treatment. Handsome results can be obtained by cutting a V groove and inserting a matching wood strip. This method is quite difficult. 14–4b. THIN STRIPS OF VENEER (real wood) edge banding already coated with adhesive are available.

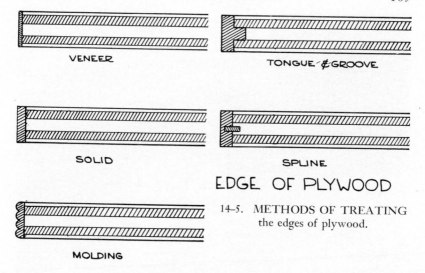

VENEER

TONGUE & GROOVE

SOLID

SPLINE

EDGE OF PLYWOOD

14-5. METHODS OF TREATING
the edges of plywood.

MOLDING

advantage, however, is that the exposed edge is unnattractive. Of course, this exposed edge can be covered with filler during the finishing process to blend with the remainder of the piece. Fig. 14–5. There are several better methods of covering it, however:

1. A thin veneer can be glued to the edge with a miter joint at each corner.

2. A solid piece of stock can be glued to the edge.

3. A piece of molding of any desired shape and size can be glued and/or nailed in place.

4. A solid wood piece can be joined to the edge with a tongue-and-groove joint.

5. A spline can be inserted between the plywood and solid wood edging.

Installing corner blocks and glue blocks. Corner blocks are installed on chairs, tables and other furniture pieces to strengthen corners which are the weakest points. Fig. 14–6. Select stock at least $1\frac{1}{2}''$ to $2''$ in thickness of some softwood such as pine or poplar. For square tables, cut the block as in Project 16. Make sure that the corners fit perfectly. Notch out the corner so the

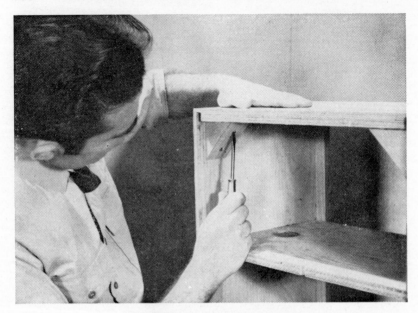

14–6. INSTALLING corner blocks.

block fits around the leg and against the rail. Drill at least two holes on either side and fasten firmly with screws.

On chairs and other objects that are not perfectly square, the correct included angle can be secured by holding a sliding T bevel over the flat pattern layout or over the object itself. Divide this angle in half for adjusting the circular saw, and cut a piece of block to fit the corner.

Glue blocks are small, triangular pieces of wood that are installed along the edges of two adjoining pieces to strengthen them. For example, when a frame is fit around the front of a case or cabinet, glue blocks are usually installed along the inside corners between the frame and case. Cut these three-cornered blocks in the same manner as corner blocks. Apply glue to the two edges and clamp in place with hand screws, or install nails or brads.

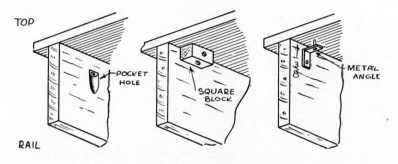

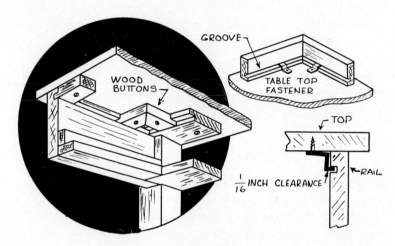

14–7. FASTENING tops to tables.

Fastening tops to tables and desks. There are several methods of permanently fastening the top to a piece of furniture that is made with leg and rail construction. Fig. 14–7.

1. To install flathead screws, drill a tapered hole from the inside of the rail to the upper edge.

2. Cut four wood cleats about ¾″ square to go along the sides and ends. Drill a series of holes from two directions in the piece. Fasten the cleat first to the rail, and then fasten the top by installing screws from the bottom of the cleat.

3. Cut a groove around the inside of the rail about ½" down from the upper edge. Use metal fasteners that slip into this groove, and screw them to the top.

4. The same method described in No. 3 can be followed by cutting a slightly wider groove. Then cut small blocks of wood, called buttons, with a rabbet on the ends to slip into the groove. Screw the buttons to the top.

Other methods are shown in Fig. 14–7.

Installing commercial legs. Tapered hardwood legs can be purchased in birch, mahogany, and other woods with a brass ferrule at the bottom. Fig. 14–8 a. Brass or aluminum legs can also be purchased. Common lengths are 7, 13, 17, 22 and 29

14–8a.   TAPERED LEG.

inches. Metal attaching brackets come with each set of legs. These brackets are made so that the legs can be fastened in a vertical (straight up and down) position or at a slight taper. On some types, the bracket itself is reversed: one position for straight legs, another for slanted legs. On other types the leg can be screwed into the metal bracket at two different positions.

Installing shelves. Modern furniture is flexible and therefore most shelves are made to be adjustable. There are several methods of doing this: Fig. 14–8 b.

1. Lay out a vertical line about 1" to 2" from either edge of the sides of the bookcase or shelf. Determine the spacing between the shelves and mark the location for a series of holes. Select suitable dowel rod and cut pins about 1" long. Drill or bore holes of this same size along the inside of the sides. Always place a stop on the drill or bit to avoid cutting a hole through the sides.

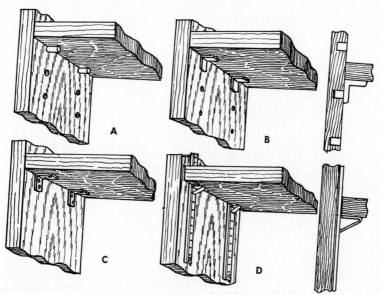

14–8b. METHODS OF INSTALLING SHELVES: (a) dowel pins,
(b) metal shelf pins, (c) fixed shelf brackets, (d) adjustable shelf brackets.

TWO GOOD MODERN TABLES, attractive for the beginner and handy to
use. IMPERIAL FURNITURE COMPANY.

CLEVER MODERN serving table. THE ROMWEBER COMPANY.

2. Follow the same method of drilling holes and install commercial adjustable shelf pins.

3. Permanently fasten the shelves with shelf brackets.

4. Use adjustable shelf brackets with snap-on clips. These can be obtained in any length. Two pieces are needed for either side. Install with screw-type nails. Cut shelves to length and then cut out small slots at the locations for the bracket strips. Ends of the shelves can be straight. For neater appearance, cut vertical grooves into which the brackets fit. Then the shelves do not have to be notched.

Making drawers and drawer guides. Drawers and drawer guides are found in desks, chests, tables and other built-ins. Fig. 14–9. Most drawers are made to fit flush in the opening. Some, however, have a lip that covers part of the drawer frame. A lip drawer has a rabbet cut about ⅜″ around the inside edge. The front of the drawer then is rounded. Fig. 13–14, page 100.

CARVED MODERN bedside tables. HEYWOOD-WAKEFIELD COMPANY.

NOTE THAT THIS CHARMING chairside table is exactly arm height. Holds lamp and ashtray. Is not "skimpy." HEYWOOD-WAKEFIELD COMPANY.

1. Determining the size of the drawer. Measure the opening (both height and width) into which the drawer will fit. There should be a clearance of about $\frac{1}{16}''$ on either side and $\frac{1}{16}''$ for height. Also measure the depth of the drawer. Fig. 14–10.

2. Choose the wood for the drawer. The front should match the rest of the project and should be as thick or slightly thicker than the other parts. Usually the front is $\frac{3}{4}''$ thick. The sides and back should be about $\frac{1}{2}''$ thick in a clear lumber such as pine, willow, oak or maple. The drawer bottom is most often made of $\frac{1}{4}''$ plywood or hardboard.

3. Select the front drawer joints. The three most common joints for joining the front to the sides are the rabbet, the drawer corner joint (rabbet and groove), and the dovetail.

a. The *rabbet* is made by cutting a recess on the inside of

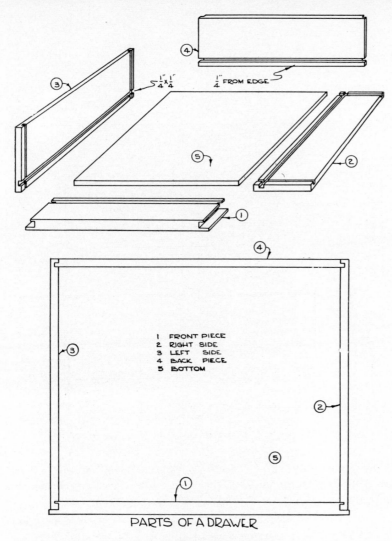

$5\frac{1''}{4} \times \frac{1''}{4}$ $\frac{1''}{4}$ FROM EDGE

1 FRONT PIECE
2 RIGHT SIDE
3 LEFT SIDE
4 BACK PIECE
5 BOTTOM

PARTS OF A DRAWER

14–9. PARTS of a drawer.

either end of the front. The depth of the rabbet should equal two thirds the thickness of the front. The width should be slightly more than the thickness of the sides to allow for clearance.

b. The drawer corner joint is often used to fasten the sides to the front because it is a strong joint that is easy to make on the circular saw. Fig. 14–11 shows this joint made with a ¾″

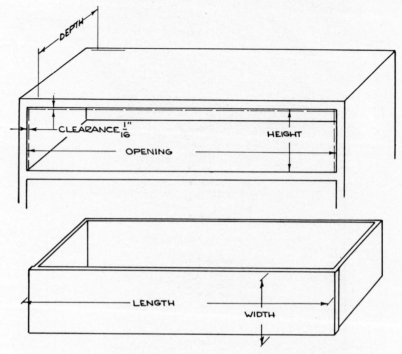

14-10.   MEASURING the size of a drawer front.

drawer front and ½″ sides. A clearance of ¹⁄₁₆″ is allowed for the front to extend beyond the sides. The steps in making this joint are as follows:

Step 1. Use a dado head that is ¼″ wide (see pages 197–198). Adjust the dado head to a height of slightly more than ¼″. Set the ripping fence to a distance of twice the width of the dado head measured from the left edge of the blade (double dado), or ½″. Cut dadoes on the inside face of the sides at the front end.

Step 2. Set the height of the dado head to an amount equal to the thickness of the sides plus ¹⁄₁₆″ (for front overlap), or ⁹⁄₁₆″. With the inside face of the front held against the fence, cut a dado across either end of the front.

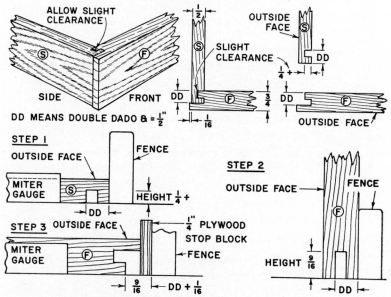

14–11. STEPS IN MAKING A DRAWER CORNER joint (rabbet and groove). Study this carefully before beginning to build a drawer.

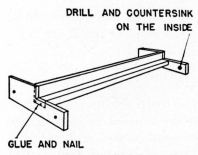

DRILL AND COUNTERSINK ON THE INSIDE

GLUE AND NAIL

14–12. SIMPLE GUIDE and runner.

Step 3. Set the dado head to a height of slightly more than ½″. Adjust the fence to a distance of ⁹⁄₁₆″ from the left edge of the dado head. Use a piece of ¼″ plywood for a stop block. Place the inside face against the table and trim off ⁵⁄₁₆″ from the inside tenon of the drawer front. The joint should slide together easily. Sometimes the joint is made with a narrow dado and thin tenon, as shown in Fig. 14–9.

c. Make a *dovetail joint* by using the portable router as described on pages 296 to 304.

4. Decide on the back drawer joints. The back can be joined to the sides with a *butt* joint, a *dado* joint or a *rabbet-and-dado*

joint. If the dado joint is used, it should be located at least $\frac{1}{2}''$ from the back edge of the drawer sides.

5. Cut the pieces for the drawer. If the drawer is to fit flush, the front is cut $\frac{1}{16}''$ narrower and $\frac{1}{8}''$ shorter than the opening measurements. If a lip drawer is being constructed, add $\frac{3}{4}''$ to this width and length. The length of the sides is found by measuring the overall depth of the drawer and then allowing for the kind of joint used in the front. The back is cut at least $\frac{1}{16}''$ narrower than the sides. Sometimes the back is cut $\frac{1}{2}''$ narrower so that the back rests on the top of the drawer bottom. The back is also cut somewhat shorter so that the back of the drawer is $\frac{1}{4}''$ narrower than the front when the drawer is completed.

6. Make the joints to join the sides to the front and the sides to the back. Cut a groove $\frac{1}{4}''$ wide and $\frac{1}{4}''$ deep, at least $\frac{1}{4}''$ from the bottom of the drawer on the inside of the front and sides. Cut the bottom itself slightly smaller than the full width and length to allow for expansion. If a center guide and slide is to be used, the bottom may have to be located higher than $\frac{1}{4}''$ from the lower edge of the drawer.

7. Assemble the drawer by fastening the sides to the front with glue and/or nails. Slip the bottom in place but *never* apply glue to the edges. Fasten the back to the sides.

Make the *drawer guides* as follows:

1. There are several kinds of drawer guides. The simplest is the guide and runner which is placed under the lower corners of the drawer. Fig. 14–12. These are constructed by cutting two pieces of stock long enough to go between the front and back rails. A rabbet which forms the guide and runner for the drawer is then cut out. These are fastened in place by gluing and/or screws.

2. The side guide and runner is made by cutting a grove along the outside of either side of the drawer. Fig. 14–13 a. This can be located anyplace on the side, usually toward or slightly above center. Two pieces of stock are then cut long enough to extend between the front and back rails. A rabbet is cut along

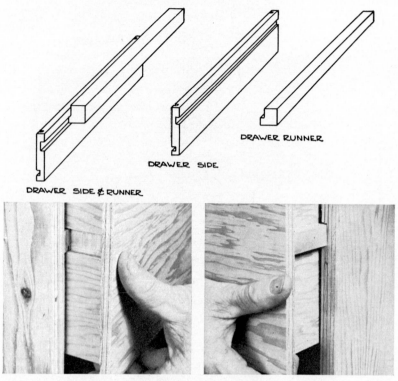

DRAWER RUNNER

DRAWER SIDE

DRAWER SIDE & RUNNER

14–13. (a) DRAWING SHOWING THE CONSTRUCTION of a side guide and runner for a desk or table. (b) A GROOVE is cut in the side of the drawer. A strip is fastened to the inside of the chest or cabinet. (c) THE PROCEDURE is reversed. Here the cabinet or chest side has a dado cut across it. A matching strip is fastened to the side of the drawer. Wax or lubricate with paraffin after finishing so that the drawer will slide easily.

the length. The tenon formed slips into the groove in the drawer side. The runner is fastened between the front and back rail on which the drawer slides or to the underside of the top of the furniture piece. Fig. 14–13 b & c show two other ways.

3. The best drawer guide is the center drawer guide and runner. The drawer guide is fastened to the frame of the chest or desk or between the front and back rails and the runner or

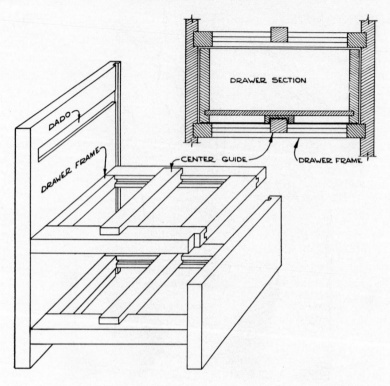

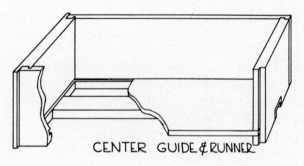

CENTER GUIDE & RUNNER

14-14. CENTER GUIDE and runner.

slide fastened to the center of the bottom of the drawer. **Fig. 14–14.** The drawer guide is simply a rectangular piece of stock usually rounded in the front. A second rectangular piece of stock has a groove cut along its length which slides over this guide. When installing the guides to a frame, such as in chest construction, a rabbet is cut out on either end of the guide or a dado on the back and a rabbet on the front, and the guide glued and/or screwed in place. The slide or runner is glued to the bottom of the drawer and oftentimes a few brads are installed to hold it firm. A notch must also be cut out of the bottom of the drawer back to provide clearance for the guide.

Hanging a door. Doors are installed principally on cabinets and desks and certain kinds of small tables. The door itself may be of solid wood or plywood on most modern furniture. It is usually of panel construction on Early American furniture. Most doors are fit flush into an opening, although in some cases a rabbet is cut around the inside edge with the door overlapping the frame. This is called a *lip door*.

FITTING A FLUSH DOOR

1. Check with a square to see that the frame of the opening is square. Sometimes the opening is slightly "out of square," in which case the door must be carefully cut to fit.

2. Measure the height at several points and cut off the top and bottom so that it will slip into the frame. It may be necessary to hold the door up to the opening several times and plane off a little to get it to fit.

3. Measure the width of the opening at top and bottom. Transfer this measurement to the door and cut to fit.

4. Sometimes, in making a double door such as is shown in the cabinet, Project No. 18, it is desirable to have the doors overlap at the center by cutting a rabbet on the front edge of one door and the rear edge of the other. In this case, allow an amount equal to one half the width of the rabbet on each of the doors.

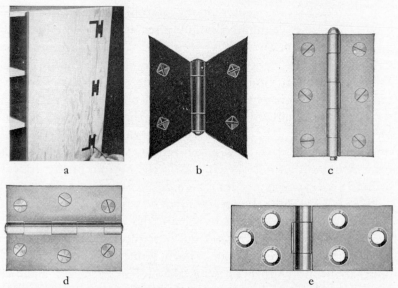

a   b   c

d   e

14-15a. SURFACE HINGES are easy to install since they require no gain. When properly selected they are ornamental. They come in styles to fit any furniture. 14-15b.   EARLY AMERICAN SURFACE HINGE.   14-15c. PLAIN FLUSH BUTT PIN. 14-15d.   TIGHT BUTT HINGE. 14-15e. TABLE LEAF HINGE.

5. Place the door in the frame opening and check it carefully. The edge away from the hinge side is frequently cut at a slight bevel so that, when it swings open or closed, the inside edge will not strike the frame, yet the door will be tight when closed. Fig. 14-15 a & b.

INSTALLING BUTT HINGES

Usually a door is hung by two hinges but, if it is to support great weight, a third is installed at the middle. The butt hinges should be proportioned to the size of the door. Fig. 14-15 c, d & e. A 1-inch butt hinge, for example, would be satisfactory for a 1- to 2-foot door, a 2-inch butt hinge for a 2- to 4-foot door, and a 3-inch butt hinge for doors that support considerable weight.

1. Place the door in the opening and put small wedges below and away from the hinge side to hold the door in place. Measure

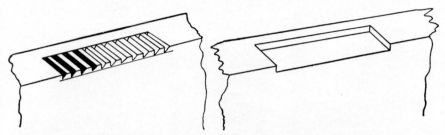

14–16. CUTTING a gain.　　　14–17. A GAIN ready to receive the hinge.

up from the bottom and down from the top and mark a line on the door and frame to indicate the top and bottom of the two hinges. Remove the door from the opening.

2. Continue the line with a try square across the edge of the frame and the door to indicate the position of the hinge.

3. Place the hinge over the edge of the door and determine how far the hinge is to extend beyond the door. Draw a line to indicate the depth of the hinge. Do this on both door and frame.

4. Measure the thickness of one leaf of the hinge and set a marking gauge to this amount. Mark a line on the door and the frame to indicate this depth.

5. Cut the gain (the opening for the hinge) by hand with a chisel as shown in Fig. 14–16. Outline the gain and then cut small notches in the stock to be removed. Trim out the gain. Fig. 14–17. If a portable router is available, this job can be done quickly.

6. Place the hinge in the door edge, drill pilot holes for the screws, and attach the hinge.

7. Hold the door against the frame, mark the position of one hole on either hinge, and drill a pilot hole. Insert one screw in each hinge.

8. Check to see if the door operates properly. If the door stands away too much from the frame side, it may be necessary to do more trimming. This should be done toward the front edge of the frame. If the door binds on the hinge side, cut a little piece of cardboard to go under the hinge. When the door operates properly, install the other screws.

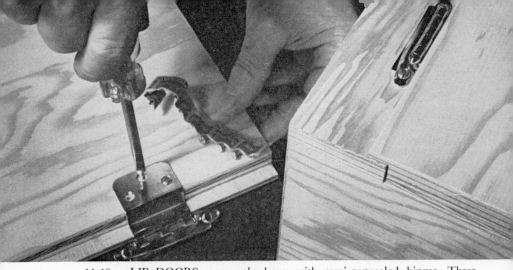

14–18a. LIP DOORS are neatly hung with semi-concealed hinges. These hinges have ½″ inset and are made for ¾″ (thick) doors rabbeted to leave a ½″ lip.

FITTING A LIP DOOR

A lip door does not require as accurate fitting, since the door itself covers part of the frame. Measure the width of the opening and add twice the amount of the lip or overhang to the width and the height of the door. Cut a rabbet equal to half this amount around three or four sides of the door. (All four sides should be rabbeted when it is a single door and only three sides when it is a double door.) The rabbet should be half or more the thickness of the stock in depth. Usually the front edge of the door is rounded on all sides. This can be done on a shaper or sander.

INSTALLING A SEMI-CONCEALED HINGE

The semi-concealed hinge is used most frequently for the lip

14–18b. MAKING A CLOSE-FITTING DOOR by rabbeting the top and bottom edges of the doors. 14–18c. CUTTING GROOVES deeper at the top than at the bottom so that the doors can be easily inserted and removed.

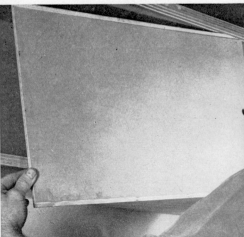

14–18d. THIS IS ONLY ONE TYPE OF COMMERCIAL TRACK that can be used to make sliding doors. 14–18e. SLIDING DOORS can be equipped with finger cups that are forced into round holes. Round pulls or rectangular grips of wood are suitable when clearance between the doors is adequate.

or overhang door. Fig. 14–18. Mark the location of the hinge on the inside of the door and install the hinges on the door itself. Hold the door with the two hinges against the frame, mark the position for the other screws, and fasten in place.

SLIDING DOORS

Close-fitting sliding doors of plywood are made by rabbeting the top and bottom edges of each door. Rabbet the back of the front door and the front of the back door. This lets the door almost touch, leaving a little gap for dust. This also increases the effective depth of the cabinet. For ⅜″ plywood doors, rabbet half their thickness. Then cut two grooves in the top and bottom

14–19. A CHEST WITH EXPOSED FRAMES. COURTESY OF W. F. WHITNEY COMPANY, INC.

14–20. THE INSIDE OF A CHEST, showing the frames and drawer guides. On this chest, moldings will be fastened to the front and the drawer fronts will cover the frames.

of the cabinet ½″ apart. Always seal the edges and back of the doors with the same material as the front so that the doors will not warp. Fig. 14–18 b. To make the doors removable, cut the bottom grooves ³⁄₁₆″ deep and the top grooves ³⁄₈″ deep. After the doors are finished, they can be inserted by slipping them into the excess space in the top grooves. Then they are dropped into the bottom grooves. Fig. 14–18 c. A metal, plastic, or wood track can also be installed above and below for the sliding doors. Fig. 14–18 d. Hardboard can also be used for sliding doors. A hole can be drilled near the center right end to serve as an opener. A recessed metal fitting or a surface piece can also be used as a handle. Fig. 14–18 e.

Making chests. Chest construction is a type of carcass work which includes making a case, drawers, and drawer guides and runners. Fig. 14–19. In making a chest, proceed as follows:

1. Determine the width, height and depth of the chest. Cut the sides, top, and bottom. Sometimes a bottom piece is unnecessary.

2. Determine the kind of joints that will be used to join the sides to the top and bottom. The most common ones are the rabbet, miter or dado, or an adaptation of one of these.

3. Make the joints to assemble the chest. Cut a rabbet around the inside back edge of the sides, top, and bottom to install a panel.

4. Determine the location of the drawers and cut dadoes, either plain or stop, in the sides to receive the frames.

124

5. Make the frames that separate the drawers. Fig. 14–20. The frames themselves are made with a dowel butt joint, a miter butt joint, or a mortise-and-tenon joint. On superior drawer construction, these frames are made as in panel construction to prevent the accumulation of dust in the drawers. If the front of the frame is to be exposed, it should be made of the same wood as the exterior of the chest. If not, the frames can be made of some good, clear softwood. Assemble the frames. Fasten the exterior to the frames.

6. Make the drawers. Cut the stock for the drawer fronts to cover the openings. Build the drawer as desired. Make the drawer guides and runners. Install these guides and runners to fit the drawers.

7. Install the back panel.

Making chairs. Building the conventional chair is the most difficult job in furniture construction for the following reasons: None of the parts is at a right angle to the next; the front of the chair is wider than the back; the back legs are arched; and the distance across the top of the back legs is greater than the distance across the bottom. Fig. 14–21. Frequently the back rungs are cut in a slight arc for comfort.

If mortise-and-tenon joints are used for joining the legs to the rails, it means that all the shoulder cuts on the tenons must be at a slight angle in order that the sides can taper from front to back.

The first step is to lay out a seat plan, which should be full size. From this, the angle at which the rails fit into the legs can be determined. Also, a full-size plan of the back and side of the chair must be made. This will determine the angle of the mortises in the back legs. All of these angles can be determined by using a sliding T bevel on the full-size pattern and transferring the angle directly to the stock.

Installing common hardware. The directions for installing hinges will be found in the previous instructions, "Hanging a Door."

14–21a. A PHOTOGRAPH and (14–21b) complete drawing of a chair. Notice the layout that must be made for determining the correct angles for joining the parts, 14–21c. COURTESY OF THE ATLAS PRESS COMPANY.

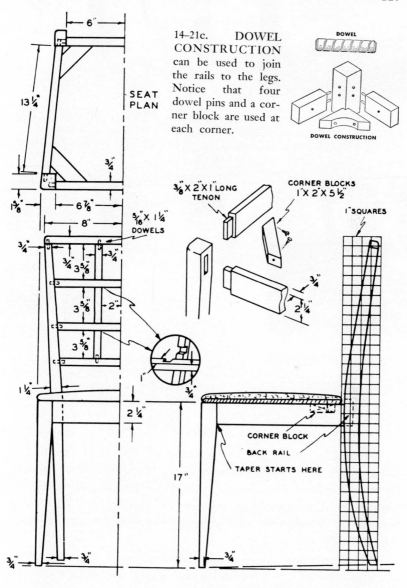

14–21c. **DOWEL CONSTRUCTION** can be used to join the rails to the legs. Notice that four dowel pins and a corner block are used at each corner.

DOWEL

DOWEL CONSTRUCTION

SEAT PLAN

$\frac{3}{8}$" X 2" X 1" LONG TENON

CORNER BLOCKS 1" X 2" X 5 $\frac{1}{2}$"

$\frac{5}{16}$" X 1 $\frac{1}{4}$" DOWELS

1" SQUARES

CORNER BLOCK

BACK RAIL

TAPER STARTS HERE

14–21b

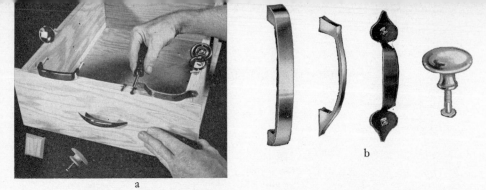

b

a

14–22a. DRAWER PULLS AND DOOR HANDLES are available in great variety. Use metal or wood to suit your project. These are designed for traditional, Early American, and modern furniture. 14–22b. TYPES OF HANDLES.

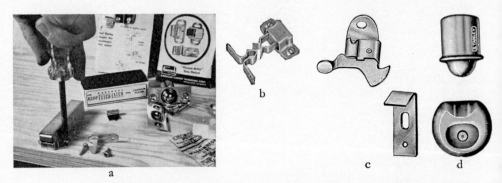

b

c

d

a

14–23a. CATCHES COME IN MANY VARIETIES. The touch type being installed here allows the door to open at a touch. The magnetic catch, extreme left, has no moving parts. 14–23b. SPRING-TYPE CATCH. 14–23c. ELBOW CATCH. 14–23d. BALL-TYPE FRICTION CATCH.

DRAWER AND DOOR PULLS AND KNOBS

These are usually located in the exact center of the drawer front or are installed by pairs, centered vertically on the drawer front and spaced far enough apart to be convenient in use. In most cases, drawer pulls are installed by drilling or boring a hole completely through the drawer front and installing screws from the back side. Fig. 14–22.

Door pulls and knobs are usually located quite close to the opening edge of the door and at a position convenient for use. These are installed in much the same manner as drawer pulls and knobs.

Catches

There are several types of catches available, including the friction, clip, ball, and magnetic. Fig. 14–23. These are all in two parts, one to fit on the door and the other to fit on the furniture piece itself. Catches should usually be installed near the handle, for smoother operation.

Locks

There are many different kinds of drawer and cabinet locks that can be purchased. Modern and Early American furniture usually require a concealed type of lock that is fit in or on the back of the door.

14–24. TABLE LEAF support.

Table leaf hinges and supports

The hinges used for drop table leaves are often of a special type to enable the leaf to drop back and under the table top. The table leaf support is available in many sizes, the width of the rail determining the maximum size that can be selected. Fig. 14–24.

ASSEMBLING FURNITURE

The steps in assembling a project are determined largely by how complicated it is. On simple projects, all parts can be assembled at one time. On more complicated ones—such as a table with four legs, rails, and a top—it may be a two- or three-stage job. It is often better to glue the two legs and a rail to form the

15–1. PROJECT clamped up.

sides or ends as a sub-assembly and later to glue these to the other two rails. Then the top is fastened in place.

Follow these steps:

1. Get all parts together and check to see that they are completed, including sanding. Make sure that you have identification marks on all pieces so that you know exactly how they are to go together. Check this and see that all joints fit properly.

2. Decide on whether the project is to be assembled with glue, screws, or nails. Most furniture pieces have screws and glue as part of the assembly.

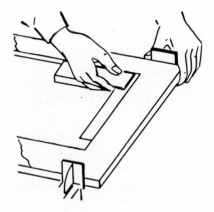

15-3.   CHECKING   ACROSS
THE CORNERS for squareness.

15-2. CHECKING AN ASSEMBLY
with a square.

15-4.   CHECKING   WITH   A
STRAIGHT-EDGE for levelness.

3. Cut a number of scrap pieces of stock that will be used to protect the wood from being marred by the clamps.

4. Get out the clamps and adjust them to the correct openings.

5. If sub-assemblies are to be glued up, decide on which parts are to be assembled first.

6. Make a temporary assembly of the parts to see that the piece will clamp up properly. Fig. 15-1. At this point check with a square and rule to see that the parts are at correct angles to each other, are parallel and level. Fig. 15-2. This can usually be done by measuring at various points. Fig. 15-3 and Fig. 15-4. Sometimes it may be necessary to do a little hand trimming or to shift the clamps.

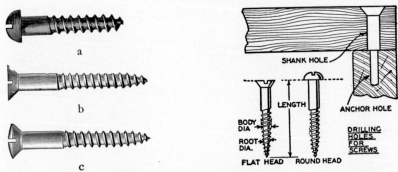

15-5. TYPES OF SCREWS: (a) roundhead, (b) flathead, and (c) ovalhead.
15-6. DRILLING HOLES for wood screws.

7. If screws are to be used, select the right ones by consulting the chart. Fig. 15-7. In most cases, the size of the screw is shown on the drawing or print; for example, No. 9 R.H. 1¼, which means that the screw is No. 9 gauge size, roundhead, and 1¼ inches long.

8. When assembling with glue, mix only the amount needed at one time. Many kinds must stand for 10 to 15 minutes before they can be used. Cover the top of the workbench with paper. Lay the clamps out in proper position. Have the scrap blocks handy and a rubber mallet ready. Also have a square and rule nearby.

9. Carefully apply the glue to the joints. Be careful not to put on too much. Apply a little extra glue on the end grain, which soaks it up.

10. Quickly assemble the parts, place the scrap pieces over the project, and apply the clamps. Do not apply too much pressure. Then quickly check with a square and rule to see that everything is true. If necessary, a clamp can be shifted or a joint can be tapped with a rubber mallet to bring it into place.

11. When the project is clamped together, remove the excess glue and store the part or piece where it can dry without being bumped. If it is a sub-assembly, after these parts are dry, complete the entire assembly.

Length	Shank Number																
	0	1	2	3	4	5	6	7	8	9	10	11	12	14	16	18	20
¼ inch				3	4	5	6										
⅜ inch		1	2	3	4	5	6	7									
½ inch			2	3	4	5	6	7	8								
⅝ inch				3	4	5	6	7	8	9	10						
¾ inch							6	7	8	9	10	11					
⅞ inch							6	7	8	9	10	11	12				
1 inch							6	7	8	9	10	11	12	14	16		
1¼ inch								7	8	9	10	11	12	14	16	18	
1½ inch									8	9	10	11	12	14	16	18	20
1¾ inch									8	9	10	11	12	14	16	18	20
2 inch										9	10	11	12	14	16	18	20
2¼ inch											10	11	12	14	16	18	20
0 to 20 Diameter Dimensions in Inches at Body	.060	.073	.086	.099	.112	.125	.138	.151	.164	.177	.190	.203	.216	.242	.268	.294	.320

TWIST DRILL AND BIT SIZES FOR DRILLING SHANK AND ANCHOR OR PILOT HOLES

	0	1	2	3	4	5	6	7	8	9	10	11	12	14	16	18	20
Shank Hole Hard & Soft Wood	1/16	5/64	3/32	7/64	7/64	1/8	9/64	5/32	11/64	3/16	3/16	13/64	7/32	1/4	17/64	19/64	21/64
Anchor or Pilot Hole Soft Wood	1/64	1/32	1/32	3/64	3/64	1/16	1/16	1/16	5/64	5/64	3/32	3/32	7/64	7/64	9/64	9/64	11/64
Anchor or Pilot Hole Hard Wood	1/32	1/32	3/64	1/16	1/16	5/64	5/64	3/32	3/32	7/64	7/64	1/8	1/8	9/64	5/32	3/16	13/64
Auger Bit Sizes for Countersunk Heads			3	4	4	4	5	5	6	6	6	7	7	8	9	10	11

15-7. SCREW CHART.

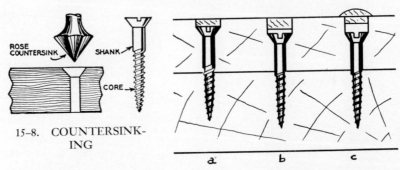

15-8. COUNTERSINK-
ING

15-9. THREE METHODS of covering the heads of screws: (a) with plastic wood; (b) with a plain wood plug, and (c) with a fancy wood plug.

Screws. Corner blocks are usually installed with screws. Screws are used to fasten the top of a project to the bottom and also can be used to fasten trim or a frame to the front of a bookcase, chest, or cabinet.

Screws can be purchased in flat, round, or oval heads. Fig. 15-5 a b c. The roundhead screws often are blued while the flathead are of bright steel or brass. Screws are available in lengths from ¼″ to 5″ and in diameters from 0 to 24 gauge. Note that the same *length* screw can be purchased in several different *diameters*. If screws are to be recessed below the surface of the wood, it is necessary to counterbore a hole. In installing screws, two holes are necessary, the hole in the first piece of wood, called the *shank* or *clearance hole*, and a hole in the second piece, called the *pilot hole*. Fig. 15-6. The correct size drill to use for these two holes is shown in Fig. 15-7. Drill the clearance hole in the first piece; then hold this piece over the second and, with a scratch awl, mark the location of the pilot hole. If installing flathead screws, countersink the upper surface so the head of the screw will be flush. Fig. 15-8. If you have used the counterbore, fill the hole after assembly with plastic wood or a plain or fancy wood plug. Fig. 15-9 a b c.

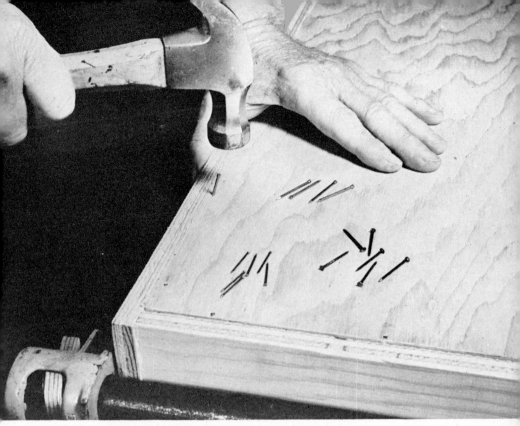

15-10. NAILING A BACK PANEL into the rabbet using 1" brads or 4d finishing nails.

Nails. There is only a limited use for nails in furniture construction. Fig. 15-10. In some cases, however, simple, modern furniture is assembled with nails. The only ones used are *finishing nails* and *brads*. The most common sizes are shown in Fig. 15-11. When joining parts with nails, always select a nail that is at least twice as long as the thickness of the first piece. If nailing is to be done in hardwood, drill a small pilot hole in both pieces to within one half the depth of the nail length. When installing nails, drive the nail into the wood until it is within a short distance of the face of the stock; then drive the head slightly below the surface with a nail set. Brads are used most often to join back panels to furniture pieces.

FINISHING NAILS AND BRADS

FINISHING NAILS

Size	Length	Gauge	Diameter Head Gauge
3d	1¼"	15½	12½
4d	1½"	15	12
6d	2"	13	10
8d	2½"	12½	9½
10d	3"	11½	8½

BRADS

Length in inches	Gauge (Available in following range)
½"	20
⅜"	20
½"	20 to 16
⅝"	20 to 16
¾"	20 to 16
⅞"	20 to 16
1"	20 to 14
1¼"	18 to 14
1½"	17 to 12
1¾"	15 to 12
2"	16 to 12
2½"	13 to 10
3"	12 to 11

Decimal equivalent of gauge number is:

21 = .032	13 = .092
20 = .035	12 = .106
19 = .041	11 = .121
18 = .047	10 = .135
17 = .054	9 = .148
16 = .063	8 = .162
15 = .072	7 = .177
14 = .080	

15-11. FINISHING nails and brads.

Section IV
Woodfinishing

PREPARING WOOD FOR
FINISHING

16–1. HAND SANDING a project after assembly.

When the project is assembled and has been allowed to dry properly, considerable time should be spent in preparing the piece for finishing in order to secure excellent results. *The first step is to remove all excess glue.* Use a sharp chisel to remove carefully all traces of glue around the joints. If any glue was spilled on the surface, remove by scraping. Never attempt to remove glue by sanding alone, since this will often force the glue into the wood and make an imperfection.

The second step is to inspect the surface carefully for dents or irregularities. A small dent in the wood can be raised by applying hot water to the area and allowing it to stand for some time. If the dent cannot be raised or if a hole or similar irregularity exists, it can be filled with stick shellac or plastic wood. *Stick shellac* is available in many different colors, can be heated with Bunsen burner or other gas flame, and the soft shellac dropped in the irregularity. *Plastic wood* can be applied from the can or tube. The craftsman can also make a filler by *mixing fine sawdust* from the sander *with liquid glue.* This will often match the original wood surface better than either of the other two preparations.

The third step is to scrape and/or sand the surface thoroughly. Fig. 16–1. A thoroughly sanded piece is one from which all machine marks, scratches, or imperfections have been removed. The final sanding is usually done with 2/0 or 3/0 paper. Always remember to work *with the grain*, never against it. The following information covers the basic abrasives used in woodworking.

Abrasives used in woodworking. There are three basic kinds of abrasives used in woodworking:

1. *Flint*, a greyish material made of soft sandstone, is good only for simple hand sanding and does not stand up well.

2. *Garnet*, a reddish-brown, hard, natural mineral, is excellent for hand sanding and for some kinds of power sanding.

3. *Aluminum oxide*, an artificial abrasive, either reddish-

brown or white in color, is used almost exclusively in commercial furniture making. It is excellent for all power sanding operations.

GRADES OF ABRASIVES

There are two methods of marking abrasives. One method is to number the abrasive according to the size screen through which it was graded. This method is used primarily for aluminum oxide. The other method is to give the abrasive a size number. This method is most often used for flint or garnet. Here is a comparison of the two:

	ALUMINUM OXIDE	FLINT AND GARNET		ALUMINUM OXIDE	FLINT AND GARNET
Very Fine	240	7/0	Medium	100	2/0
	220	6/0		80	0
				60	1/2
				50	1
Fine	180	5/0	Coarse	40	1 1/2
	150	4/0		36	2
	120	3/0		30	2 1/2

BACKING

The backing for the abrasive may be paper or cloth. Most abrasives have a paper back but the cloth is best for power sanding operations, especially belt sanding.

TYPES

Abrasives are available in many different types. Use 9" x 11" sheets for hand sanding. Cut for the finishing sander. Use narrower rolls for making belts for belt sanders and wide rolls for making discs for disc sanders. Of course, most manufacturers of sanders have prepared belts and discs of various grades to fit their machines.

GENERAL INSTRUCTIONS FOR FINISHING WOODS

The finishing process varies with the kind of wood and the appearance desired. Fig. 17–1. Today the finisher has many choices of materials, some of which have greatly simplified his job. He can use not only the standard wood finishes such as shellac, varnish, or lacquer, but many specialized commercial finishes that have been especially designed to simplify the finishing process. One excellent finish, for example, which adds great

17–1. TO PRODUCE LIGHT FURNITURE like this, it has been necessary to bleach the wood. COURTESY OF THE WIDDICOMB FURNITURE COMPANY.

beauty to the natural wood, is a three-step process that can all be applied with cloths. No brushes or mixing containers are needed. Dust does not effect the finish. It is simple and foolproof and has been used very successfully by the author on many of the projects in this book. Complete directions can be obtained from the manufacturer. (See item A under "Finishing Supplies" in the *Appendix*.)

While the procedure varies for each different kind of wood, the general method to follow in applying standard wood finishes is as follows. (Complete directions for doing each step are given in one of the later sections.)

1. *Bleaching*. The first step in many light finishes is to bleach the wood. Many natural or darker finishes do not require bleaching.

2. *Staining*. This adds color to the wood and enhances the grain. In some light and natural finishes no stain is applied. Use either a water or an oil stain.

3. *Filling*. Fillers add color and close the pores of the wood. Closed-grain woods, like pine, cherry, poplar, fir, and cedar, require no fillers. Others, like birch, gum, and maple, require a liquid filler. (White shellac is good.) Open-grain woods such as oak, mahogany, and walnut require a paste filler. For some natural finishes, both the filler and stain are eliminated. For many blond, bleached, or "decorator" finishes, the filler can be white lead, white zinc, or a natural paste filler colored with yellow ochre, raw sienna, burnt sienna, or even red, black, green, or blue.

4. *Sealing*. A sealer is applied over stain and/or filler to prevent the color from bleeding into the finish. A good sealer for most finishes is the shellac wash coat. This is a mixture of seven parts alcohol to one part shellac, using a four-pound cut of shellac. If a lacquer finish is to be applied, a regular lacquer sealer can be used in place of the wash coat of shellac.

5. *Applying the finish*. A shellac, varnish, or lacquer finish can be applied after sealing. Usually, two or more coats are required. Always sand the surface with 5/0 paper after each finish.

To give a rubbed finish to varnish or lacquer, rub on pumice or rottenstone after the second and third coats. Apply shellac and varnish finishes with a brush. Lacquer can be applied with a brush but is more satisfactory if sprayed. After the second and final coat, all finishes can be made smoother by first rubbing with pumice stone in oil and then rottenstone in oil, using a felt pad. A final coat of paste wax can be applied over any finish to protect it.

Some sample finishes. While specific finishes cannot be given for all woods, here are a few common ones:

OAK

1. *Golden oak.* Bleach, apply filler of white zinc tinted with yellow ochre and raw sienna, seal, and apply several coats of lacquer.

2. *Wheat oak.* Bleach, stain with a wheat-colored oil stain, apply natural paste filler tinted lightly with raw sienna and burnt sienna, seal, and lacquer.

3. *Limed oak.* Bleach, apply sealer, white paste filler or white lead, seal, and lacquer.

MAHOGANY

1. *Natural.* Apply the three-step cloth finish. (See item A under "Finishing Supplies" in the *Appendix.*)

2. *Harvest wheat.* Bleach, stain with wheat-colored oil stain, fill with paste filler colored with same colored stain, seal, and lacquer.

3. *Red mahogany.* Apply red mahogany stain, wipe off, leaving dark areas in corners and recesses, seal, and lacquer.

WALNUT

1. *Natural.* Apply wash coat of shellac, fill with walnut filler, seal, and apply several coats of spar varnish.

2. *Harvest.* Bleach, fill with light brown filler, seal, and apply several coats of spar varnish. Add flat varnish if desired.

PINE

1. *Honey*. Make honey-colored stain by mixing one part light oak oil stain to five parts turpentine. Add several drops of red color in oil. Apply to the surface. Add sealer and then several coats of shellac or varnish.

2. *Knotty pine*. Add raw sienna and burnt sienna to naphtha. Then mix with linseed oil. Apply to the surface and wipe off. Seal and apply several coats of lacquer.

FIR PLYWOOD

Natural finish. Follow these four steps:

1. Thin one part interior white undercoat with one part turpentine or paint thinner. After it has been applied 10 or 15 minutes, or when it becomes tacky, wipe thoroughly with a dry cloth. Sand lightly.

2. Apply a coat of sealer, using white shellac.

3. Add color by using tinted interior undercoat, enamel, or color in oil. Apply thinly and wipe to proper color depth.

4. Apply a coat of flat varnish.

FINISHING SUPPLIES

Finishing supplies needed depend upon the kind of finishes required. A few of the more common ones are listed here:

1. *Brushes*. There are many styles, including flat, round, and oval. The best have a chisel-shaped point. The sizes vary from 1″ to 4″ in width but an average of 2½″ is good for most work. An excellent medium-hard bristle is made from Chinese boar hair set in rubber. For varnishing, softer bristles such as fitch hair are good, while camel's hair brushes are desirable for hand lacquering.

It is important to care properly for the brushes you use. Keep varnish brushes in a solution of half turpentine and half varnish. Keep shellac brushes in alcohol, and lacquer brushes in lacquer thinner. Always suspend the brushes in solvent, never allowing them to rest on the bottom of the container. To do this, drill a hole in the handle and insert a wire that will suspend the brush in the container.

Always clean the brushes after they have been used for the last time—first with solvent, then with soapy water. Rinse thoroughly in warm water. Dry and wrap in waxed paper.

2. *Turpentine.* Turpentine is made of resin drippings from pine trees and is used as a solvent and thinner for varnish, paints, and enamels.

3. *Linseed oil.* Linseed oil is available in raw state or as boiled linseed oil. The boiling improves the drying qualities.

4. *Alcohol.* Alcohol is used as a thinner and solvent for shellac.

5. *Benzine.* Benzine is used as a solvent and as a cleaning fluid.

6. *Pumice.* Pumice is a white powder made from lava. It is one of the buffing and polishing compounds needed for smoothing finishes. No. 1 is for coarse rubbing and No. FF or FFF for fine rubbing.

7. *Rottenstone.* Rottenstone is a reddish-brown or greyish-black substance for smoother rubbing than pumice.

8. *Rubbing oil.* This should be a good quality petroleum or paraffin oil.

9. *Steel wool.* Steel wool, sometimes used in place of sandpaper, is used for rubbing after certain finishing operations. It is available in four grades: 0—coarse, 00—medium, 000—fine, and 0000—extra fine.

10. *Wet-dry abrasive paper.* Waterproof aluminum-oxide paper in grades 240 or 320 is used with water for sanding between finishing coats.

FINISHING PROCEDURE

Following are detailed directions for the different steps in the finishing process:

Bleaching wood. Many modern furniture pieces that have an extremely light finish require bleaching. The major disadvantage of bleaching is that it weakens the wood cells and removes many of the natural oils. Also, many woods will not bleach evenly, resulting in light and dark areas that become more pronounced than when in the natural state. It is necessary, however, to bleach woods to secure the light finishes such as blond oak or harvest-wheat mahogany.

For simple bleaching of small articles, a mixture of oxalic acid crystals and hot water is effective. This should be brushed on the wood, allowed to remain 10 to 15 minutes, and then a hypo brushed on such as that used in photography work (3 ounces sodium hyposulphate to one quart of water). Neutralize by applying a mild solution of borax. To bleach furniture of any size it is far better to use a commercial bleach. There are two kinds. One has a "one" and "two" solution requiring the first to be applied to the wood, followed a short time after by the second solution. The second kind has a "one" and "two" solution that are mixed together just before applying.

Always apply commercial bleaches with a rope brush. Follow the directions given by the manufacturer. *Wear rubber gloves* and always put the bleaching materials in glass or crockery containers only. Also bleach *from the top down*, since the second application will usually lighten the wood still more.

Bleaching raises the grain and makes it necessary to do further sanding before proceeding with the finishing.

TWO MODERN PIECES dependent upon the proper finish for a handsome effect. THE WIDDICOMB FURNITURE COMPANY. IMPERIAL FURNITURE COMPANY.

Applying stains. Stains add color to wood and bring out the grain. While there are many kinds, the two most common are *oil* and *water stains.* Oil stains can be purchased commercially in colors such as light and dark walnut, light and dark oak, mahogany, and cherry. Almost any color is available. Oil stains can also be made by adding colors in oil to linseed oil and turpentine as follows: raw sienna and burnt sienna to make various shades of oak; raw sienna and yellow ochre to make limed oak; raw sienna, burnt sienna, and burnt umber to make various shades of mahogany; burnt umber and red to make various shades of walnut. Other colors in oil that are useful are black, Prussian blue, green, orange, plain red, and yellow.

147

Water stain is available in ready-mixed form or can be made by mixing powdered stain with hot water.

OIL STAIN

1. Mix the desired amount of oil stain in a porcelain or glass container. Oil stain will cover about 300 to 350 square feet per gallon.

2. Apply a thin coat of linseed oil to the end grain to prevent the wood from soaking up too much stain.

3. Select a clean brush of the desired size and dip it about one third into the stain. Start at the corners or the lower surfaces and work in and up. Use light strokes, brushing the stain evenly. Always begin an unfinished area and work toward the finished part. Apply stain to a surface, wipe softly with a clean cloth, and allow to dry 24 hours before proceeding.

WATER STAIN

Water stain raises the grain and therefore it is a good idea to sponge the wood surface lightly with water first, then sand with 5/0 sandpaper.

Apply the water stain in the same general manner as oil stain. Sponge the end grain just before the stain is applied to keep it from darkening too much. Allow water stain to dry from 10 to 12 hours. Sand lightly.

Applying fillers. Fillers are used to fill the wood pores and to add beauty to the wood. For open-grain woods, a commercial paste filler is best. This can be purchased in the natural color and mixed to various shades or in the color desired. White lead and zinc are also used as wood fillers, as they come from the can. These can also be tinted and are especially useful for modern bleached finishes.

PASTE FILLER

Mix the paste to the consistency of heavy cream by adding

the desired amount of turpentine. Test to see that the correct color is secured.

1. Apply the filler with a stiff brush, brushing first with the grain and then across it. Cover only a small area at a time.

2. Allow the filler to dry for a few minutes or until it loses its glossy appearance. Wipe off the excess across the grain with rough cloth or burlap.

3. Lightly rub the surface with the grain, using a piece of cheesecloth or other soft cloth to remove the excess. Do not press so hard that the filler is wiped out of the pores. After the filler has dried from six to eight hours, proceed with the finishing.

Applying a varnish finish. Varnish is a transparent finish made from gum, resins, and oils. There are many different kinds made for a variety of purposes. In furniture finishing, select a rubbing varnish or one made especially for this purpose. Complete directions are given by the manufacturer as to drying time and method of application.

The general finishing process is as follows:

1. *Secure suitable finishing conditions.* Since varnish is a slow-drying material, it is essential that the room be clean and dry and at a temperature between 70 and 80 degrees. Never varnish on a humid day or in dusty conditions.

2. *Select the right kind of varnish* and a good 1½" to 2" varnish brush. Pour the desired amount of varnish into a metal or glass container. Never varnish directly from the can. For the first coat, thin with about one fourth turpentine. When this step is completed, discard the remaining varnish mixture.

3. *Brush the surface thoroughly* to remove as much dust as possible, and then wipe with a tack rag. (This is a clean cloth dampened with turpentine into which about 2 or 3 tablespoons of varnish have been worked thoroughly. This cloth will pick up dust particles and specks.)

4. *Apply the varnish by first starting at a corner* and working inward. Dip the brush about one third into the varnish and apply it with smooth, even strokes. Start at either edge and brush to-

ward the center. Finally, when the entire surface is covered, without dipping the brush, use only the tip and brush lightly with the grain.

5. *With a small wood splinter pick out any dust specks.* It isn't necessary to rebrush these spots because varnish will fill in by itself.

6. *Allow it to dry thoroughly.* Rub with 5/0 wet or dry sandpaper, using a felt-back pad.

7. *Apply a second coat* without thinning the varnish. When it is dry, rub with pumice and water.

8. *For an extremely smooth job, apply a third coat.* Allow it to dry and rub with rottenstone and oil.

Applying a shellac finish. Shellac is a very desirable finish for many kinds of projects, although it is not waterproof. Shellac is also a good sealer over a stain or filler, and over knots before applying paint or enamel. Shellac is available in a natural yellow color or in bleached white. The orange is tougher but on many light finishes gives an undesirable yellowish cast. The standard shellac is called a "four-pound cut," which means that there are four pounds of shellac mixed to a gallon of alcohol. Another common mixture is the two-pound cut.

It is best to apply shellac in several thin coats.

1. *Mix an equal amount of four-pound cut shellac and alcohol* in a glass or porcelain container. Four-pound cut shellac will cover about 300 to 350 square feet per gallon. Select a good quality brush 1½″ to 2″ wide.

2. *Dip the brush about one third and wipe off the excess on the container.* Start near the center and top of a vertical surface or the middle of a horizontal surface. Brush out quickly in long, sweeping strokes. Do not go over the same area several times, since shellac dries very rapidly. Brush toward the edges and be careful not to allow the shellac to run over the edges and pile up. The tendency for a beginner is to put shellac on too thick.

3. *After the surface is completely covered, allow it to dry 3 to 4 hours.* Be sure to soak the brush in alcohol.

4. *Go over the surface with 5/0 sandpaper*, rubbing lightly.

5. *Apply a second coat with a slightly reduced alcohol mixture.* Allow it to dry and sand lightly.

6. *Apply a third coat with 25 per cent alcohol mixture.* After the last coat dries, rub with pumice or rottenstone in oil, using a felt pad. Wipe off lightly with benzine.

Applying a lacquer finish with a spray gun.

1. Always work in a spray booth or out of doors on a calm day. Wear a mask.

2. Check the gun. Fig. 19–1. It must be clean. Turn wide

19–1. A SMALL SPRAY GUN and compressor.

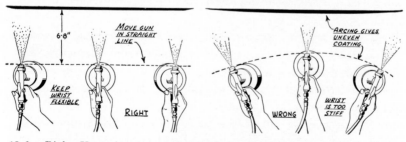

19–2. *Right:* Keep the gun moving back and forth with an even stroke at right angles to the surface. Don't tilt the gun up or down. *Wrong:* Never use an "arcing" motion.

open the adjusting screw that controls the flow of materials. Adjust the fluid flow at the pressure feed tank. Check the spreader control to make sure the spray pattern is wide enough.

3. Fill the spray can half full of lacquer and one fourth more with lacquer thinner.

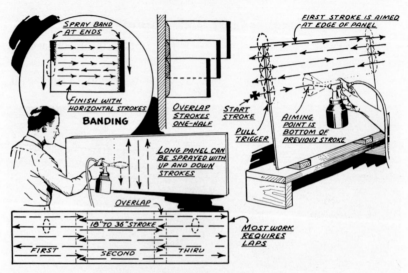

19–3. *Banding:* Vertical bands sprayed at the ends of a panel prevent overspray from horizontal strokes. Long work is sprayed in sections of convenient length, each section overlapping the previous section by 4″. When spraying a panel use alternate right and left strokes, triggering the gun at the beginning and end of each stroke. The spray should overlap one half the previous stroke.

4. Now try the spraying action on a scrap piece of wood.

5. Hold the gun about 6 to 8 inches from the work. Fig. 19–2. Move the gun with straight uniform strokes, going backwards and forwards. Never arc the gun. Keep it perpendicular to the work surface at all times.

6. Start the stroke off the work and pull the trigger when the gun is opposite the edge. Fig. 19–3. Release the trigger at the other edge but continue the stroke a few inches before reversing.

7. Clean all equipment with thinner immediately after use.

SAFETY

Safety is of prime importance in the operation of power tools.

1. *Do not use a machine until you understand it thoroughly.* Any tool with a sharp cutting edge can cause serious injury if mishandled. Many machines are equipped with guards. These guards don't prevent accidents, however, but merely indicate points of danger and must be used correctly to protect the operator. Also, it is impossible to do some operations, especially on the circular saw, with the guard in place. Therefore special care must be observed.

2. *Always wear tight-fitting clothes when working around machines.* Tuck in your tie and roll up your sleeves or wear a tight-fitting shop coat.

3. *Always keep your fingers away from the moving cutting edges.* The most common accident is caused by trying to run too small a piece through a machine.

4. *Keep the floor around the machine clean.* The danger from falling or slipping is always great.

5. *Make all adjustments with the power off and the machine at a dead stop.*

6. *Follow the suggestions for each machine given in this book.*

RADIAL ARM SAW

1. Always keep the safety guard and the anti-kickback device in position.

2. Make sure the clamps and locking handles are tight.

3. When crosscutting, adjust the anti-kickback device (sometimes called fingers) to clear the top of the work by about ⅛″. This acts as a guard to prevent your fingers from coming near the revolving saw.

4. For crosscutting, dadoing and similar operations, pull the saw into the work. *Cut on the forward stroke.*

5. Return the saw to the rear of the table after each cut.

6. For ripping, make sure that the blade is rotating upwards toward you. Use the anti-kickback device to hold the work

20–1. PARTS of the radial arm saw.

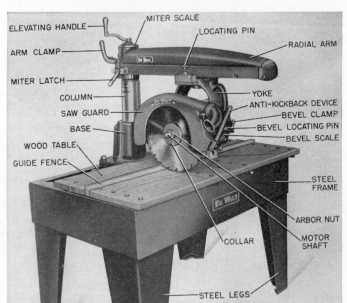

firmly against the table. Feed the stock from the end opposite the anti-kickback device.

7. Keep your hands away from the danger area—the path of the saw blade.

CROSSCUTTING

1. Mount a crosscutting or combination saw.

2. Adjust the radial arm to zero (at right angles to the guide fence), and set the motor so that the blade will be at right angles to the table top. Lock the radial arm with the arm clamp.

3. Turn the elevating handle down until the teeth are about $\frac{1}{16}''$ below the surface of the wood table. (The blade should follow the saw kerf already cut in the table.)

4. Adjust the anti-kickback device about $\frac{1}{8}''$ above the work surface.

5. With one hand hold the work on the table firmly against the guide fence. The layout line should be in line with the path of the saw.

6. Turn on the power and allow the saw to come to full speed. Grasp the motor yoke handle and pull the saw firmly but slowly through the work. Fig. 11–1, page 70.

7. When the cut is completed, return the saw behind the guide strip. Then turn off the power.

20–2. MAKING A RIGHTHAND MITER CUT. Notice that a dado can be cut at an angle in the same way. 20–3. CUTTING A BEVEL.

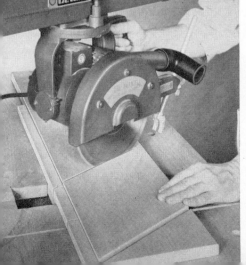
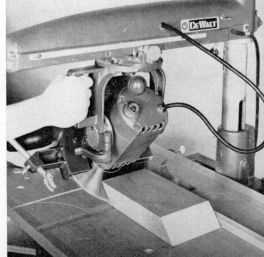

8. For miter cuts, swing the radial arm to the correct angle (usually 45°), by holding the *miter latch* down. Fig. 20–2.

9. For a bevel cut loosen the bevel clamp and tilt the motor to the desired angle. Fig. 20–3.

10. To cut dadoes, mount a dado head. To adjust for depth of cut, turn the elevating handle until the dado head touches the work. Remove the work and continue to lower the dado head to the desired depth. (Each turn of the handle lowers it $\frac{1}{16}''$.) Plain dadoes are cut at right angles or any angle just like cross-cutting. Fig. 20–4. To cut a blind dado, set the stop clamp on the radial arm so that the forward movement of the blade can't go beyond the layout line at the end of the blind dado.

RIPPING

1. Mount a combination or ripping blade. Pull the entire motor carriage to the front of the arm. Pull up on the locating pin above the yoke. Rotate the yoke 90° clockwise until the blade is parallel to the guide fence as shown in Fig. 20–5.

2. Move the motor assembly along the radial arm until the correct width is shown on the rip scale. Tighten the *rip clamp* (on opposite side of radial arm from locating pin). Lower the saw until the blade just touches the wood table.

3. Adjust the guard so that the infeed end clears the work slightly (about $\frac{1}{8}''$). Adjust the anti-kickback device so that the points rest on the work and hold it firmly against the table.

4. Turn on the power. Make sure the saw is rotating upwards toward you. Hold the work against the guide fence and feed it into the blade. Never feed the work from the anti-kickback end. Use a push stick to complete the cut.

20–4. CROSS DADOING. 20–5. Ripping.

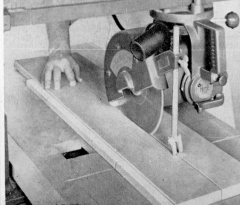

20–6. MAKING A COMPOUND MITER, or hopper, cut for a shadow-box picture frame.

5. Use the dado head for cutting a plain or blind groove.

6. Many other cuts can be made quickly. Fig. 20–6.

PLANER

The thickness *planer* or *surfacer*, as it is sometimes called, is a single-purpose machine that produces a true, smooth surface on a board. The planer will not correct *wind* or *twist*. If these exist, one surface must be finished on the jointer and then the board passed through the planer. Fig. 21–1.

Planers are made with either single or double surfacing knives. Most medium and small sizes are single, in that they surface only one side of a board at a time. It is a most useful machine especially for surfacing lumber that has been purchased rough.

Size. The size is indicated by the width and thickness of stock that can be handled by the machine. Common sizes are 13″ by 5″, 18″ by 6″, 24″ by 8″, and 30″ by 10″.

Parts. The main parts consist of a bed, movable table, a feed mechanism, and a cutting head. The table moves up and down on two screws or by sliding on a wedge-shaped casting. Fig. 21–2 shows a cross-section of the planer head. You will notice that there are two table rolls set about $\frac{1}{32}$″ to $\frac{1}{16}$″ above the level of the table. The infeed roll, directly above one of the table rolls, moves the work into the machine. It is usually corrugated and on most machines is made in segments to give a better grip. Just in

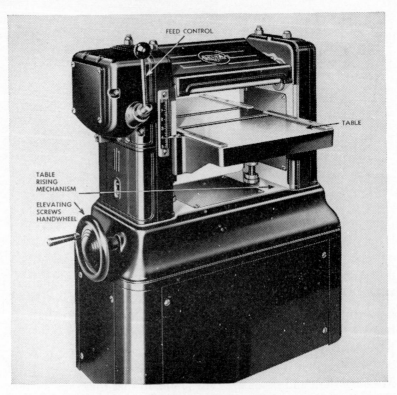

21–1. PARTS of a planer.

front of the infeed roll is a chip breaker that presses firmly on the board to prevent the knives from chipping the wood surface. The cutter head is similar to a jointer cutter head and has three, five, seven, or more knife blades. It revolves in a direction opposite the infeed roll. Next is a pressure bar which exerts pressure on the finished surface of the board to hold it firmly against the table. The outfeed roll and the table roll just below it move the smooth surface of the board through the planer.

Controls. There are only three or four simple controls on most planers: a switch to turn on the machine, a hand wheel which elevates or lowers the table, a pointer on the table indi-

PLANER HEAD

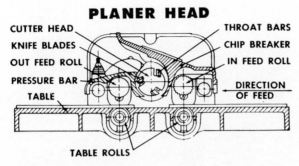

CUTTER HEAD
KNIFE BLADES
OUT FEED ROLL
PRESSURE BAR
TABLE

THROAT BARS
CHIP BREAKER
IN FEED ROLL
DIRECTION OF FEED

TABLE ROLLS

21-2. CROSS-SECTION of a planer head, with the parts named.

cating thickness on a scale attached to the base, and a feed control lever which operates the feed control. On some planers there is a control that regulates the rate of feed from slow to fast. On all power-driven machines the switch causes the cutter head to revolve but not the feed roll. The feed roll starts when the feed control lever is operated.

Safety. Follow all the basic rules for all machine tools and, in addition:

1. Keep your fingers away from the underside of the board as it is fed through the planer.

2. Never stand directly behind the board when planing.

3. Don't look into the planer as the board passes through.

4. Plane only one thickness at a time.

5. Never plane warped or twisted boards until one surface has been trued on the jointer.

6. Make sure the board is at least 2″ longer than the distance between the feed rolls.

Operation. 1. Measure the thickness of the board at its thickest point and adjust the machine to about $\frac{1}{16}″$ less than this.

2. If necessary, surface one side of the board on a jointer first.

3. Place the best or finished surface against the table with the board being fed with the grain. Stand to one side of the machine.

4. Turn on the machine and pull in the feed control. Then

21-3. FEEDING STOCK into a planer. Notice that the operator is standing to the side.

push the board into the planer. Fig. 21-3. If it should get started at a slight angle, a quick shove will straighten it. If the board sticks as it is part way through the planer, turn off the power first and then release the pressure with the elevating hand wheel.

5. When the major portion of the board has passed through the machine, walk around to the back and hold it as it comes through. On long stock it's a good idea to have a helper on the other side to guide the board at it comes off the machine.

6. After the first cut is taken, readjust the planer another $\frac{1}{16}''$ less and take a second cut until the finished size is reached.

7. If several pieces are to be surfaced, finish only one side of all pieces and then the other sides.

8. If the board being surfaced is made up of glued-up sections, always scrape the glue from the joints first. The glue will adhere to the outfeed roll, causing irregularities in the finished surface of the board. This same condition will exist if wood with too much pitch is surfaced or if old lumber with a finish on it is resurfaced. If this mistake is made, stop the machine and clean the rolls with kerosene before proceeding.

CIRCULAR SAW

The circular saw is a very versatile machine. With it many fundamental operations in woodworking can be done. Fig. 22–1. It is one of the first power machines needed in the shop and can do not only cutting operations of all kinds but, with a molding head, can also do shaper work.

Size. The size of the circular saw is indicated by the diameter of blade recommended for its use. Typical sizes are the 8″ or 10″. These saws are made in either bench or floor type. The large saws frequently have two arbors on which two different blades can be mounted. As one blade is turned into position, the other is below the table, not running. This is called a *universal-type saw*. Most saws, however, have a single arbor and are called *variety saws*. On some the table tilts to do such operations as chamfering, beveling, mitering, etc. These are called *tilt-table saws*. Fig. 22–2. Most saws are *tilt-arbor saws*—that is, the arbor tilts while the table remains permanently fastened in the horizontal position. On some saws the blade tilts to the right and on others to the left.

22–1. THIS OPERATOR practices good technique with the circular saw.

Blades. There are five basic kinds of saw blades. In selecting a blade, first make sure that you secure one of the correct diameter with the correct size hole in it. Never attempt to install a blade that has too large a hole.

The five kinds of blades are:

1. The *cutoff* or *crosscut*, which has teeth similar to the hand crosscut saw and which is used primarily for trimming stock to length and squaring operations. Fig. 22–3 a.

2. The hollow ground (planer) saw used for fine cabinet work. Fig. 22–3 b.

3. The rip saw with chisel-like teeth, which is used for ripping operations. Fig. 22–3 c.

4. The combination saw, which has a combination of ripping and crosscut teeth and is used as a universal-type blade for all kinds of cutting. Fig. 22–3 d.

5. The "easy-cut" saw or P.T.I., which has only a few large teeth around the blade and is considered to be the safest one,

22–2a.   A TILT-TABLE SAW.

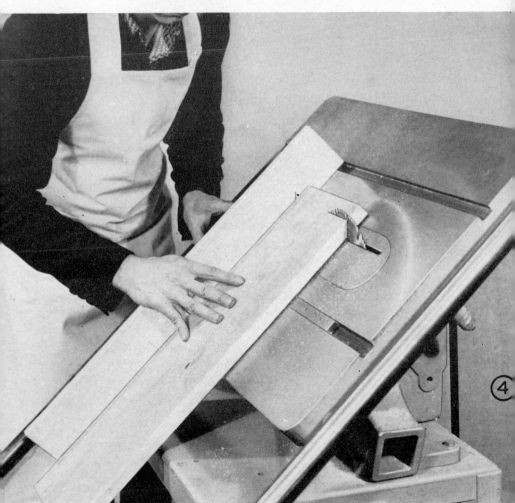

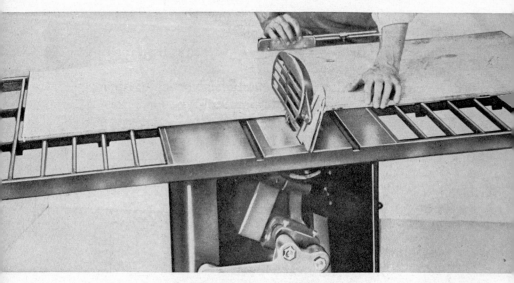

22–2b. A TILT-ARBOR SAW. Notice the difference in cutting a bevel. See Fig. 22–2a.

since it practically eliminates kickback. It does, however, make a rather wide saw kerf and does not cut so smoothly as the cutoff, hollow ground, or combination saws. Fig. 22–3 e.

Accessories. In addition to standard equipment, a *dado head* can be purchased that will cut all widths of grooves or dados. This will be described later. A *molding head* is also available for most saws and, with the proper kinds of blades, many different moldings and irregularly shaped edges can be cut. The molding head on the circular saw will do many of the same operations as the shaper.

Parts. Study the parts as shown in Fig. 22–4. Notice that this is a tilt-arbor saw. The table top has two grooves cut in it into which the miter gauge fits. These are parallel to the saw blade. The miter gauge comes equipped with a stop which can be adjusted for any length to do cutting of duplicate parts. A fence clamps to the table for all ripping operations. Also available are extensions which can be fastened to the sides of the table top and

22-3. KINDS OF BLADES: (a) cutoff or crosscut, (b) hollow ground (planer), (c) rip, (d) combination, and (e) easycut.

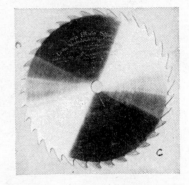

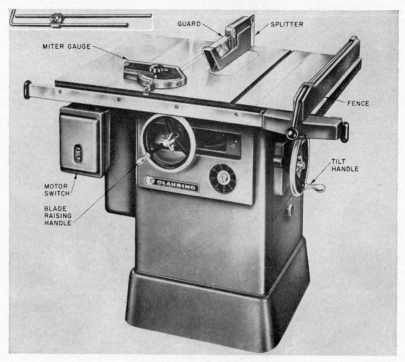

22–4. PARTS OF A CIRCULAR SAW. Inserts shows the stop rod that fits
into the miter gauge.

are especially convenient when cutting long or large stock such
as a sheet of plywood. An opening in the center of the table
is covered by a throat plate. A guard, which drops over the blade,
is always fastened to the back or side of the table. This should
be kept in place whenever possible. There are, of course, many
operations for which the guard cannot be retained. *Most of the
illustrations in this book show the saw without a guard so the
reader can see the operation more clearly.* There is also a slitter,
which is usually a part of the back of the guard. This fits directly
back of the saw blade and is slightly thicker than the blade. It
keeps the saw kerf open as the cutting is done.

Adjustments

INSTALLING OR REMOVING A SAW BLADE

1. Remove the throat plate. This usually snaps in or out of position.

2. Select a wrench to fit the arbor nut. On most saws the arbor has a lefthand thread and must be turned clockwise to loosen. However, some saws have a righthand thread. If so, you must turn it counterclockwise to remove. Always check the thread before loosening. If the nut doesn't come off easily, force a piece of scrap wood against the blade to keep the arbor from

22–5. REMOVING a blade.

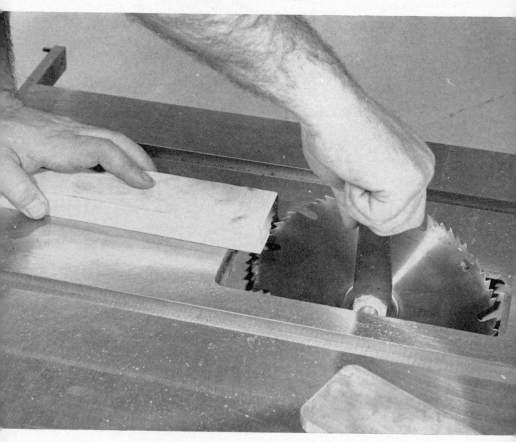

turning. Fig. 22–5. With another piece of wood strike the end of the wrench to loosen the nut.

3. Remove the nut and the collar and take off the old blade.

4. Replace the blade in the correct position, usually with the manufacturer's name toward the nut end of the arbor. Replace the collar and nut. Since it is a lefthand thread, the nut cannot come off. Tighten it down firmly, but not too tight. Replace the throat plate.

RAISING THE SAW BLADE

There is a wheel or lever on the front of the machine to raise or lower the blade. Often, in addition, there is a lock that must be loosened when making this adjustment. To raise the blade to the proper position, hold a square against the table and side of the blade and carefully turn the blade until the top tooth is the exact height. For most cutting, the blade should be adjusted ⅛″ higher than the thickness of the stock. On many joint cuts, however, the exact blade height must be set.

TILTING THE SAW BLADE

A lever or handle on the left side of the machine tilts the blade. A pointer or scale on the front indicates the degree of tilt. There is usually a lock to hold the blade in position when it is tilted.

ADJUSTING THE FENCE

A ripping fence is fastened to the table for all ripping operations and for many other cutting jobs. It is usually placed to the right of the blade. To adjust the blade to correct position, move it to the approximate location. Hold a rule or try square at right angles to the fence and carefully measure the distance from the fence to one tooth bent to the right. Fig. 22–6. On some machines there is a pointer on the fence and a scale on the front of the table to indicate the width of cut. This should be checked frequently to make sure it is accurate.

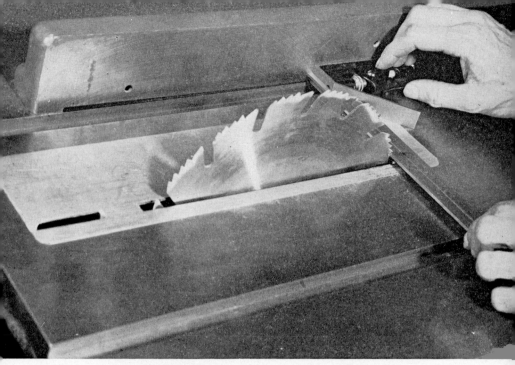

22–6. ADJUSTING the fence to secure the correct width of cut.

Adjusting the miter gauge

The miter gauge, which is used for all crosscutting operations, can be used in either groove of the table but usually is placed in the groove to the left of the blade. There is a pointer and scale on the miter gauge for setting it to any degree right or left. Most gauges have an automatic stop position at 30, 45, 60, and 90 degrees.

Safety. Follow the general safety practices given for all machines. In addition, remember the following:

Avoid kickback

Kickback results from one or more of the following:
1. Cutting irregular-shaped stock.
2. Using a blade that is dull.
3. Using the fence as a stop block.
4. Cutting without a slitter.

5. Allowing a small piece of wood to drop into the revolving blade.

Kickback is the most dangerous thing that can happen. Even a small 8″ saw can produce kickback that will send a large board flying at tremendous speed back past the operator. It is not uncommon for a glass to be broken 20 feet across a room.

STAND CORRECTLY

Stand a little to the side, but never directly back of the blade.

USE A PUSH STICK

Always push the stock through with a push stick when there is less than 6 inches between the blade and the fence.

OBSERVE PROPER PROCEDURE

1. Never use the fence for a stop when crosscutting.
2. Always keep the guard and slitter in place unless the particular kind of cutting makes it impossible.
3. Always adjust the saw to protrude only about ⅛″ above the stock being cut.
4. Never reach over a revolving saw but bring the cut piece back around the side of the machine.
5. Keep your fingers away from the saw blade at all times.

Ripping. Install a ripping, combination, or easycut blade for these operations.

CUTTING WIDE STOCK TO WIDTH

1. When the board to be cut is 6 inches or wider, it is considered a wide cut. Adjust the fence to the correct position and the blade to the correct height.
2. Turn on the machine, place the board over the table, apply pressure against the fence with the left hand, and push the board forward with the right. If the board is longer than 6 or 8 feet, you should have a helper standing behind the saw to hold

the piece up after it goes
through the blade. If a
helper is not available, make
use of a roller stand as shown
in Fig. 22–7.

3. Feed the stock at an
even speed into the blade
about as fast as it will cut.
You can tell if you are over-
loading the saw by its sound.
Hold your right hand close
to the fence as you push the
end of the board through
the saw. Fig. 22–8.

4. As the cut is com-
plete, let the pieces fall to
the front of the machine.

5. If extremely thick or
hard wood is being cut, it is
often necessary to cut part
way through the board, invert the board, and complete
the cut. See "Resawing."

CUTTING NARROWER STOCK TO WIDTH

1. When cutting stock
narrower than 6 inches, ob-

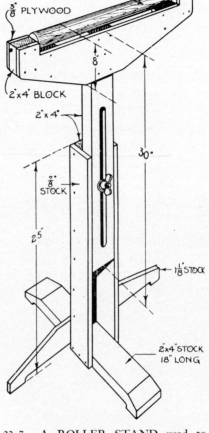

22–7. A ROLLER STAND used to
support long stock for ripping.

serve the same general practices as in starting the cut. On wide
stock, it is good practice to have a push stick hanging on the side
of the saw so that you don't take a chance and cut without it.

2. As the end of the board reaches the front of the table, have
a push stick handy to take the place of your right hand, guiding
the board between the blade and the fence. Fig. 22–9. *Never under any circumstances cut narrower stock without a push stick.*

3. If very narrow stock is being cut, it may be a good idea to cut half the length of the stock, pull it back out, reverse it and complete the cut from the other end.

RESAWING

1. Resawing on a circular saw can be done only if the width of the board is less than twice the capacity of the saw. For example, a 7″ board can be resawed on an 8″ circular saw. If the board is wider than that, a kerf can be cut on either side on the circular saw and the resawing completed on a band saw.

22–8. CUTTING WIDE BOARDS to width.

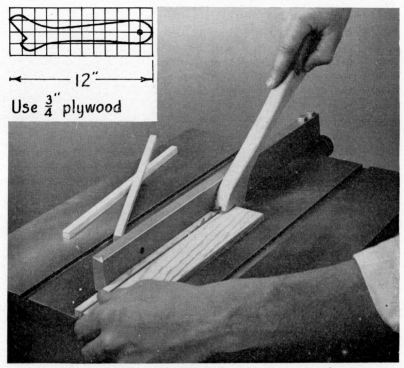

Use $\frac{3}{4}''$ plywood

12"

22-9. USING A PUSH STICK to cut narrow stock.

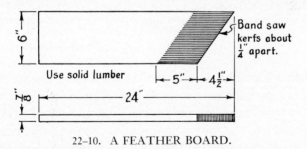

6"

Band saw
kerfs about
$\frac{1}{4}''$ apart.

Use solid lumber

5"

$4\frac{1}{2}''$

$\frac{7}{8}''$

24"

22-10. A FEATHER BOARD.

2. For resawing, it is a good idea to make a feather board to help to guide the stock. Cut a bevel at about 30 degrees across the end of a piece of scrap stock; then make a series of saw kerfs with the grain, about 6" long and about $\frac{3}{8}''$ apart. Fig. 22-10.

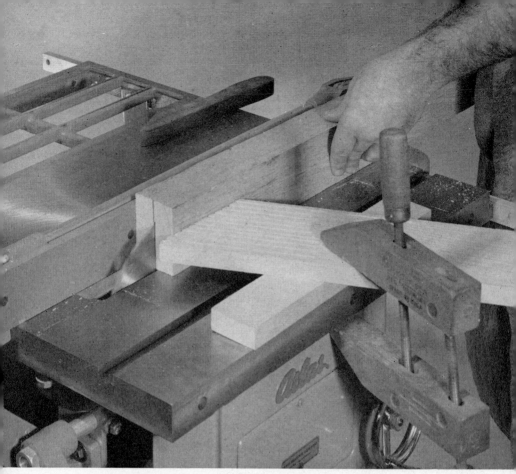

22-11. RESAWING with the help of a feather board. Notice that this holds the stock firmly against the fence at the same time freeing the operator's hands.

The feather board helps to hold the stock firmly against the fence at all times during the cutting. It is needed because the operator must use both hands to guide and push the board. Clamp this board to the table to apply slight pressure to the stock. Fig. 22–11. Adjust the blade to equal about half the width of the board to be resawed. Push the board through the saw, return it, reverse it, and cut the other half.

Crosscutting. Install a crosscutting, hollow-ground, or combination blade. Use the miter gauge for all crosscutting operations. To give added support, some operators like to fasten permanently a long support board to the miter gauge. Always remove the ripping fence for these operations. Carefully mark a line across the face and both edges of the stock so that the mark can be easily seen during the cutting. This is important in sawing accurately.

CUTTING SHORT BOARDS

Place the gauge in the groove in the side toward the longest portion of the board. Fig. 22–12. Hold the stock firmly against the gauge and advance it slowly into the blade. Never drag the cut edge back across the blade.

22–12. CROSSCUTTING short pieces.

CUTTING LONG PIECES

If the board is longer than 6 feet, have a helper support the other end.

CUTTING PLYWOOD

Because of its size and construction, plywood is a special cutting problem. Adjust the blade to clear barely the top of the plywood and place the stock with the good side up. There are three ways to do the cutting:

1. The miter gauge can be reversed in the groove when the cut is started, to guide the stock for as long a cut as possible. Fig. 22–13. Then the gauge can be removed and slipped into its regular position to complete the cut.

2. Another suggestion for sawing plywood is to clamp a straight-edged board on the underside of the plywood. This will act as a guide against the edge of the table. Fig. 22–14.

3. The ripping fence can be used as a guide in cutting plywood to size.

22-13. STARTING A CUT on a piece of plywood with the miter gauge reversed.

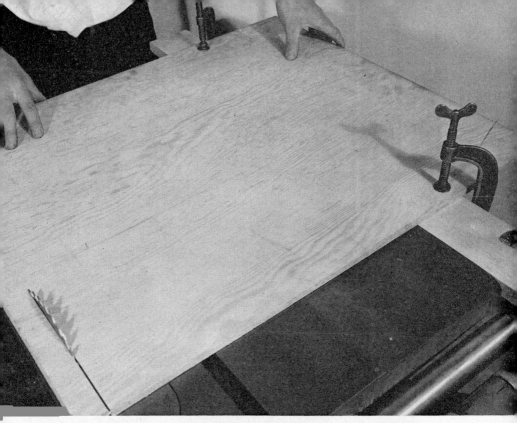

22–14. CLAMPING a piece of scrap stock to plywood to act as a cutting guide.

Cutting identical or duplicate pieces to length

There are many ways of cutting identical pieces to length:

1. For cutting many short pieces, clamp a stop block to the ripping fence in front of the cutting edge of the blade. Adjust this fence to cut the proper length of stock. By placing the end of the board against this stop, you can cut the correct length and there will be plenty of clearance between the fence and the finished pieces to prevent kickback. Fig. 22–15.

2. A second method is to adjust the stop on the gauge for the correct length of the cut. Fig. 22–16.

3. A third method is to clamp a stop block to the auxiliary board fastened to the miter gauge. Fig. 22–17.

4. A fourth method is to clamp a stop block to the table. Fig. 22–18.

22–15. CUTTING identical pieces to length with stop block clamped to fence.

22–16. USING THE STOP ROD on the miter gauge to cut identical pieces to length.

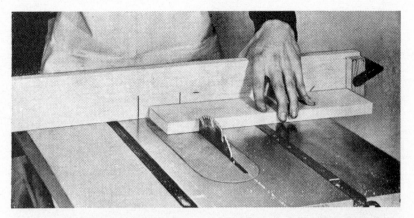

22–17. USING A STOP BLOCK on an auxiliary board fastened to a miter gauge to cut identical pieces to length.

22–18. USING A STOP BLOCK fastened to the table.

Special cuts.

CUTTING A BEVEL OR CHAMFER WITH THE GRAIN

Tilt the blade to the correct angle for the chamfer or bevel.

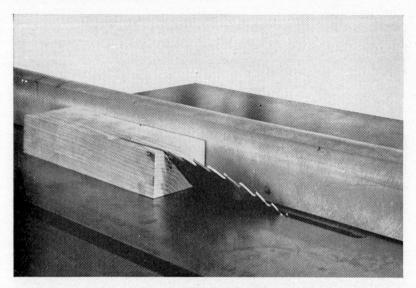

22-19. CUTTING A BEVEL with the grain.

22-20. CUTTING A BEVEL across the grain.

Place the fence on the tilt side of the table. Adjust the height of the blade to clear the top of the board slightly. Hold the work firmly against the fence as the cut is made. Fig. 22–19.

CUTTING A BEVEL OR CHAMFER ACROSS GRAIN

Adjust the blade to the correct angle and place the miter gauge in the groove on the side toward which the blade tilts. Hold the stock firmly against the gauge to make the cut. Sometimes it's a good idea to clamp the stock to the gauge for making this kind of cut. Fig. 22–20.

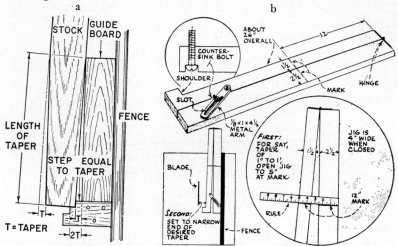

22–21a. A SIMPLE GUIDE BOARD for cutting tapered table legs. Cut the notches about ¼" deep and the width of the taper. 22–21b. AN ADJUST-ABLE JIG for cutting tapers. On this type the exact taper per foot is set at the 1' mark.

CUTTING A TAPER

A tapered jig should be used. This can be a simple piece of stock with a block nailed to it or an adjustable jig as shown in Fig. 22–21. The jig should be made exactly 2' long. Then determine the amount of taper per foot in inches. The taper jig is then set to twice this amount. Fasten the fence in place with the taper starting at the correct point on the stock. Hold the stock

22-22. CUTTING A TAPER with an adjustable jig. A simple way to adjust the jig is to draw a line along at the limit of cut. Then adjust the jig until this line is parallel to the fence.

firmly against the jig and the jig against the fence. Cut the taper as in ripping. Fig. 22–22.

Joint cuts. All cuts for making joints should be done with a crosscut, hollow-ground, or combination blade, since it is important to have a very smooth cut. Almost all cuts for joints must be made with the guard and slitter removed. *Therefore it is extremely important to observe all safety precautions.*

CUTTING A RABBET

Lay out the width and depth of the rabbet on the end or edge of stock so that the lines can be easily seen during the cut-

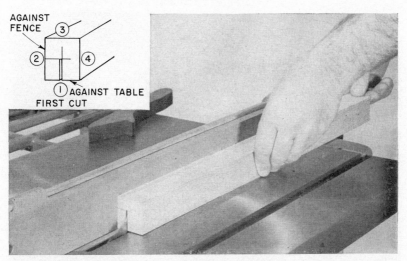

AGAINST FENCE ③
② ④
① AGAINST TABLE
FIRST CUT

22–23. MAKING THE FIRST CUT OF A RABBET with the grain. After the cut is started, hold the work against the fence with your left hand and push it along with a push stick. Notice that side No. 1 is against the table and side No. 2 is against the fence.

ting. Adjust the saw blade to a height equal to the depth of the rabbet. If the rabbet is cut with the grain, place the stock face down on the table with the edge against the fence and make the first cut. Fig. 22–23. If the rabbet is cut across grain, place the stock face down and hold against the miter gauge with the end firmly against the fence. Fig. 22–24. For the second cut, adjust the blade to a height equal to the width of the rabbet and adjust the fence with the saw blade just inside the waste stock. Fig. 22–25. Hold the surface away from the rabbet firmly against the fence and carefully make the second cut. If the surface or edge of the board that was on the table is held against the fence for the second cut, when the saw cut is made, the strip of wood will kick back with considerable force.

CUTTING A MITER

Miter cuts are usually made at a 45-degree angle, although they can be made at any angle. If any shape other than a rec-

22–24. MAKING A FIRST CUT of a rabbet across the grain.

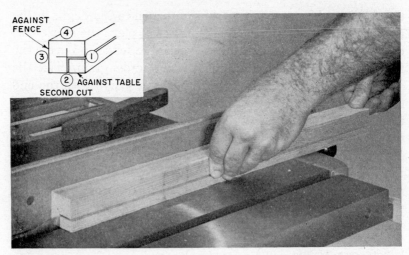

22–25. MAKING THE SECOND CUT of a rabbet with the grain. With this method the waste stock falls to the right of the blade without binding or kickback. Notice that side No. 2 is against the table and that side No. 3 is against the fence.

tangle must be cut, find the
correct angle of the miter by
dividing 180 degrees by the
number of sides and subtract-
ing from 90 degrees. When
cutting mitered corners for
picture frames, follow the
sketch shown in Fig. 22–26,
to determine the over-all
length of the sides. Determine
the length of the glass or pic-

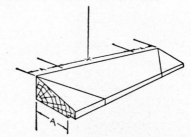

LENGTH OF GLASS OR PICTURE

22–26. THE LAYOUT FOR CUT-
TING a picture frame.

ture. Add to this length twice the width of the frame, measured
from the rabbet edge to the outside edge. Layout this measurement along the outside edge of the stock.

Making a flat miter cut: Adjust the miter gauge to the correct
degree, usually 45 degrees.

22–27. MAKING A FLAT MITER cut.

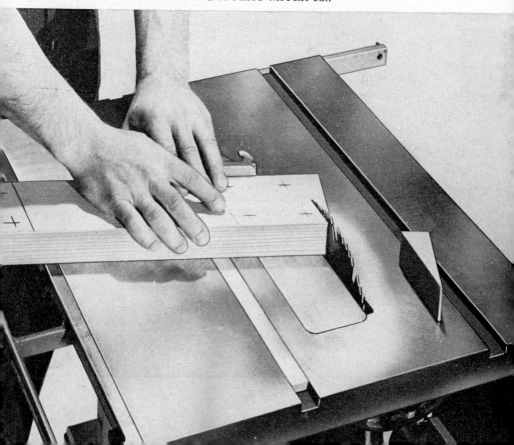

22–28.   SAW CUT FOR A SPLINE for a flat miter joint.

If two miter gauges are available, the cutting will be simplified. Adjust both gauges to turn inward toward the saw blade. Place a stop rod on the left miter gauge to equal the exact length of the sides to be cut. Hold the stock firmly against the right miter gauge and cut the first miter from the inside edge toward the corner. Fig. 22–27. To make the second cut, hold the mitered end against the stop rod and cut as before.

To install a spline in a flat miter cut, cut a scrap piece of wood at an angle of 45 degrees, which can be used as a jig. Adjust the height of the blade to equal the desired depth of the spline cut. Adjust the fence so the cut will be in the correct position, from right to left. Hold the stock firmly against the jig as shown in Fig. 22–28, and cut the groove for the spline.

Making a miter on edge: Tilt the saw blade to an angle of 45

22–29. MAKING A MITER CUT for a miter joint on edge.

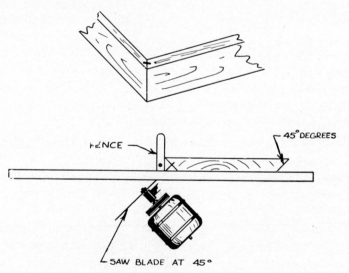

22–30. SAW CUT FOR A SPLINE for a miter joint on edge.

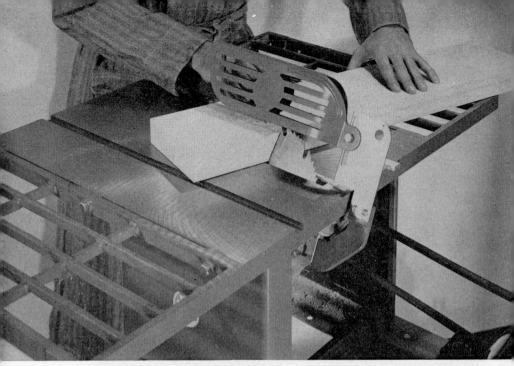

22-31. MAKING A COMPOUND MITER, or hopper, cut. See page 416 in the appendix for correct settings for blade tilt and miter angle.

degrees and set the miter gauge at 90 degrees. Place the miter gauge in the groove so the blade tilts away from it. Adjust it to the correct height, and make the miter cut as shown in Fig. 22–29. See page 187.

To install a spline in a miter on edge, set the fence as shown in Fig. 22–30. Adjust the height of the blade and cut the groove as shown.

Making a compound miter cut: This is used in making many modern picture frames. Adjust the miter gauge to the correct angle and the saw to the desired degree. Fig. 22–31. Then make a trial cut of the two pieces on scrap stock. Carefully check the corners.

Putting a feather across a miter corner: Make a small jig, similar to the one in Fig. 22–32, that will support the corner of the frame. Adjust the blade to the correct height and set the fence with the cut being made in the center across the corners.

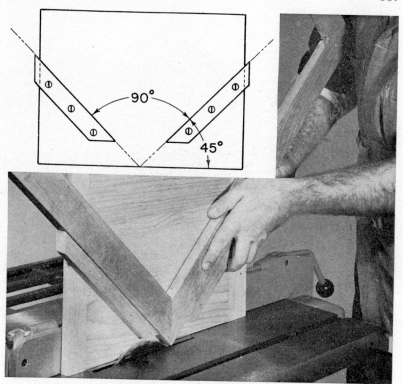

22–32. MAKING A SAW CUT across the corner of a frame to install a key or feather. Notice the jig for holding the stock firmly in position.

CUTTING A TENON

There are two common methods of cutting the tenon: (a) Cut all pieces to the desired size and length. (b) Lay out the tenon on either end. Usually there are eight tenons to be cut in making simple tables, chairs and other four-legged objects.

Method A

1. Set the fence with the distance from the left edge of the saw to the fence equal to the length of the tenon.

22–33. MAKING A SHOULDER CUT on a tenon using the fence for a stop.

   2. Adjust the height of the saw equal to the thickness of the stock to be removed.

   3. Hold the pieces against the miter gauge and make the shoulder cut. Fig. 22–33. If the tenon is perfectly centered, the stock can be reversed and the other side of the tenon cut. This may be on one, two, three, or four sides, depending on the type of tenon.

   4. Make all shoulder cuts on all pieces.

   5. Readjust the fence so the distance from the right side of the saw to the fence will remove the correct thickness of the material from one side of the tenon. Adjust the saw blade equal to the length of the tenon. *Make the cheek cuts.* This should not be done freehand on pieces less than 4″ wide, since it can be a very dangerous operation. Fig. 22–34. *For added protection, use*

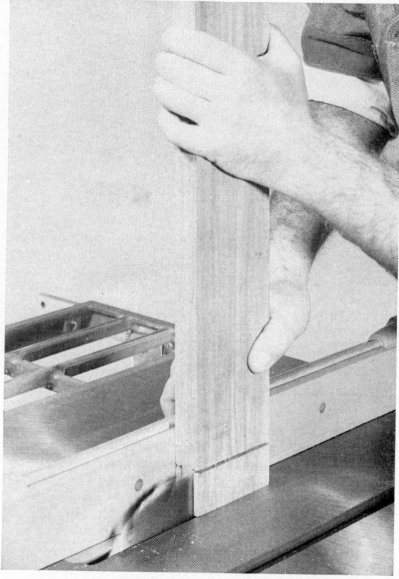

22-34. MAKING THE CHEEK CUT freehand. Special care must be exercised when cutting a tenon in this manner.

22–35. MAKING THE CHEEK CUT using a feather board as a safety device.

the feather board as shown in Fig. 22–35. The danger can be minimized by using a jig similar to that shown in Fig. 22–36 a, which will keep the operator's fingers away from the saw. A commercially made tenoner attachment simplifies this operation and makes it safe. Fig. 22–36 b.

Method B

1. Place a dado head on the saw and adjust it to a height equal to the thickness of stock to be removed on one side of the tenon. See method C, under Cutting a Groove, for the use of the dado head.

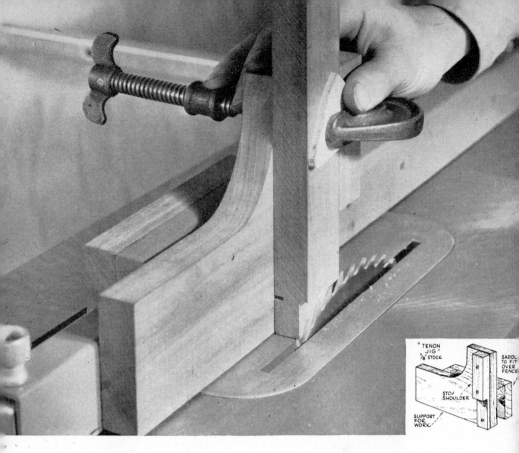

22–36a. **MAKING THE CHEEK CUT** using a wooden jig. 22–36b. A
TENONING JIG is an accessory for making tenons and grooves. This one
will take stock up to 2¾″ thick and any width within the capacity of the saw.

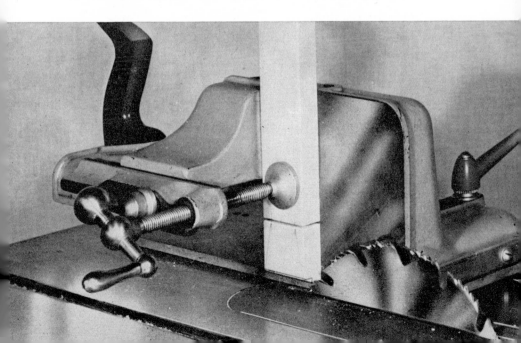

22-37. CUTTING A TENON, using a dado head.

2. Adjust the fence so the distance from the left edge of the dado to the fence is equal to the length of the tenon.

3. Hold the stock firmly against the miter gauge with the end held against the fence. Make the first cut, return the stock to the original position, and move it to the left to make succeeding cuts until one side is finished. Fig. 22–37. Repeat on the other sides.

Method B-B

The same procedure as in Method B can be followed with

a single saw blade, trimming off the waste stock with a hand chisel.

CUTTING A GROOVE

A groove is a rectangular opening cut with the grain of wood. There are three simple ways of doing this operation.

Method A. With a single saw blade.

Adjust the blade to a height equal to the depth of the groove. Adjust the fence to cut to one side of the groove. *Make the first cut.* Readjust the fence to cut to the other side of the groove and *make the second cut.* Fig. 22–38. Set the fence at several positions, making several cuts in the waste stock. Clean out the groove with a hand router or chisel. Fig. 22–39.

22–38. CUTTING A GROOVE.

22-39. CUTTING A DADO with a single saw blade. Notice that several passes have been made through the waste stock. The dado can be completed with a hand chisel or router plane.

Method B. Using wobble washers.

Wobble washers replace the regular washers that hold the saw blade on the arbor. These can be set so the single saw blade wobbles and cuts a groove of a specific width. There are marks on the washers for setting the width of cut. Adjust the blade to the correct height. Set the fence and make the cut. *This is somewhat dangerous because the saw blade does not run smoothly.*

22-40. THE TYPICAL DADO HEAD consists of two ⅛" outside blades, one ¹⁄₁₆" thick chipper blade, two ⅛" thick chipper blades and one ¼" thick chipper blade. With this assortment you can cut grooves from ⅛" to ¹³⁄₁₆" in intervals of ¹⁄₁₆".

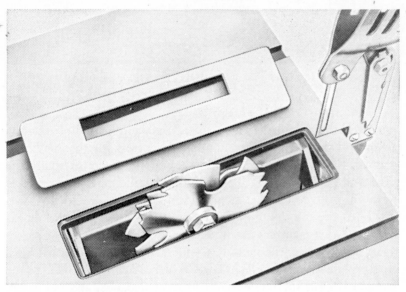

22-41. A SPECIAL THROAT PLATE is needed for installing a dado head.

Method C. With a dado head.

Using the dado head is the safest and fastest method of cutting grooves. This consists of two combination-type blades with cutters placed between them. Fig. 22-40. Remove the throat

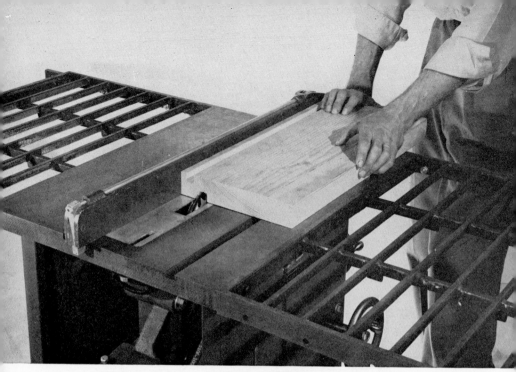

22-42. CUTTING A GROOVE with a dado head.

plate and the saw blade. Place one of the dado head blades on the arbor and then the correct number of cutters for that width of groove. Fig. 22–41. Finally, add the second blade. (Usually the blades and cutters are $\frac{1}{16}''$, $\frac{1}{8}''$ and $\frac{1}{4}''$ wide, making it possible to cut a groove of any standard width.)

Turn the cutters until the points are evenly spaced. For example, if three cutters are used, they should be set 120 degrees apart. This makes the dado head operate smoothly. Put a special throat plate made for a dado head in place. Adjust the dado to the correct height, the fence to the correct distance, and cut as before. Fig. 22–42.

CUTTING A STOPPED GROOVE

A stopped groove is cut only a portion of the length of the stock, usually toward the center. Fasten hand screws to the fence to control the length of the cut. Turn on the machine, hold one end of the stock against the first clamp, and lower it into the saw. Push the stock along until it strikes the second clamp. Carefully raise the stock. Fig. 22–43.

CUTTING DADOES

Plain dado. A dado is a groove cut across grain. It can be done in any of the ways described for cutting a groove. The fence can serve as a stop block and the work held against the miter gauge. When cutting a regular dado, pass the stock completely across the cutter and remove. Fig. 22–44. Do not draw the board back across the dado head. This is a very important precaution to take in using the dado head.

Blind dado. A blind dado or gain is cut only partly across the board. Follow the directions described under dado joints in the section on "jointery," in laying out and cutting the hole at the end. Clamp a stop block to the fence to control the length of the dado. Cut the dado as before until the board hits the stop

22-43. CUTTING A STOPPED GROOVE. Notice the use of hand screws as stop blocks to control the length of cut.

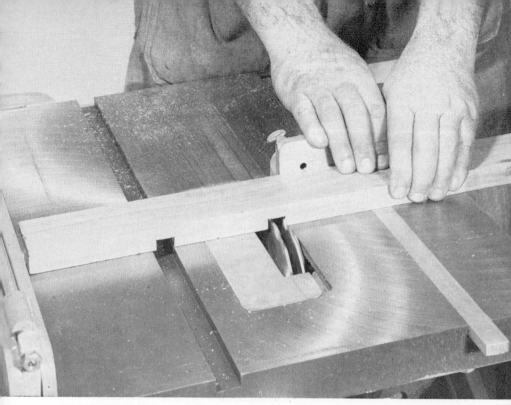

22-44. CUTTING A PLAIN DADO.

block. Fig. 22–45. Then slowly raise the board or turn off the machine and remove the board.

Corner dado. Make a simple jig which is simply a V block for holding the stock at an angle of 45 degrees to the table. Cut the dado as shown in Fig. 22–46.

CUTTING LAP JOINTS

End-lap and half-lap. The end-lap and half-lap joints are actually two tenons with the stock removed from only one side. Lay out the stock to be removed from only one side. Lay out the stock to be removed on each side and cut the pieces exactly as you would two tenons—shoulder cuts first and then cheek cuts.

Cross-lap and edge-lap. Cross-lap and edge-lap joints are cut similar to a dado, except that the lap joints are usually wider. Make the layout and cut by one of the methods described for cutting grooves or dadoes.

22-45. CUTTING A GAIN OR BLIND DADO. Notice the stop block clamped to the table to control the length of the dado.

22-46. CUTTING A CORNER DADO, using a V block to hold the stock.

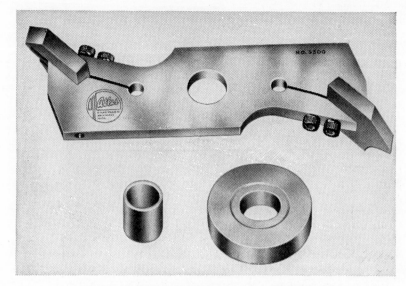

22-47. A MOLDING HEAD for a circular saw.

Middle-lap. In this joint, one member is cut like a tenon and the second like a dado. Follow the directions for making each of these two kinds of cuts.

Using a molding head. The molding head with cutters can be installed on a circular saw to do many of the operations that would normally be done on a shaper. Figs. 22–47 and 22–48.

22-48. TYPES OF CUTTERS and kinds of moldings that can be made.

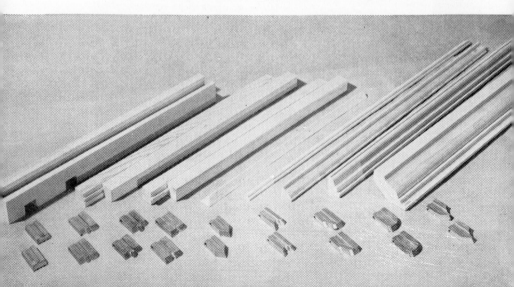

22-49. INSTALLING a molding head.

Remove the throat plate from the saw blade and replace with a molding head that has cutters of the desired shape clamped in place. Fig. 22-49. When possible, clamp a board slightly thicker than the width of the molding head to the fence. Fasten it high enough so that the stock to be cut *will just slip underneath it.* The fence can then serve as a guide and guard. Adjust the fence the correct distance from the molding head and set the molding head to the correct height. *Make a test run on a piece of scrap stock.* Fig. 22-50. Readjust if necessary. When doing the actual

22–50. USING a molding head. Notice that a feather board is used to hold the stock against the fence.

cutting, feed the board slowly. If an edge is to be shaped on all four sides, cut the end grain first and then the edge grain.

BAND SAW

The band saw is a simple machine to operate. It gets its name from the fact that *the cutting blade is a continuous band of metal*. It is designed to cut curves and irregular shapes but can perform much straight cutting.

THE BAND SAW

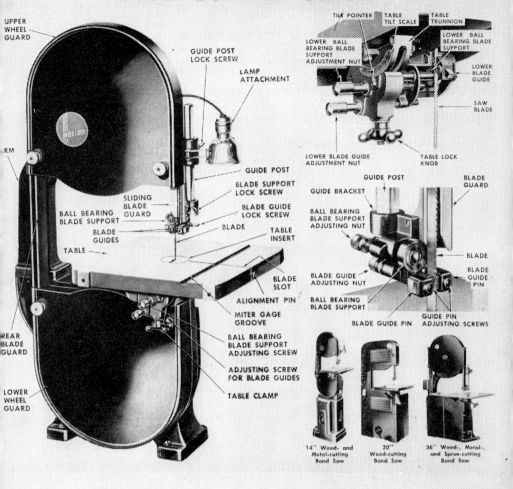

UPPER WHEEL GUARD

GUIDE POST LOCK SCREW

LAMP ATTACHMENT

TILT POINTER

TABLE TILT SCALE

TABLE TRUNNION

LOWER BALL BEARING BLADE SUPPORT ADJUSTMENT NUT

LOWER BALL BEARING BLADE SUPPORT

LOWER BLADE GUIDE

SAW BLADE

RM

GUIDE POST

BLADE SUPPORT LOCK SCREW

SLIDING BLADE GUARD

BLADE GUIDE LOCK SCREW

BALL BEARING BLADE SUPPORT

BLADE

BLADE GUIDES

BLADE

TABLE INSERT

TABLE

LOWER BLADE GUIDE ADJUSTMENT NUT

TABLE LOCK KNOB

GUIDE POST

BLADE GUARD

GUIDE BRACKET

BALL BEARING BLADE SUPPORT ADJUSTING NUT

BLADE

BLADE GUIDE PIN

BLADE GUIDE ADJUSTING NUT

BALL BEARING BLADE SUPPORT

BLADE GUIDE PIN

GUIDE PIN ADJUSTING SCREWS

BLADE SLOT

ALIGNMENT PIN

MITER GAGE GROOVE

BALL BEARING BLADE SUPPORT ADJUSTING SCREW

ADJUSTING SCREW FOR BLADE GUIDES

TABLE CLAMP

REAR BLADE GUARD

LOWER WHEEL GUARD

14" Wood- and Metal-cutting Band Saw

20" Wood-cutting Band Saw

36" Wood-, Metal-, and Sprue-cutting Band Saw

23–1. PARTS of a band saw.

Size. The size of the band saw is determined by the diameter of the wheel. A 14″ to 24″ size is most common. The size is also indicated by the distance from the top of the table to the bottom of the upper guide. This limits the thickness of stock that the machine can cut.

Parts. The band saw consists of a frame on which two wheels

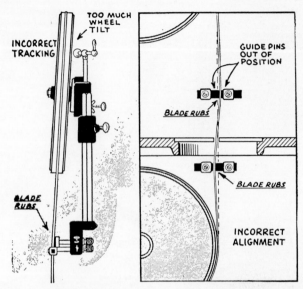

23-2.   DRAWING   SHOWING   INCORRECT
TRACKING and alignment of a band saw blade.

are mounted. Fig. 23–1. The lower wheel is connected to the source of power and the upper wheel can be moved up or down and tilted for adjustment. The table is fastened to the frame and can be tilted 45 degrees in one direction and, on some types, a few degrees in the other direction. Two guide units, above and below the table, keep the blade aligned for cutting. Fig. 23–2. The upper one can be moved up and down as the thickness of stock varies. Guards should cover both upper and lower wheels and all parts of the blade except that doing the cutting.

Adjustments. The adjusting handles, wheels, and guides are shown in Fig. 23–3. Here are some of the common adjustments:

INSTALLING A NEW BLADE

1. Remove the guards, the throat plate, and the pin or set screw in the table slot. Loosen the upper wheel, open the upper and lower guides, and move the thrust bearing or guide wheels back.

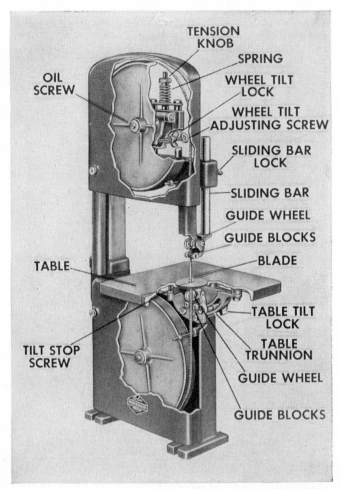

OIL SCREW

TENSION KNOB

SPRING

WHEEL TILT LOCK

WHEEL TILT ADJUSTING SCREW

SLIDING BAR LOCK

SLIDING BAR

GUIDE WHEEL

GUIDE BLOCKS

TABLE

BLADE

TABLE TILT LOCK

TILT STOP SCREW

TABLE TRUNNION

GUIDE WHEEL

GUIDE BLOCKS

23-3. A CUTAWAY SHOWING THE PARTS and adjusting handles of another jig-saw model.

2. Uncoil the saw blade and slip it through the slot of the table and then over the two wheels. Make sure that the teeth point downward toward the table. Tighten the upper wheel slightly. Turn the upper wheel over by hand to see if the blade

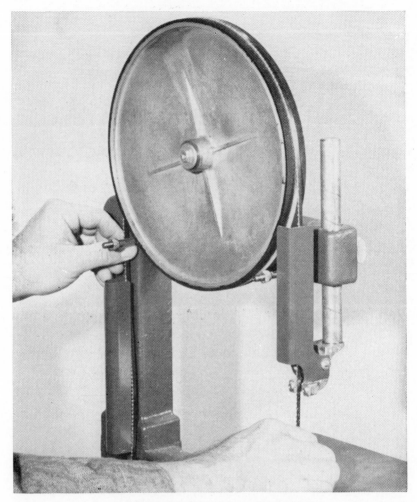

23-4. INSTALLING a new band saw blade.

stays in the center of the wheel. If it tends to move to one side or
the other, loosen the nut that controls wheel tilt and tilt the
wheel until the blade stays on center. Lock the tilt in position.
Apply additional tension to the blade. Fig. 23-4. The amount of
tension will vary with the width of the blade.

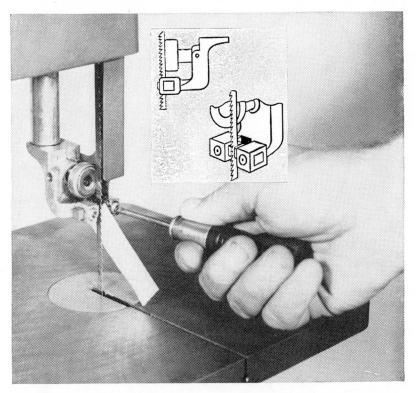

23-5. ADJUSTING the guide slides on a band saw.

ADJUSTING THE GUIDE SLIDES OR PINS

Place a piece of paper around the blade and press in the guide slides. Fig. 23-5. The front of the guide slides should be even with the bottom or gullet of the teeth. It may be necessary to move the guide assembly forward or back to make this adjustment. Now lock the guide slides in position and remove the paper. This will provide just the right amount of clearance. Do this for both the upper and lower guides, making sure that both are aligned vertically. Now move the thrust bearing or guide

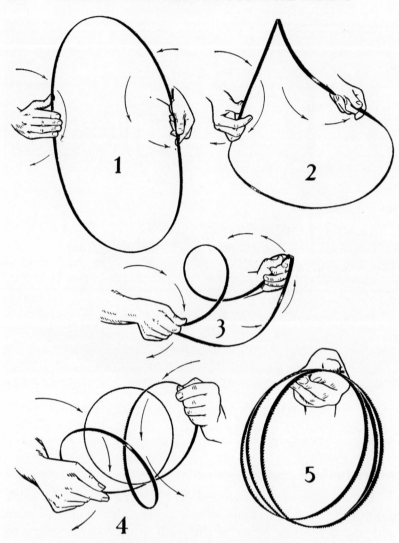

23-6. FOLDING a band saw blade.

wheel forward or back until it just barely clears the back of the blade. When the machine is operating but not cutting, the guide

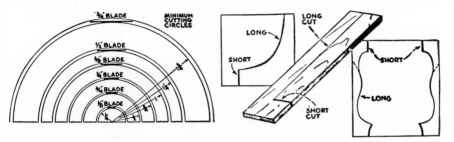

23–7.   MINIMUM CUTTING CIRCLE for band saw blades. 23–8.   AL-
WAYS MAKE SHORT CUTS before long ones.

wheels should stand still. If they revolve continuously, the back
of the blade will crystallize. Replace the throat plate, the set
screw, or pin, in the table and the guards.

FOLDING A BAND SAW BLADE

In changing a band saw blade, fold the old blade and hang it
on a rack. Turn the blade with the teeth pointing upward and
make an oval shape with it, arms outstretched. Now hold the
blade and twist as shown in Fig. 23–6. The blade will fold into
three circles.

Safety. The band saw is one of the safest machines to use in
the shop. Follow the general safety procedures for all machines.

Basic procedures. 1. Before operating the band saw, check
to see if the correct size blade is on the machine. A *small blade* is
needed to cut sharp curves and a *larger one* for large circles and
straight sawing. Fig. 23–7. A ⅛″ or ¼″ blade is satisfactory for
most cutting.

2. Check to see that the blade is square with the top of the
table. Raise the upper guide out of position and check with a
square.

3. *The correct cutting position for righthand operators* is to
face the blade, standing slightly to the left of it. Guide the stock
with the left hand and apply forward pressure with the right.

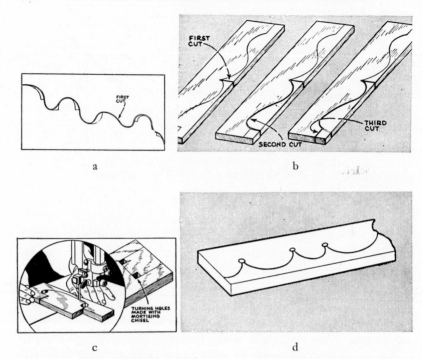

a   b

c   d

23–9. (a) ROUGH OUT THE MORE COMPLEX CUTS before making the finished cut. (b) BREAK UP THE COMPLICATED CURVES into several simpler cuts. (c) USE TURNING HOLES that are a part of the design. (d) HERE, DRILLED HOLES are used to simplify the cutting.

4. *Follow these simple suggestions for all cutting:*

a. Change the position of the upper guide before each cutting so that it just clears the upper surface of the stock.

b. Check your layout before cutting. Sometimes you will find that you have the layout on the wrong side of the stock and that the stock will hit the arm of the band saw as the cutting is done.

c. *Always make the short cuts before the long ones.* When stock is cut from two sides, cut the short side first so that there will be a minimum of backing out. Then cut the long sides. Fig. 23–8. Whenever possible, *cut out through* the waste stock rather than *backing out.*

d. Make straight cuts before curved ones. This will make the problem of backing out simpler.

e. "Break up" complicated curves and drill clearance holes. If it is a complex curve, such as the side of an Early American bookcase or spoon rack, decide how the cuts are to be made and drill a clearance hole at the sharp corners in the waste stock. Fig. 23–9. This will make it possible to cut out the design as several simpler pieces.

f. *Check the band saw blade for leading.* This condition causes the blade to pull to one side or the other, thus cutting a slight taper. It is difficult if not impossible to cut a straight line when this condition exists. It may be caused by a slight burr on one side of the blade; there may be more set to the teeth on one side than on the other; the guides may be too loose or out of line; or the blade may be too narrow. To correct the first two conditions, hold an abrasive stone lightly against the side toward which the blade leads. For the other conditions, readjust the guide block or change the blade.

Straight cutting. While the band saw was primarily designed for cutting curves and circles, many straight cutting jobs can be done. The advantage of the band saw is that, if you want to, you can do this cutting freehand, following a guideline.

CUTTING FREEHAND

Lay out a guideline in the stock. Guide one edge of the stock with the left hand and apply slow, even pressure with the right. Do not be in a hurry. It requires some skill and patience to cut a straight line. Fig. 23–10.

CUTTING WITH THE RIPPING FENCE

Some band saws are equipped with a ripping fence. If one is not available, a scrap piece of stock with a straightedge can

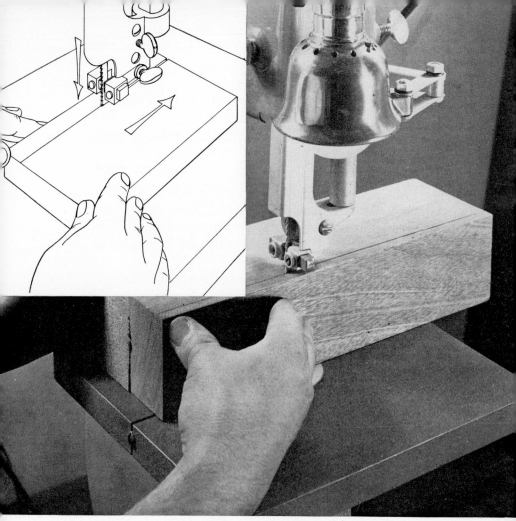

23-10. DOING FREEHAND straight cutting.

be clamped to the table. Make sure that it is parallel to the blade. Follow the same technique as with a circular saw. Fig. 23-11.

RESAWING

Cutting stock to narrower thicknesses is a common operation. The widest possible blade must be installed for this. There are several ways to guide the stock. The best way is to clamp a pivot pin to the table as a guide. This is especially desirable because, if the saw tends to lead to one side or the other, the board can be shifted. Fig. 23–12. A ripping fence can also be used but is not satisfactory if the blade tends to lead. When extremely wide stock is to be resawed, it is sometimes wise to make a starter cut from either edge with the circular saw. The disadvantage is, of course, that the circular saw makes a wider kerf.

When feeding the stock through the band saw, hold it firmly against the fence or guide pin. Do not overload the blade. If the lumber is rather green, apply some beeswax to the blade.

23–11. RESAWING, using a ripping fence.

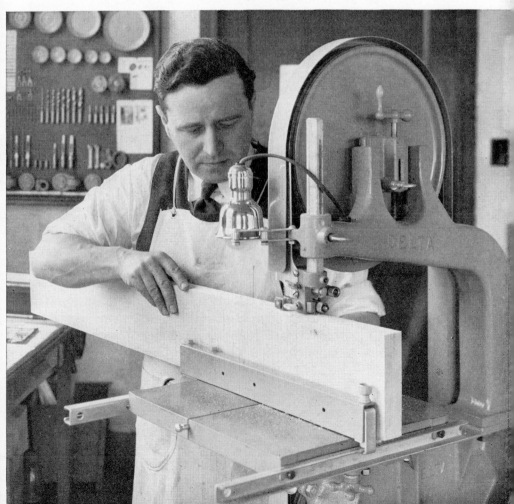

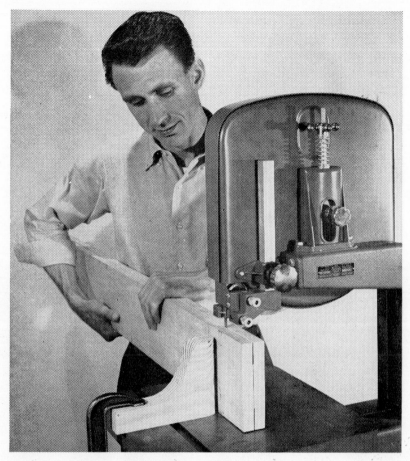

23-12. RESAWING with the aid of a pivot block.

Cutting triangular pieces

Tilt the table to an angle of 45 degrees and fasten the ripping fence to it so it just clears the blade. Start with square stock to cut triangular pieces. Fig. 23–13. This is especially useful in cutting glue blocks used for strengthening adjoining surfaces. The same technique can be followed for cutting quarter-round molding from round stock. This technique can also be applied to cutting a slight kerf across the ends of square or round stock in preparation for wood turning or for cutting octagon shapes. A simple V-type jig can be made to perform these same operations with the table in the normal position.

23–13. CUTTING TRIANGULAR PIECES with the table tilted 45 degrees.

CUTTING COMPOUND CURVES

Compound sawing is done in making book ends, bases for lamps and other decorative shapes that are cut on two adjoining surfaces. The cabriole leg found in traditional and French Provincial furniture is a good example. The most common method of cutting is shown in Fig. 23–14.

Step 1. Make a pattern of the design on heavy paper. Square up the stock and then lay out the pattern for the design on the two adjacent sides.

Step 2. Make the inside and outside cuts from one side, being careful to keep in the waste stock.

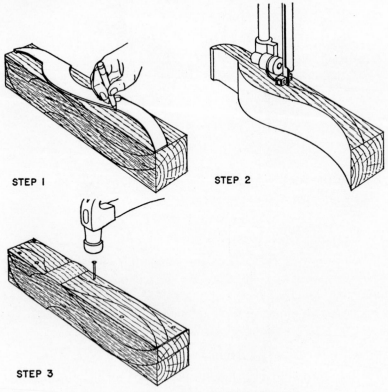

STEP I

STEP 2

STEP 3

23–14. CUTTING A CABRIOLE LEG.

Step 3. Nail the waste stock back in position. Make sure you keep the nails in the waste stock. Turn the leg a quarter turn and repeat the cutting. Some operators like to make the first two cuts almost to the end and then back out the blade. Then turn the stock a quarter turn and repeat the cutting.

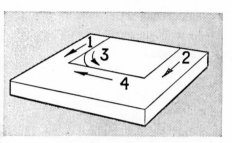

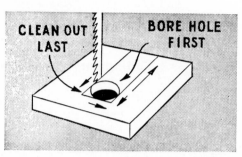

23–15. STEPS IN CUTTING a square opening. Cut No. 3 continues all the way to the corner at right, where cut No. 4 starts.

23–16. TO CUT A LONG, THIN OPENING, bore a hole at the end of the opening and cut up to it.

CUTTING A SQUARE OPENING FROM THE EDGE

Make straight cuts to the bottom of the opening on either side, backing out the blade. Then start at one side and cut an arc across the waste stock to the bottom of the other. Fig. 23–15. Complete the cut across the bottom.

CUTTING LONG, THIN OPENINGS

Drill a hole at the end of the long, thin opening and then make the straight cut. The end must be trimmed out with a hand chisel, rasp, or other tool. Fig. 23–16. A square hole can be cut at the end with a mortising attachment.

OTHER KINDS OF STRAIGHT CUTTING

Many other kinds of straight cutting can be done in the same manner as with the circular saw. The band saw is like a tilt-table saw rather than a tilt-arbor. Here are some of the operations: *squaring an end* with a miter gauge, *cutting angles* with a miter gauge, *making a compound angle, cutting several pieces to identical length* (there is no need for a clearance block since the blade cuts in one direction and will not kick back), *cutting bevels and chamfers, cutting a miter joint, cutting a cross-lap joint,* and *cutting an open mortise-and-tenon joint.*

Cutting curves and irregular shapes

CUTTING SHALLOW CURVES

Most curves are shallow and can be cut freehand. Cut up to the layout line and guide the stock with the left hand, applying even pressure with the right. The cut should be made just outside the layout line. Fig. 23–17.

23–17. CUTTING CURVES freehand.

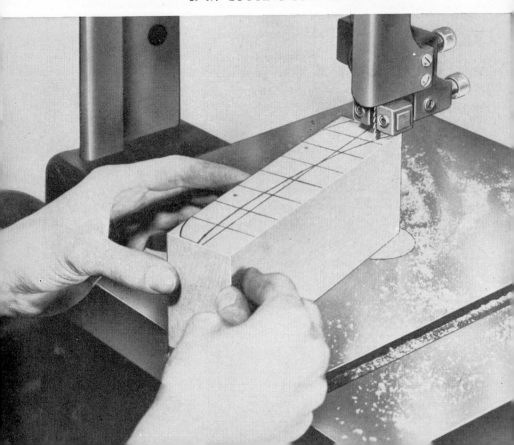

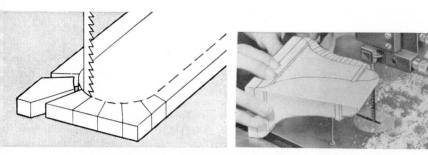

23–18. (a) CUTTING A SHARP CURVE by first making several relief
cuts. (b) THIS SHOWS THE USE OF RELIEF CUTS in making compound
cuts for book ends. Notice how the work is held level with a common nail.

23–19. CUTTING A CIRCLE freehand.

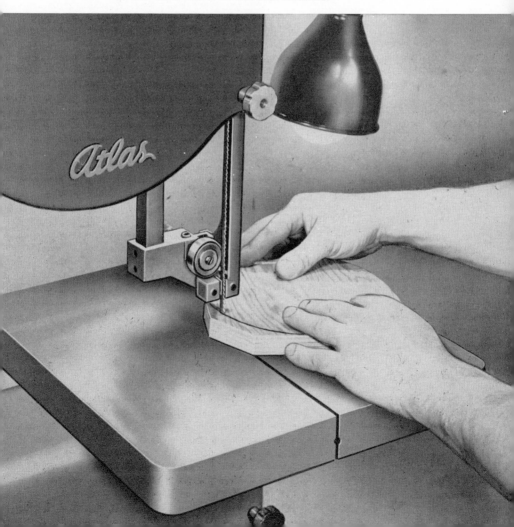

Cutting sharp curves

Remember to install a blade narrow enough to make the cut. If a wider blade is on the machine, sharp curves can be cut by first making many relief cuts to within $\frac{1}{32}''$ of the layout line. Fig. 23–18. The stock will then fall away as the curve is cut.

Cutting complex curves

Break up the complex curve into several small cuts.

Cutting circles

A circular piece can usually be cut freehand, although it is somewhat difficult. Fig. 23–19. If many circular pieces are to be

23–20. A JIG for cutting circles.

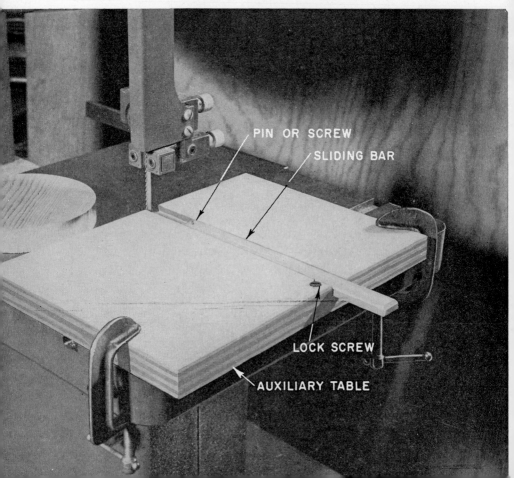

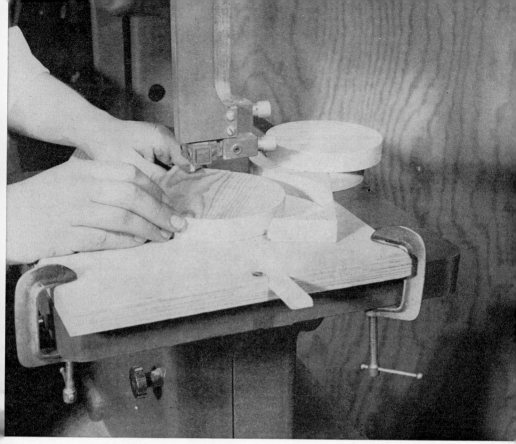

23-21. USING A JIG to cut circles.

cut, make a simple wood jig. Cut a piece of ¾ inch plywood slightly smaller than the table. Fasten cleats to two sides. Cut a groove or dado at right angles to the blade with the center of the groove at the front of the teeth. Fig. 23-20. Cut a small hardwood stick or aluminum bar that will just slip into the groove and be flush with the top of the wood table. Place a sharp pin or screw at the end of the sliding bar. It's a good idea also to put a small flathead screw next to the bar so that when it is tightened down the bar will not move. Remember that the pin must be at right angles to the blade and in line with the front. Now adjust the pin equal to the radius of the desired circle. Turn the board slowly as the circle is cut. Fig. 23-21.

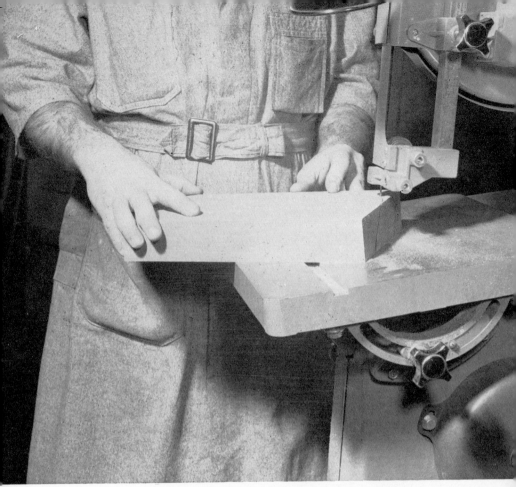

23–22. CUTTING A BEVELED CIRCLE freehand.

Beveled circles can be cut by tilting the table. Fig. 23–22.

CUTTING SEGMENTS OF A CIRCLE

Use the temporary wood table and attach an arm to it at right angles to the saw blade. Cut a pattern of the segment of the circle needed. Attach another arm to this. Place two wood screws through the pattern from the underside with the sharp points exposed. Now fasten the end of the arm of the pattern to the arm of the table with a single screw located at a point equal to the radius of the arc. Cut the stock, holding the material over the pattern. This same technique can be followed for cutting the arc of a corner. Fig. 23–23.

CUTTING CURVED RAILS OR SEGMENTS

When it is necessary to cut pieces or segments of a circle for constructing a round table or curved fronts of drawers, lay out a line on thick stock equal to the curve and cut the first curve freehand. Then fasten a pivot block or ripping fence to the table

23–23. CUTTING A ROUNDED CORNER using a jig.

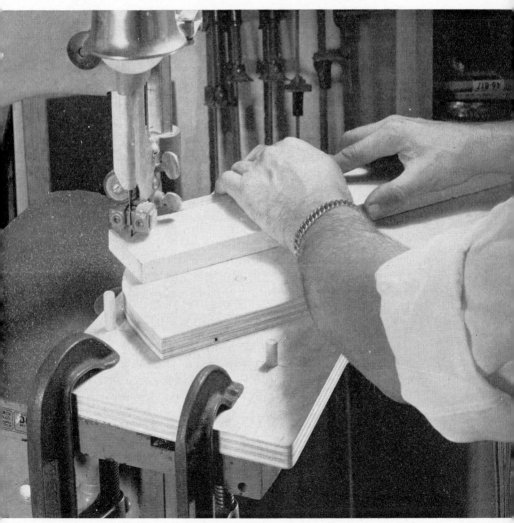

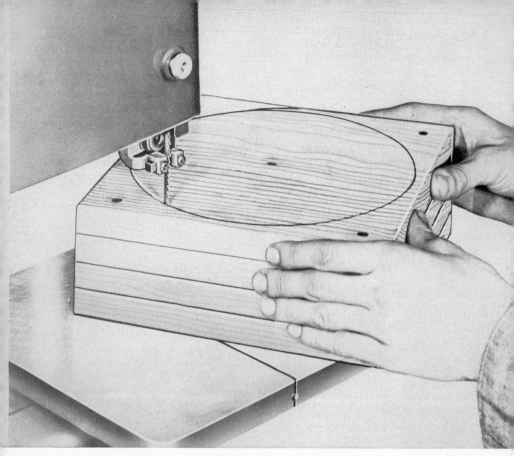

23-24. CUTTING DUPLICATE PARTS by fastening the pieces together in the waste stock with nails

a distance from the blade equal to the thickness of the segments desired. Hold the stock against the fence or pin in making this cut.

Cutting duplicate parts

When two or more pieces of the same design must be cut, a simple procedure is to lay out the design on the first piece and then nail the two or more pieces together, fastening them together in the waste stock. Fig. 23–24. Another method is to cut the shape in thick stock and then saw it up into the desired number of pieces. Fig. 23–25.

23-25. CUTTING DUPLICATE PARTS by first cutting thicker stock to shape and then re-sawing to desired thickness.

CUTTING BEFORE TURNING ON THE LATHE

Before doing any turning on the lathe, the band saw often can be used to rough out the shape. This saves time and makes the turning much easier. For example, suppose you want to turn a ball-shaped object on the lathe. First carefully square up the stock. Draw a center line around the adjoining sides. Then carefully lay out the profile for the ball on two adjoining surfaces. Do the compound cutting as described early in this section. After the ball has been roughed out, the finished turning can be done on the lathe. Always rough out large square stock to an octagon shape on the band saw before doing the turning.

CUTTING OFF ROUND STOCK

The simplest method for cutting off round stock is to hold it in a V block. Another method is to drill a hole lengthwise in a piece of scrap stock and shove the round stock through this. It is very dangerous to cut a piece of round stock freehand. Fig. 23-26.

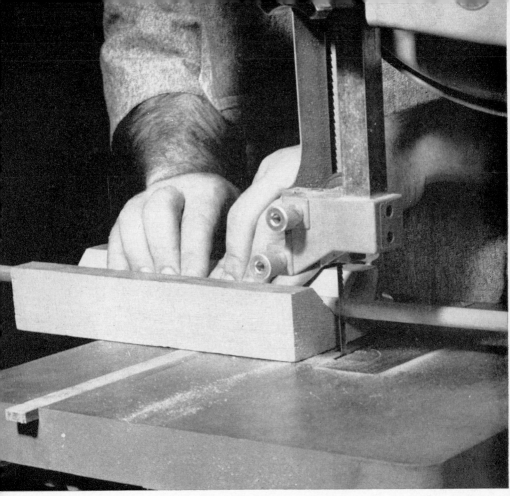

23-26. CUTTING OFF ROUND STOCK, using a V block.

CUTTING GROOVES IN DOWEL ROD

Dowel rod with slight grooves holds better for gluing because the glue can penetrate along the entire length. Tilt the table at an angle of about 15 degrees and turn the miter gauge to the same angle. Now hold the dowel rod against the miter gauge and push it into the saw to the desired depth. The saw will automatically cut a spiral groove along the rod.

JIG SAW

The jig or scroll saw, as it is sometimes called, is used primarily for all kinds of internal and external irregular cutting. It is one of the simplest and safest machines and will be found most useful in making any parts that involve intricate cutting.

Size. Size is indicated by the distance from the blade to the back of the overarm, the usual size being 18″ to 24″. An 18″ machine will cut to the center of a 36″ circle.

The types of jig saw vary from simple vibrator to the larger, regular jig saw. Fig. 24–1.

Parts. The main parts of the jig saw include a base and overarm. A driving mechanism changes rotary action to reciprocal or up-and-down motion. A table is fastened to the base which can be tilted 45 degrees to one side. On some models the table can also be turned 90 degrees, and then tilted, for cutting long stock.

There are an upper and a lower chuck which hold the saw blade. The lower chuck is connected to the crosshead which forces it to go up and down. Fig. 24–2. The upper chuck operates on a spring in the plunger. There is also a guide which can be moved up and down to hold the blade in position and to keep the work solid. Some larger jig saws are equipped with an air blower which keeps the sawdust away from the blade and layout line. Most saws operate from an electric motor with a step-pulley arrangement providing for four different speeds ranging from about 600 to 1600 rpm.

Adjustments

TILTING THE TABLE

A knob or lever located beneath the table can be loosened

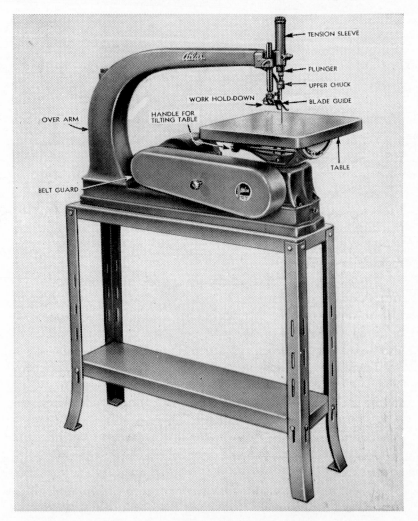

24-1. PARTS of a jig saw.

and the table tilted the desired degree for cutting bevels, chamfers, and other angular work. A pointer and gauge indicate the degree of tilt.

SWIVELING THE TABLE

On larger jig saws, the table can be turned 90 degrees by loosening two cap screws that hold the frame to the crankcase.

24–2. CHUCKS OF A JIG SAW. Notice that the lower chuck can be turned a quarter turn by loosening a set screw.

No.	Width	Thickness	No. of teeth per inch
58	.020	.070	32
59	.020	0.70	20
60	.020	0.70	15
61	.020	.085	15
64	.020	.110	20
65	.028	.250	20
77	.010	.048	18
81	.010	.070	14
82	.010	.055	16
83	.010	.045	18
84	.008	.035	20
85	.019	.050	15
86	.019	.035	12
87	.020	.070	7
88	.020	.110	7
91	.020	.110	15
92	.020	.110	10
93	.028	.187	10
94	.028	.250	7
95	.016	.054	30
96	.016	.054	20
97	.020	.070	15
98	.020	.085	12
703	.025	.187	9
704	.035	.250	7

REMOVING THE OVERARM

For some jobs in which a saber blade is needed, the overarm is removed. Several cap screws hold this to the base.

ADJUSTING THE BLADE GUIDES

On larger machines, the blade guide can be opened or closed for different thicknesses of blades, or the guide can be turned to the correct slot. The guide should just clear the blade, and the front of the guide should be at the bottom of the teeth.

ADJUSTING THE GUIDE ASSEMBLY

The whole guide assembly can be moved up or down by loosening the thumb screw that holds it in place. This guide assembly should always be adjusted so that the holddowns keep the work firmly on the table.

Blades. There are three major types of blades. Fig. 24–3 a b c.

1. *Jig-saw blades* are usually single-tooth and are used for cutting wood. These are fastened in both upper and lower chucks.

2. *Jeweler's saw blades*, sometimes called *piercing blades*, are made for cutting metal. They are excellent for cutting metal parts for hardware or trim.

3. *Saber blades* are larger, shorter blades that are fastened only in the lower

24–3. BLADES FOR THE JIG SAW: (a) jig saw blade; (b) jeweler's blade; and (c) saber blade.

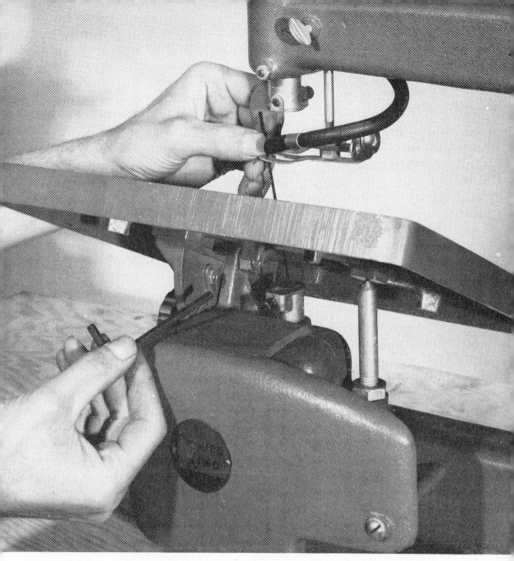

24-4. INSTALLING A BLADE using an Allen wrench to tighten the chuck.

jaw, between the V jaws. They are commonly used for rapid cutting on thick stock and for internal openings.

INSTALLING A JIG-SAW BLADE

The regular jig-saw and jeweler's blades are installed in the following manner:

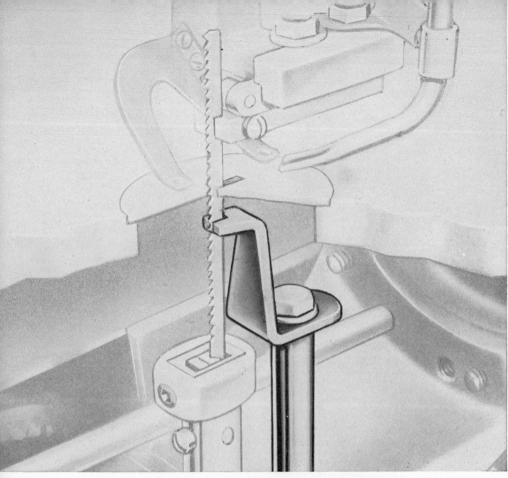

24-5. INSTALLING A SABER BLADE. Notice that the lower chuck has been turned a quarter turn and the blade fastened in the V jaws. An extra blade-support bracket has been fastened in place. See page 235.

1. Tip the table so you can work on the chuck easily. It may be desirable also to remove the throat plate. The chuck is opened or closed with either a thumb screw or a set screw. (The latter requires an Allen-type wrench. Fig. 24-4.)

2. Fasten the blade about ⅜″ deep in the lower chuck and lock it firmly. Loosen the plunger in the overarm and push it down. Pull the upper chuck down over the blade about ⅜″ and lock firmly. Make sure the guide is adjusted to clear the blade

slightly. Push up on the plunger to apply pressure to the spring and tighten the nut that holds it in the overarm.

3. Turn the machine over by hand to be sure it runs smoothly. Replace the throat plate and adjust the table.

For saber blades, proceed as follows:

On larger machines the lower chuck can be turned a quarter turn. Loosen the set screw that holds the chuck to the shaft, turn it a quarter turn, and retighten. Fasten the saber blade in the V chuck and tighten it. Sometimes a lower guide attachment is fastened in place to help support the blade. Fig. 24–5. On machines on which the lower chuck cannot be turned, the blade is fastened at right angles to the overarm and the cutting done from the side.

Safety. Observe all regular safety procedures. When this is done the jig saw is a very safe machine to use.

Basic procedures. 1. *Assume the correct cutting position.* Always stand directly in front of the blade with both hands

JIG- OR SCROLL-SAW BLADE SIZES

MATERIAL	SPEED	KIND AND SIZE OF BLADE IN THICKNESS, WIDTH AND NUMBER OF TEETH PER INCH
Softwood	Fast	For stock ⅛″ or less in thickness use a jig saw blade— .010—.045—18
		For stock ¼″ or more in thickness use a jig saw blade— .020—.110—10
Hardwood	Medium	For stock ⅛″ or less in thickness use a jig saw blade— .010—.055—16
		For straight cutting on stock ¼″ or more in thickness use a saber blade—.028—.250—20
Jewelry Metals	Medium	Use a jeweler's blade. No. 1/0 for light work and No. 2 for heavier stock.

24–6. JIG- OR SCROLL-SAW BLADE chart.

resting comfortably on the table. Guide the work with both hands, applying forward pressure with the thumbs.

2. *Select the correct size and type of blade.* This depends on the material to be cut, its thickness, and the details of the design. Fig. 24–6. The blade should always be the largest one that will do a good job. *Three teeth should be in contact with the work* at all times while the cutting is being done. Thin blades tend to break too easily or become clogged.

3. *Check all adjustments.* Make sure the blade is tight in the chuck, that the table is set at right angles to the saw blade, that the saw guides are adjusted properly, and that the holddown is in a position to keep the work firmly against the table.

4. *Lay out and plan your work before cutting.* Have a clean accurate layout that can be easily followed. When doing complicated cutting, make short cuts first and then long. Be careful when cutting corners. This is when blades usually break. If the

24–7. CUTTING external curves.

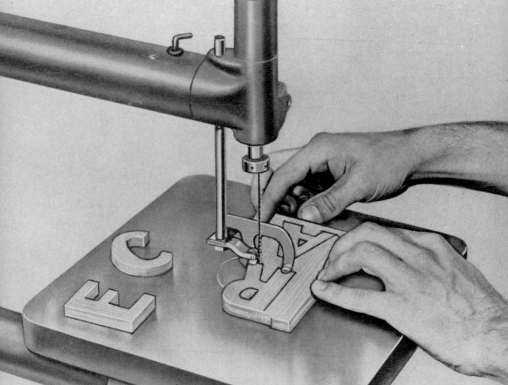

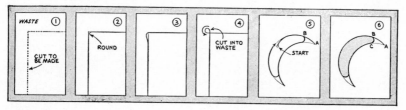

24-8. METHODS OF CUTTING to a corner and of cutting internal openings.

job is very intricate, rough cut the pattern to the approximate shape and then cut it to the finished line.

Cutting external curves. Install the correct size and kind of blade and adjust the holddown to the correct position. Place the work on the table with the forefinger over it on either side and the other fingers on the table. Apply forward pressure with the thumbs. Fig. 24–7. Start in the waste stock and come up to the layout line at a slight angle, applying as much pressure as necessary to keep the cutting going without vibration.

A smooth cut is obtained only when the work is carefully guided. Do not twist the blade, as it is easily broken. When cutting sharp curves, apply almost no forward pressure and turn the work slowly. Fig. 24–8. When it is necessary to cut to the end of a long, thin opening, cut to the corner, back out the blade a short way, and "nibble out" the corner until the work can be turned. On certain types of wood, a little soap or wax applied to the blade will help the cutting.

Cutting duplicate parts. If it is necessary to cut two or more parts to the same shape, it is a good idea to fasten them together with nails in the scrap stock and cut as before.

Cutting internal openings. Bore a hole in the waste stock large enough for the blade. Sometimes it is wise to make the hole a part of the design. For example, if a rectangular opening with rounded corners is needed, bore four holes of the desired radius, one at each corner. Fig. 24–8. If a jig-saw blade is used, remove the throat plate, slip the work over the table, put the

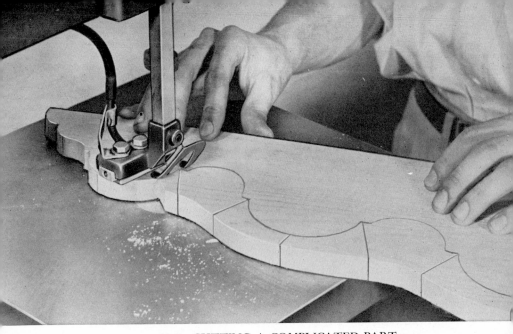

24-9. CUTTING A COMPLICATED PART.

24-10. CUTTING AN INTERNAL OPENING with a saber blade. Notice that a hole has been drilled in the waste stock to admit the blade.

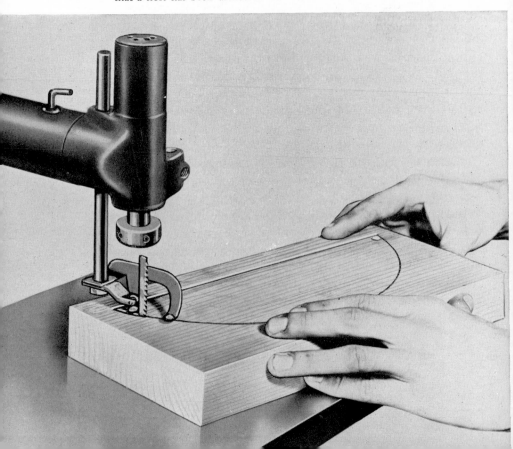

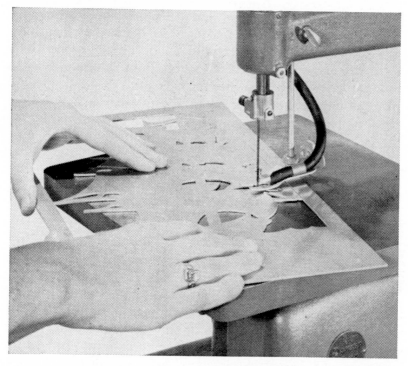

24–11. CUTTING METAL on the jig saw.

blade through the opening, and fasten it in the upper and lower chucks. Replace the throat plate. If a saber blade is used, it can, of course, be fastened in the machine first and the work placed over it. If the opening is unusual in design, it may be necessary to rough out the waste stock first and then cut up to the finished line. Fig. 24–10 shows the method of cutting an internal curved opening.

A bevel or chamfer can be cut by tilting the table the desired degree.

Straight cutting. Straight cutting can be done by fastening a fence to the table to guide the work.

Cutting metal hardware and fittings. A most important use for the jig saw in furniture making is the cutting of fittings such as escutcheon holes, drawer pulls, reinforcement corners, and other decorative metal pieces. For these jobs be sure to install a rather fine jeweler's blade. Set for high speed. Fig. 24–11. Small files can be purchased that fasten in the V chuck to finish the metal edges.

JOINTER

The jointer performs planing operations. It is one of the machines most often used in the shop and, while it does not do a large number of operations, it does these very frequently.

On this machine a series of rotating cutters shear off small bits or chips of wood to produce a smooth surface. The circular head usually has three blades. *The most common operations* are surfacing a board and planing an edge or end. *Some less common processes* include cutting a rabbet, bevel, chamfer, and taper.

Size. The size of the jointer is indicated by the length of the knives. The most common size for small shops is the 6″ or 8″. Since the great majority of operations are performed on the edge of stock, this size is plenty large enough.

The length of the bed also affects the usefulness of the jointer, since a longer bed provides better support.

Parts. The jointer consists of a *frame or base with two tables* —the *front or infeed table* and the *rear or outfeed table*. Fig. 25–1. On most machines, both of these tables are adjustable, although there are some on which only the infeed table can be raised or lowered.

The cutter head is the heart of the jointer and consists of the head itself and three or more knives. This assembly usually operates on two roller bearings.

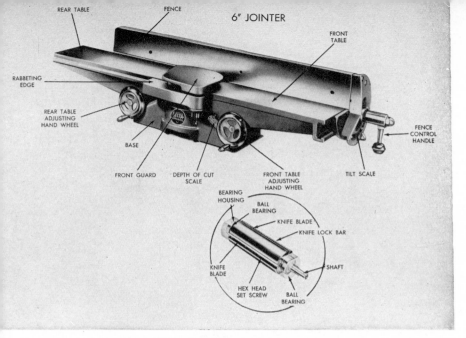

25–1. PARTS of a jointer.

The fence provides support for the work while it is fed through the machine. It can be adjusted at various angles, usually up to 45 degrees both ways from the vertical position.

The guard is a protective device covering the cutter head. It either swings out of the way or lifts up. Most operations, except rabbeting and certain tapering, should be done with the guard in place.

The jointer should be operated at about 4000 rpm.

Adjustments

ALIGNING AND ADJUSTING THE OUTFEED TABLE

1. The top of the outfeed table must be the exact height of the cutter blades. When the table is too low, the board drops down as it passes the cutter head, making a recess at the end. If the table is too high, the board will be slightly tapered. Turn the cutter head until one blade is at its highest point. Fig. 25–2.

2. Release the table lock screw on the right side of the

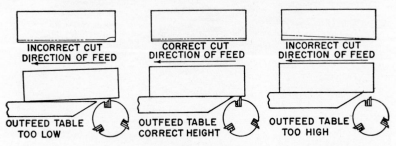

25-2. ADJUSTING THE HEIGHT of the outfeed table.

jointer. Turn the knob down until the outfeed table is lower than the cutter blade; then turn it up slowly until the table is in line with the highest point of the cutter blade. To check, place a straightedge on the outfeed table with one end projecting over the blade. Turn the cutter head over by hand to check. Tighten the lock nut. Once the outfeed table is set, it does not require changing except for special jobs. If the outfeed table is the fixed kind, raise or lower the cutter head until it is even with the outfeed table.

ADJUSTING THE INFEED TABLE

The infeed table must be about $\frac{1}{32}''$ below the cutter head for light cuts and about $\frac{1}{16}''$ to $\frac{1}{8}''$ below for rough cuts. Loosen the lock on the right side of the front table, then turn the handle beneath the table to raise or lower it. There is a pointer and scale indicating the depth of cut which must be checked periodically for accuracy.

ADJUSTING THE POSITION OF THE FENCE

1. To adjust the fence, loosen the knob or lever that holds it in position and set it at a 90-degree angle. To check this, hold a square against the table and fence. Fig. 25-3. The fence can be moved in or out. Never expose any more of the blade than is necessary.

25–3. CHECKING THE FENCE for squareness.

2. The fence can also be tilted 45 degrees to right or left. This can be set on the tilt scale and can be checked with a protractor head of a combination set or sliding T bevel. There is a pointer and scale to indicate the tilt.

Safety. There are certain special precautions that must be observed when using the jointer. Some of these apply to all machine operations. Others are specific to the jointer.

1. *Always keep the knives of the jointer sharp.* Dull knives tend to cause kickback and also result in poor planing. See "Sharpening Machine Tools."

2. *The fence should be tight.* Never adjust the fence while the jointer is running.

3. *See that the guard is in place and operating easily.*

4. *Always allow the machine to come to full speed before using it.*

5. *Do not plane any surface or edge less than 12" in length.* Also, be sure that the stock is over ½" thick and ¾" wide. *More accidents are caused by failure to observe this rule than for any other reason.*

6. *Stand to the side of the jointer, never directly behind it.* In case of kickback you will be out of the way.

7. *Cut with the grain, never against it.*

8. *Always use a push stick when surfacing thin stock.*

9. *Do not try to take too heavy a cut.*

Basic procedures. 1. Check the fence for squareness and the infeed table for depth of cut before turning on the machine. If the jointer has been used for some other operation, make a trial cut after resetting it.

2. Adjust the *depth of cut* with these things in mind:

a. The amount of stock to be removed. Take a light cut for such operations as face planing or end planing and a slightly heavier cut for edge planing. The amount of wood in contact with the blade should determine this.

b. The kind of wood. Use a heavier cut on softwoods and a lighter cut on hardwoods.

c. The kind of planed surface. Take a heavier cut for removing stock and a lighter cut for finishing.

3. Change the position of the fence periodically to distribute the wear on the jointer blades.

4. When duplicate parts are needed, do the jointery operations first; then cut the stock into the desired pieces.

5. If you are righthanded, stand to the left of the jointer with the left foot forward and the right foot back and beneath the infeed table. Move your body along as you do the planing operation.

6. Always check a board for warp and wind first. Place a concave surface down for the first cuts. If the board has wind, balance it on the high corners to take the first cuts.

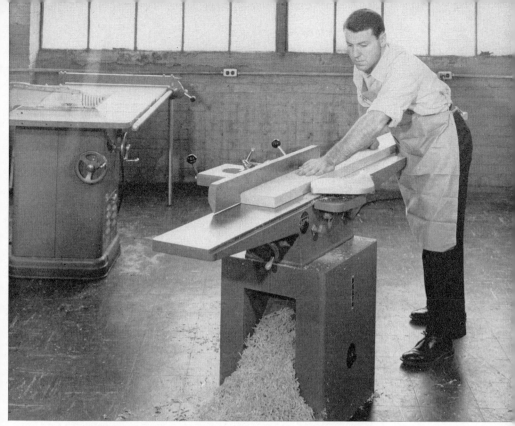

25-4. FACE PLANING, or surfacing, on an 8" jointer.

Planing a surface

1. Check the board for warp and wind and for direction of grain. Adjust for a light cut.

2. Hold the board firmly on the infeed table with the left hand toward the front of the board and the right hand on the board over the rear of the infeed table. Apply equal pressure. Fig. 25-4.

3. Turn on the machine and allow it to come to full speed.

4. Move the stock forward and at the same time keep your left hand back of the cutting. When about half to two thirds of the board has passed the cutter head, move the left hand to the board over the outfeed table.

5. As most of the board passes over the cutter, move the

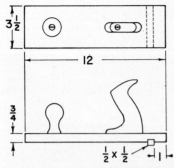

25–5. (a) THIS PUSH BLOCK MAKES use of an old plane knob and handle. (b) USING A PUSH BLOCK.

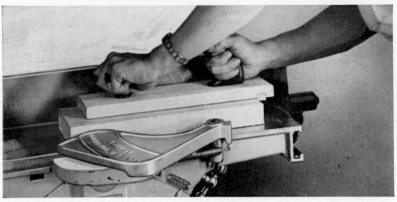

right hand to the board over the outfeed table to finish the cut.

6. If the board is less than 2″ thick, use a push block to push the board through. *Under no circumstances use your fingers.* Fig. 25–5 a and b.

Planing an edge. The most common use for the jointer is planing or jointing an edge. An edge is said to be jointed when it is at right angles to the face of the board and is true along its entire length. Fig. 25–6 a, b, c.

1. Check the fence for squareness. Generally, for safest operation, it is better to set the fence as close as possible to the left side of the machine.

2. Select the best edge and determine the grain direction.

3. Adjust for proper depth of cut. If ¼″ of stock is to be removed, it is best to do it in at least two ⅛″ cuts or, for a smoother edge, in four ¹⁄₁₆″ cuts.

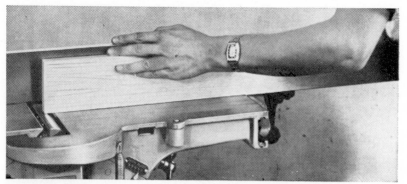

a

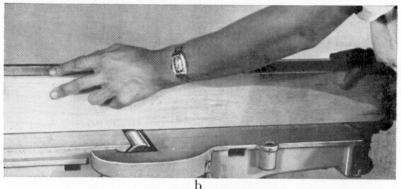

b

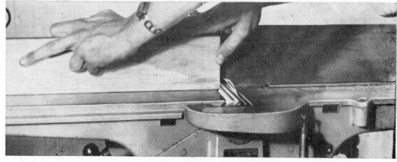

c

25–6. THREE STEPS IN JOINTING an edge or surface.

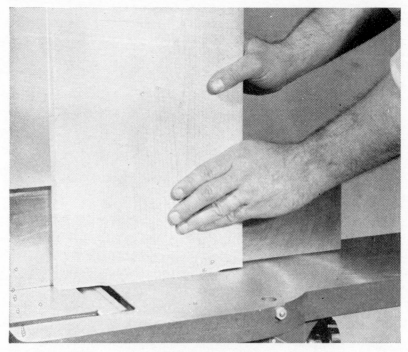

25-7. PLANING end grain.

4. Hold the stock firmly against the infeed table and fence. The smoothest surface of the board should be against the fence.

5. For the righthanded person, the left hand is a guide and the right hand is the one that pushes the stock across the cutter head. Move the left hand along with the board and, when the major portion is over the outfeed table, move the right hand. Do not push the board too fast as this will make a rippled edge.

Planing end grain. *Remember, never plane end grain less than 10" wide.* The reason this is so dangerous is that the cutters must shave off the ends of the fibers, which are tough. *Always set the machine for a very light cut for this operation.* Fig. 25–7.

1. If both edges of the board are surfaced, proceed as fol-

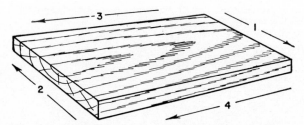

25–8. THE CORRECT STEPS in squaring up stock on
a jointer.

lows: Take a light cut of about 1″ in length along the end grain.
Reverse the board and finish the cut. Make sure you hold the
board firmly over the outfeed table as the end of the cut is made.
Fig. 25–8. As in hand planing, running the board completely
across would split out the edge.

2. If only one edge of the board is surfaced, the jointing
can be done from the finished edge all the way across, since a
splinter can be removed when the rough edge is later surfaced.

Cutting a bevel or chamfer.

1. Adjust the fence to the correct angle. Since the fence
can be tilted to the right or left, the cuts can be made with the
fence tilted either way.

2. Check the fence with a protractor or sliding T bevel.

3. Proceed with the cutting as for edge planing. Examine
the cut after each pass to see how much more must be removed.
When chamfering or beveling the ends and edges of a board,
do the ends first and then the sides. Fig. 25–9.

Cutting a stop chamfer. A stop chamfer can be cut only on
jointers on which the outfeed table can be lowered.

1. Lower both tables an amount equal to the depth of the
chamfer. This can be checked by placing equal-sized blocks of
wood on the tables and checking with a level. The distance can

25–9. CUTTING A BEVEL or chamfer. See page 249.

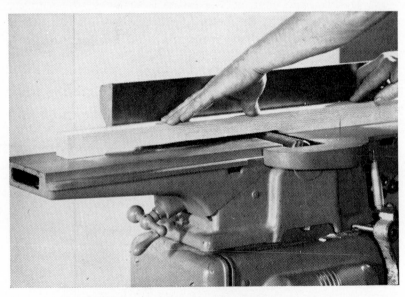

25–10. CUTTING A RECESS in a board.

be measured from the top of the cutter to the bottom of the level when the level is true.

2. With the power turned off, hold the stock with the end of the chamfer over the cutter and clamp a stop block over the outfeed table. Hold the stock with the beginning of the chamfer over the cutter and clamp a stop block over the infeed table at the end of the board.

3. Adjust the fence to an angle of 45 degrees. Turn the cutter over by hand to make sure that it does not strike the fence.

4. Turn on the machine. Hold the end of the stock against the stop block on the infeed table and slowly lower it into the cutter. Push the board along until it strikes the stop block over the outfeed table. Then carefully raise the board.

5. With the fence set at right angles, follow the same general procedure for cutting a recess in a board. Fig. 25–10.

Cutting a long taper.

1. If the taper to be cut is shorter than the length of the infeed table, lower this table an amount equal to the taper. Mark the beginning of the taper around each piece. Move the fence as close to the left side of the jointer as possible and remove the guard.

2. *Turn on the machine.* Place the portion of the piece that is to be untapered on the outfeed table and lower the board, with the starting line directly over the cutter. Push the board along

25–11. DIVIDE A LONG TAPER into two parts. See page 252.

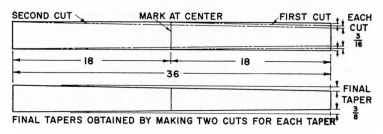

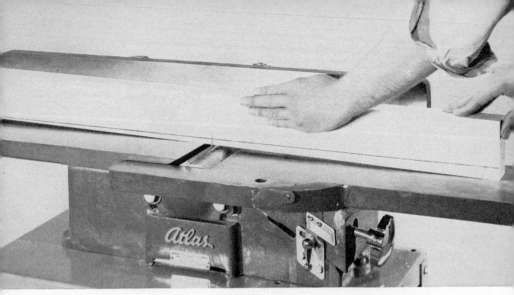

25-12. MAKING THE FIRST CUT on a long taper.

to complete the tapered cut. *For most work a push stick should be used.*

3. If the piece to be tapered is longer than the infeed table, divide the tapered section into two or more parts. (*For example,* if the tapered portion is 24″, divide it into 12″ sections.) If the amount of taper is ¼″, adjust the machine to a ⅛″ cut. Fig. 25-11. Make the first cut from the halfway point and then make a second cut starting at the beginning of the taper. Fig. 25-12.

Cutting a short taper. A short, sharp taper should be cut in a slightly different manner.

1. Lay out the location of the taper around the stock. Lower the front or infeed table an amount equal to the taper. Remove the guard and fasten a stop block to the infeed table so that the front of the taper will just touch the cutter.

2. Turn on the machine and stand facing the outfeed table, just opposite from the way you would normally stand.

3. Hold the end of the stock against the stop block. Lower the stock and then draw it toward you to cut the taper. Sometimes it is a good idea to slip a block of wood under the stock on the outfeed table to help to guide it as the taper is cut. Fig. 25-13.

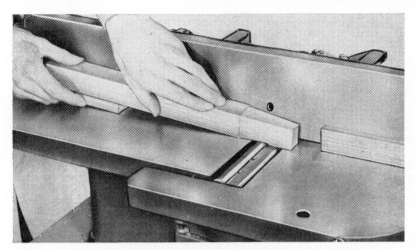

25–13. CUTTING a short taper.

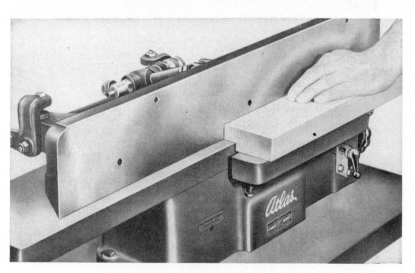

25–14. CUTTING a rabbet. See page 254.

Cutting a rabbet. One of the best ways to cut a rabbet with the grain is on the jointer.

25-15. MAKING THE CHEEK CUT on a tenon.

1. Adjust the fence to an amount equal to the width of the rabbet.

2. Lower the infeed table an amount equal to the depth of the rabbet. If the rabbet is quite deep, it may be necessary to cut it in two passes, in which case half the depth is set.

3. Remove the guard. Hold the stock firmly on the infeed table and move it along slowly. Fig. 25–14.

4. Many types of simple moldings can be cut in this way.

Cutting a tenon. Lay out the tenon and make the cheek cut on the circular saw.

1. Adjust the fence to equal the length of the tenon.

2. Lower the infeed table to equal the amount of stock to be removed on either side of the tenon.

3. Hold the end of the tenon firmly against the fence and move the stock past the cutter.

4. Since the cutting is being done across grain, care must be taken to work slowly. Fig. 25–15.

DRILL PRESS

The drill press is one of the most versatile machines in the woodworking shop, since it can be used not only for drilling and boring all sizes of holes but also, with attachments, can serve as mortising machine, router, shaper, planer, and sander.

Size. A drill press can be either a *bench* or *floor type*. The size is indicated by the largest diameter of stock through which a hole can be drilled. For example, a 15″ drill press measures 7½″ from the center of the chuck to the column.

Parts. The major parts are shown in Fig. 26–1. The *base* is heavy cast iron. The *column* is of ground steel, and the *table*, which fastens to the *table bracket*, can be locked in any position. The *head* contains all the operating mechanism. The *spindle*, which revolves, can be removed and other kinds installed. For most work a spindle with a *Jacobs chuck* is satisfactory. The *depth gauge and stop* will control the amount or depth of the drilling. Most machines have *stop nuts* and a *pointer* to control the amount of movement. The tension for the feed is applied with the *feed handle*. If the machine is to double as a shaper and router, it should have a *hi-lo attachment* so that speeds from 200 to 5000 rpm can be secured. Fig. 26–2.

Adjustments.

INSTALLING A DRILL OR BIT

To fasten a drill or bit in a chuck, open the chuck slightly more than the diameter of the tool. Insert the tool firmly in the chuck and tighten with a key. Remove the key immediately. Never attempt to fasten a tapered shank drill or bit or a squared shank in a chuck. Fig. 26–3.

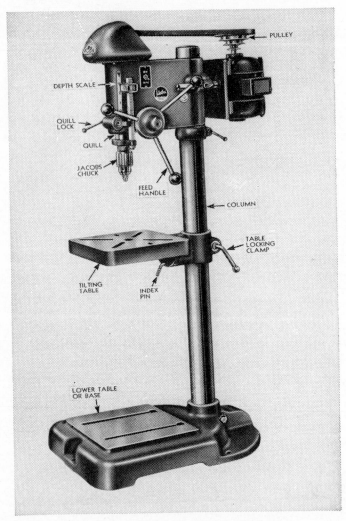

PULLEY

DEPTH SCALE

QUILL
LOCK

QUILL

JACOBS
CHUCK

FEED
HANDLE

COLUMN

TABLE
LOCKING
CLAMP

TILTING
TABLE

INDEX
PIN

LOWER TABLE
OR BASE

26–1. PARTS of a drill press.

REMOVING THE CHUCK

It is necessary to remove the chuck for operations other than drilling, since the chuck should never be used for any cutting that exerts side thrust. Place the wedge provided for this between the chuck and the collar. Tap the wedge with a brass hammer as you hold the chuck in your left hand. Fasten an adapter in the chuck's place to hold the router, shaper, planer, or sanding tool. Fig. 25–4. On some machines, the whole chuck and spindle assembly are a single unit. To remove this, remove the guard and then loosen the set screws that hold the spindle in the quill. Insert the new spindle.

ADJUSTING THE TABLE

Raise or lower the table by first loosening the clamp that holds it tight to the column. Always place the table with the clearance hole directly under the chuck. The space between

26–2. A HI-LO ATTACHMENT for the drill press.

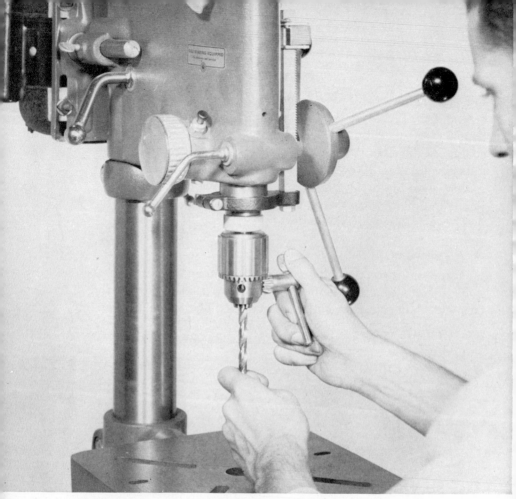

26–3. INSTALLING A DRILL in a chuck.

chuck and table should be slightly more than the length of the cutting tool, plus the thickness of the stock and a backup scrap block. To tilt the table, pull out the pin that locks it to the table bracket, loosen the nut, and then tilt the table to the desired angle. Most tables have holes drilled for setting the table with the pin at 45 degrees to right and left and at 90 degrees.

Adjusting the belt

Loosen the thumb screw that holds the motor bracket in place. Move the motor slightly so the belt can be moved to a new position, then apply pressure to the motor bracket to secure belt tension. Tighten the thumb screws. Fig. 26–5.

ADJUSTING THE FEED TENSION

Turn the housing on the feed tension spring in a counter-clockwise direction until there is enough tension to raise the quill quickly and evenly when the handle is depressed.

Safety. The safety practices for the drill press are the same

26–4. REMOVING A CHUCK from the spindle with a wedge and hammer.

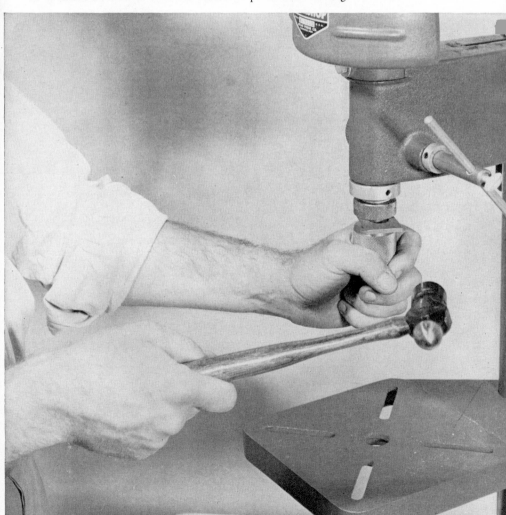

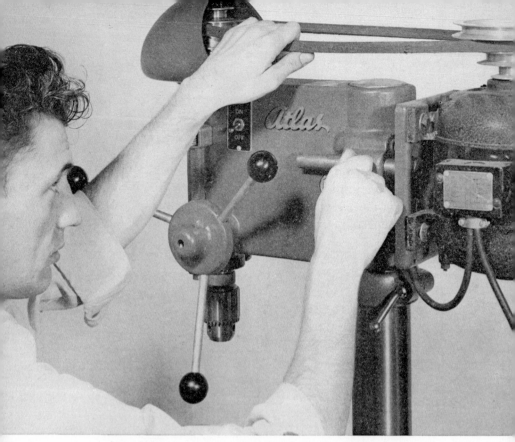

26–5. ADJUSTING belt tension.

as for all other power tools, plus those additional ones that must be observed when using it as some other machine. In addition, observe the following:

1. *Keep your fingers away from the revolving tool.*

2. *Never remove chips with your fingers.*

3. *Always make sure that the stock is properly clamped whenever clamping is necessary.*

4. *Always remove the chuck key immediately after installing a tool.*

5. *Keep the cutting tools sharp.*

Basic procedures.

1. Always make sure that the drill press is set to the proper

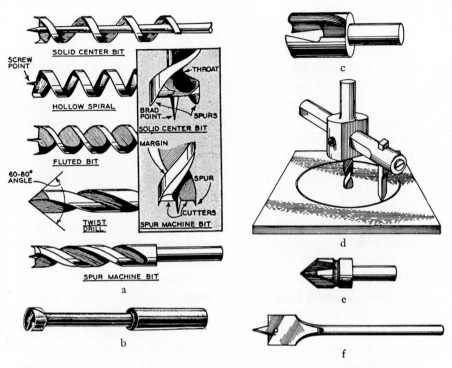

26-6. (a) TYPES OF CUTTING TOOLS for use on the drill press: solid center (or single-twist auger) bit, hollow-spiral auger bit, fluted (or double-twist) bit, twist drill and spur machine bit. (b) MACHINE FOERSTNER. (c) PLUG CUTTER. (d) HOLE CUTTER. (e) COUNTERSINK. (f) SPEED BIT.

speed. In general, maintain a slow speed for large drills and bits and higher speed for small ones. Bits up to about ½″ in size should be operated at a speed of between 2000 to 3000 rpm, bits from ½″ to 1″ at about 1000 to 2000 rpm, and above 1″ at about 300 to 500 rpm. For shaper operations, a speed of 4000 to 5000 rpm is required.

2. Whenever necessary, clamp the work securely. For most drilling and boring of small holes, the work can be held in place with the hand. For other operations, however, hand or C clamps should be used.

3. Install the correct kind of tool for the work. There are many styles of wood bits, of which the most common are the auger, the Foerstner, the expansion, and the spur machine. Fig. 26–6. The auger bit is made in either a single or a double twist. The one to use on the drill press must be made especially for that purpose. Never attempt to use a hand-type auger bit. The machine auger bit must have a straight shank and a brad-type point. It is possible, however, to adapt a hand auger bit to machine use by cutting off the square shank and filing the spur point to the brad point. Foerstner bits are used for boring shallow holes. These, too, should have straight shanks. Expansion bits and hole cutters are used for cutting large holes. Twist drills, the same as those used in metalworking, can be used for drilling small holes. If a set is to be used exclusively for woodwork, the points should be ground to an included angle of 60 to 80 degrees. All bits or drills must have straight shanks.

Boring small holes in flat stock. To bore a hole 1¼″ or smaller in size, use an auger bit. Locate the center of the hole and mark it with a center punch or scratch awl. Insert the bit in the chuck. Place a piece of scrap wood on the table and adjust the machine to correct speed. Fig. 26–7. Turn on the machine and slowly bring the point of the bit into the stock. Hold the stock firmly and apply even pressure to the handle. Fig. 26–8. If the stock is hardwood or the hole deep, rack up the bit once or twice to remove the chips before finishing the hole. Always bore through the hole and into the scrap wood. If no backup board is used, the wood will split out as the bit goes through the stock.

Boring large holes in flat stock. Holes larger than 1¼″ must be cut with an expansion bit or a hole cutter. Adjust the cutter until the distance from the center to the spur is equal to the radius of the hole. Fasten the stock to be cut on the table with a piece of scrap stock underneath. It is often necessary to clamp the work for this operation because the cutter is a single-point tool and has a tendency to rotate the work. Make sure that the

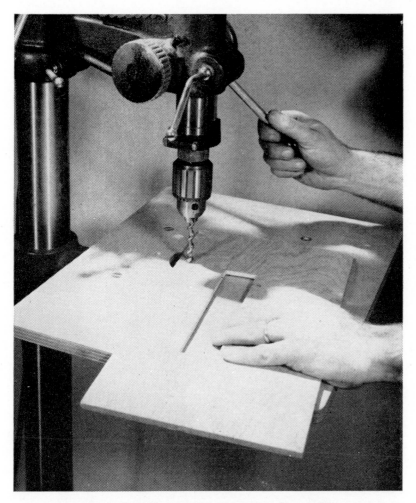

26–7. BORING SMALL HOLES in flat stock.

center of the cutter is directly over the center of the hole. Fig. 26–9. Maintain a low speed and apply slow, even pressure. Thin stock cracks easily when doing this job. The hole cutter can be used to cut small wheels for toys and other objects.

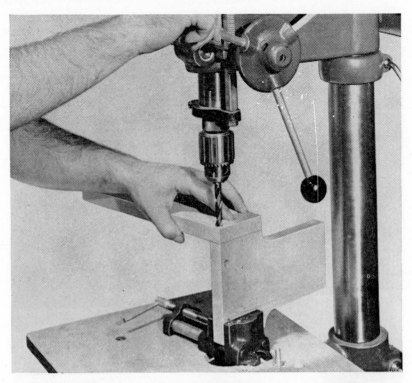

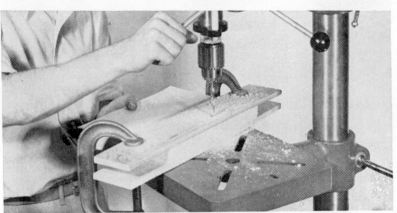

26–8. DRILLING HOLES in two or more pieces, using clamps

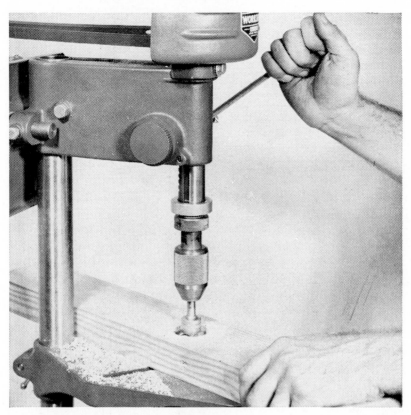

26-9. BORING LARGE HOLES in flat stock with a machine expansion bit.

Boring deep holes. On most drill presses the spindle will move only 4″ and therefore, for holes deeper than that, other methods must be used. *If the hole is less than 8″,* one of the following methods can be followed:

1. Clamp a piece of scrap stock to the table of the drill press. Select the correct size bit, install it in the chuck, and bore a small hole. Lower the table to accommodate the stock to be drilled. To line up the hole in the scrap stock with the chuck, it may

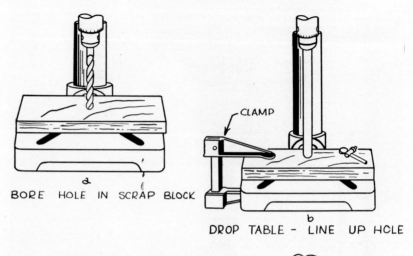

BORE HOLE IN SCRAP BLOCK

DROP TABLE - LINE UP HOLE

26–10.   BORING   A   DEEP
HOLE: (a) boring a hole in scrap
stock, (b) aligning the hole in the
scrap stock with the chuck, (c)
boring the second hole after the
first is completed with a guide pin
inserted in the scrap stock.

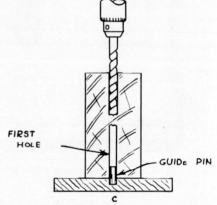

be necessary to remove the bit and replace it with a long piece
of dowel rod. Replace the auger bit and bore the hole to the
maximum depth. Then cut a short piece of dowel rod and put
it in the hole in the scrap stock, turn the material to be bored
over, with the hole over the dowel rod, and bore the other half
of the hole. This will assure the meeting of the holes in the center.
Fig. 26–10 a b c.

2. A second method is to turn the table parallel to the col-

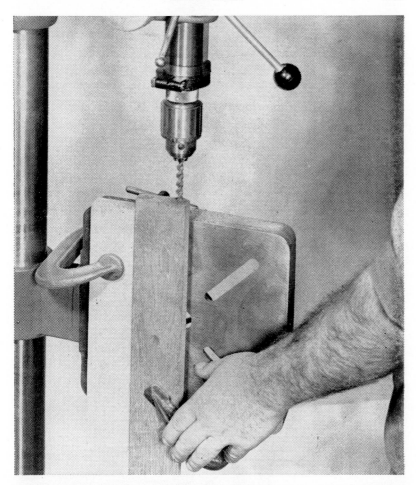

26-11. BORING DEEP HOLES with the table turned on edge. This same technique can be followed for boring holes for dowel joints in leg and rail construction.

umn. Fig. 26–11. Fasten a temporary fence to the table with the hole to be bored aligned with the bit. Then bore from both ends.

If a hole longer than 8″ is to be bored, an extended auger bit can be made by brazing a rod to its shank and one of the above procedures followed, moving the stock as needed.

Boring equally spaced holes along a surface or edge.

1. Clamp a temporary wood fence on the table as shown in Fig. 26–12. Clamp a stop block to the fence in such a position that the bit is directly over the location for the last hole. Then cut several identical blocks equal in length to the distance be-

26–12. BORING EQUALLY SPACED HOLES using a fence as a jig as described in step 2, page 270.

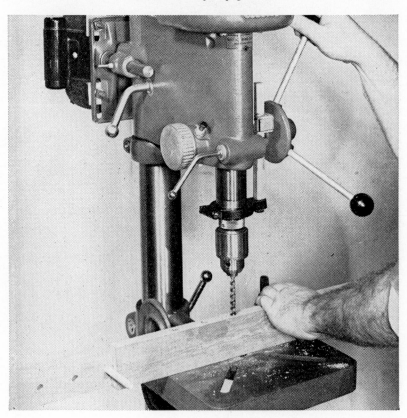

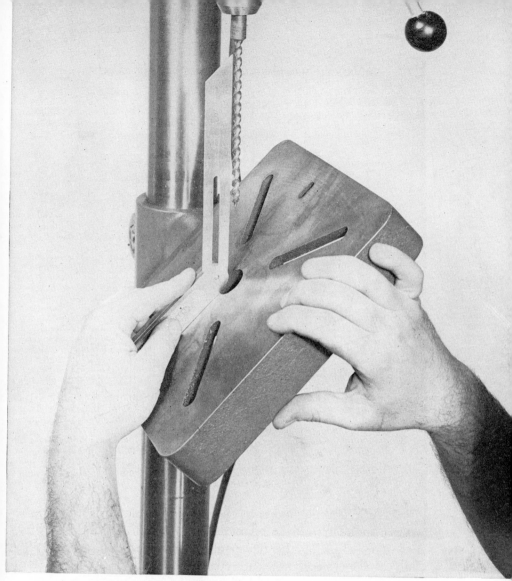

26–13. CHECKING THE ANGLE of the table with a sliding T bevel. See
page 272.

tween the holes. Place the blocks against the stop block and the
end of the work against these blocks. After the first hole is bored,
remove one of the blocks and push the work along to the next
block, bore that hole, remove the block, and proceed.

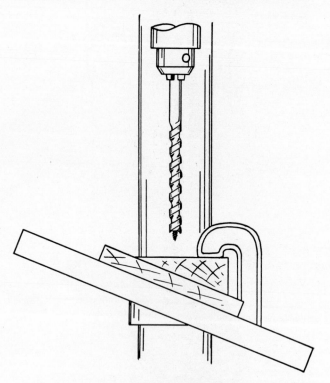

26–14. BORING A HOLE at an angle with a piece of scrap
wood over the stock.

2. A second method is to clamp to the table a fence with a series of holes in it. Place a pin in the first hole and hold the work against it, adjusting the fence to bore the first hole correctly. Move the pin to each hole and repeat.

Boring holes at an angle. Tilt the table to the correct angle. This can be checked with a sliding T bevel or protractor head as shown in Fig. 26–13. Clamp the work to the table and proceed. If the hole is fairly large, it may be necessary to cut a piece of scrap stock which has the same angle as the table. Fig. 26–14. This is then clamped to the stock directly over the hole. This makes it possible to start the hole on a flat surface.

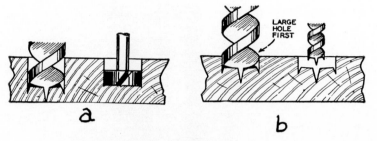

26-15. COUNTERBORING. (a) Use a large auger bit or a Foerstner bit. (b) Counterboring and boring a small hole for installing screws.

Enlarging smaller holes and counterboring. One method of enlarging smaller holes is to use a Foerstner bit. A second method is to secure a piece of dowel rod equal in diameter to the hole already bored. Fasten this over the spur of the larger auger bit as a guide. Counterboring is enlarging only part of a hole. Fig. 26-15. This is often done in furniture construction when heads of screws must be covered. Of course, it's better practice to bore this hole first and then the smaller hole for the screw.

Boring holes for dowel joints.

Edge butt

Lay out the location of the dowel hole. Fasten a temporary fence to the table so that the point of the auger bit lines up with the center of the edge. Hold the stock firmly against the fence and bore the hole. It is good practice to hold the face surface of both boards against the fence. The hole should always be about ⅛" deeper than the rod to be used. A dowel jig can be used as a guide instead of the fence.

Corner butt

Bore the holes in the edge grain in the same manner as described in the step above. Turn the table at 90 degrees to the horizontal and bore the holes in the end grain.

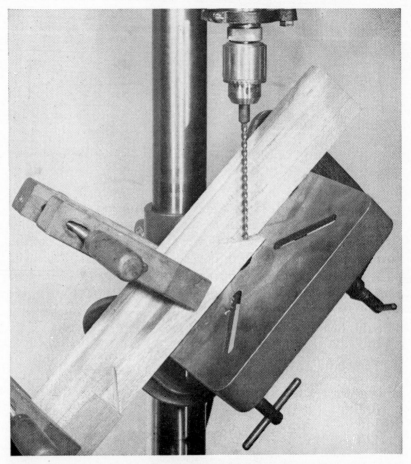

26–16. ONE METHOD OF BORING A HOLE for a miter joint with dowels. Notice that the table is tilted to 45 degrees.

MITER JOINT

Method A. Tilt the table to an angle of 45 degrees. Clamp a temporary fence to it. The edge of the stock should be centered under the chuck. Clamp a stop block to this fence so that the position for the first hole is directly under the chuck. Adjust for

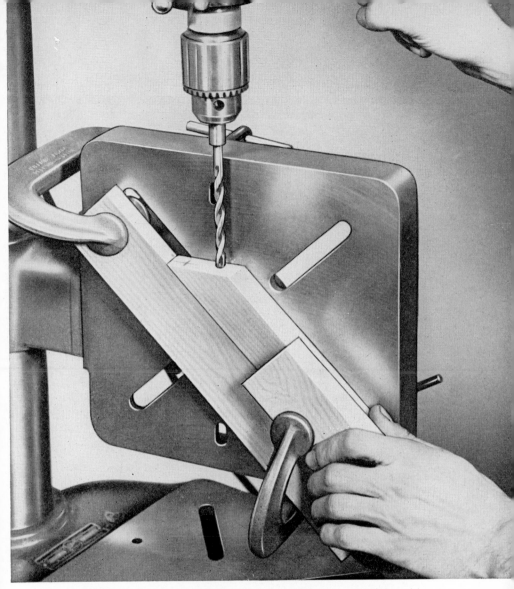

26–17. A SECOND METHOD OF BORING A HOLE for a miter joint with dowels. Here the table is turned to a vertical position. See page 274.

the correct depth of hole. Bore this hole on all the pieces. (*For example*, in making frames there would be eight holes.) Then readjust the stop block and bore all the second holes in each piece. Fig. 26–16.

26–18. DRILLING HOLES IN SMALL ROD, using a V block.

Method B. Turn the table to a 90-degree position. Clamp a fence to the table at an angle of 45 degrees and proceed as shown in Fig. 26–17.

Boring holes around a circle. Clamp a temporary wood table that has a sharp brad point in the center over the table. Locate this point a distance from the chuck equal to the radius of the circle around which the holes are to be bored. Place the work over this brad point and bore the first hole, swing the work to the next position, and repeat.

Boring holes in round stock.

1. For small round stock, fasten a V block to the table with the center of the V directly under the center of the chuck. Drill the hole. Fig. 26–18.

26–19. BORING HOLES AROUND THE EDGE of a disc using a V block to hold the work.

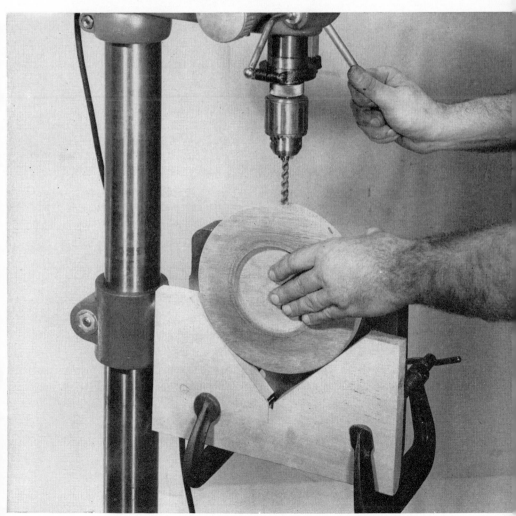

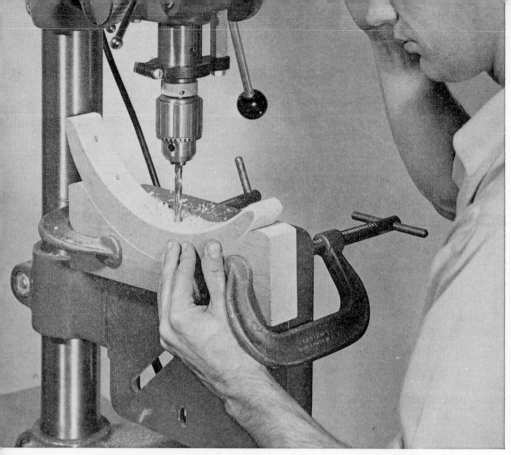

26–20. DRILLING HOLES in an irregularly-shaped piece.

2. A second method is to tilt the table at 45 degrees and clamp a fence to it with the corner formed directly under the center of the chuck.

3. To drill or bore holes in the center of wood balls or beads, cut a double V at right angles in a piece of scrap stock. Fasten this to the table with the crossed centers directly under the chuck.

4. If holes must be bored in the edge of a circular piece, turn the table at 90 degrees, clamp a large V block in place, and bore the holes. Fig. 26–19. The same technique can be followed in drilling holes in odd-shaped pieces. Fig. 26–20.

Drilling holes for wood screws. Select the correct size drill for the wood screws. Drill the pilot hole through the first piece and into the second piece to the desired depth. Drill the shank clearance hole through the first piece. For flathead screws, use an 82-degree, rose type countersink to enlarge the end of the shank hole. If the screw is to be covered with a plug, bore the

26–21. USING a plug cutter.

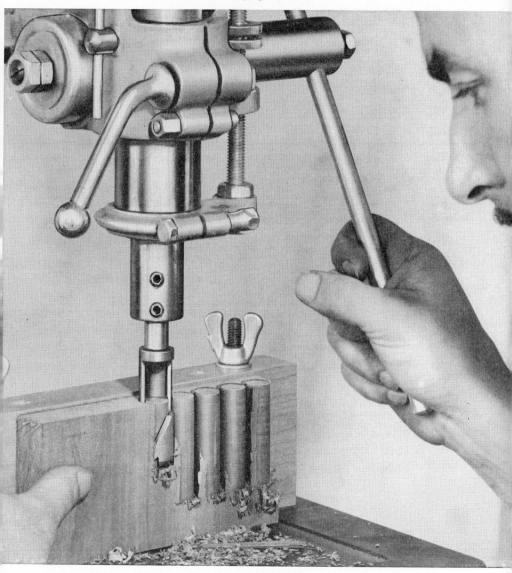

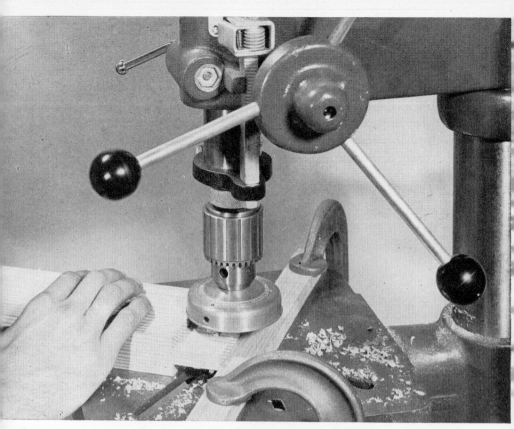

26–22. USING a planer attachment.

hole for this first, then the clearance hole, and finally the pilot hole.

A second method of drilling holes for screws is to drill the clearance hole first. Then hold the first piece over the second and mark the location for the pilot hole with a scratch awl.

Cutting plugs. Insert the plug cutter in the chuck. Place a piece of scrap wood on the table. This will prevent the plug cutter from burning. Place a piece of wood of the desired kind over this and cut the plugs. Maintain a slow spindle speed of 1200 rpm. Try to match the direction and kind of grain of the plug to the place where it will be used. Fig. 26–21.

Cutting a mortise. A mortising attachment can be fastened to the drill press to cut a mortise. See the section on Mortisers and Mortising Attachments. Page 289.

Using a shaper attachment. The drill press can be quickly converted into a shaper. Attach an auxiliary wood table and fence to the table. Replace the chuck with a shaper cutter adapter. The head assembly can be kept in its normal position or it can be inverted so that it is below the table. Adjust the speed to 5000 rpm. Attach the cutters and perform the shaper operations as described in the section on the Shaper. Page 280.

Using a router attachment. Replace the chuck with a router bit adapter. Fasten in place an auxiliary wood table. Adjust to 4000 rpm and perform the router operations as described in the section on the Routers and Routing Attachments. Page 297.

Using a planer attachment. Fasten a planer attachment to an adapter. Install a temporary wood table and fence. Adjust the speed to between 3000 and 5000 rpm. Feed the stock to be sur-

26–23. USING a sanding attachment.

faced in and against the revolving cutter with the grain. Fig.
26–22. After each cut, move the fence in order to take the next
cut.

Using a sanding attachment. For sanding the face of a
board, fasten a rotary sander attachment to the adapter and adjust
to a speed of 3500 rpm. To sand the edge of stock, fasten a drum
sander attachment to an adapter and fasten a temporary wood
table in place. Fig. 26–23. Adjust to a speed of about 1200 rpm.

SHAPER

The shaper is used primarily for cutting moldings and edge
designs, for cutting various types of joints, and for grooving,
fluting, and reeding. It is one of the most dangerous machines
in the shop and therefore should be treated with utmost respect.
It will, however, provide that added touch of craftsmanship to a
piece of furniture. With attachments the drill press can also
serve as a shaper. See pages 279 and 289.

Size. The size is determined by the size of the table and the
diameter of the spindle. Fig. 27–1. Most small shapers are a single
spindle, while the large production types frequently have two
spindles.

Parts. The shaper consists of a base to which a table is attached, and a spindle that operates at a speed of between 5000 to
10,000 rpm. Usually the spindle moves up and down to make
adjustments, although sometimes the table moves. A fence can
be attached to the table for most shaping. Most shapers are
equipped with a reversing switch. In normal use the shaper
should operate in a counterclockwise direction, with the work
fed from right to left. For many jobs, though, it is better to reverse this so the work is fed from left to right.

Cutters. There are two common types of cutters—the clamp

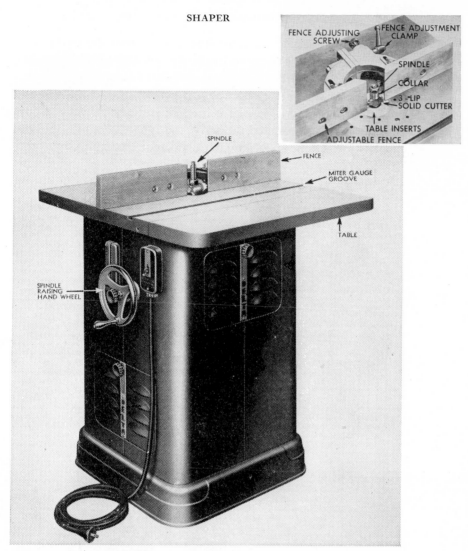

27-1. PARTS of a shaper.

with removable blades, and the formed cutters. Fig. 27–2 a, b. Whenever possible, only formed cutters should be used because they are the safest. These can be purchased in many different shapes. Fig. 27–3. The clamp type is dangerous because it has

only two blades, which can become loose. The safety cutter head
has three blades but these, too, may fly out if not kept tightened.

Safety. *Remember that the shaper is the most dangerous machine to use in the shop* because it operates at a high speed and
because cutters are exposed for most operations. Always be sure
that the cutter is installed properly, that guards are in place, and
that the job is done according to the correct procedure.

27–2. TYPES OF SHAPER CUTTERS: (a) clamp type with removable flat
blades, and (b) formed shaper cutters.

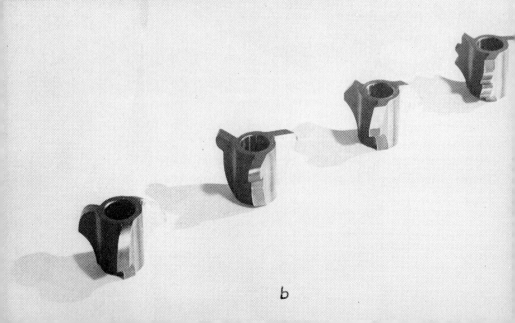

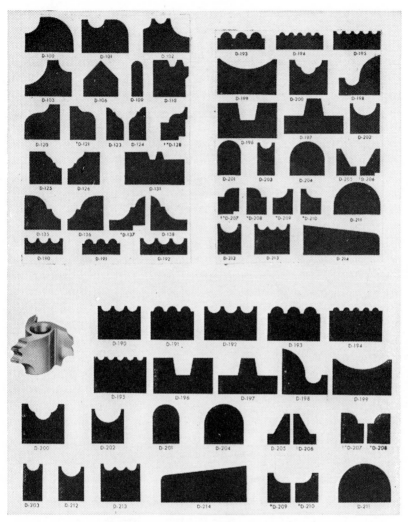

27-3. SHAPES AVAILABLE in formed shaper cutters.

Basic procedures.

INSTALLING THE CORRECT CUTTER

On most shapers there is a flat portion on the spindle just be-

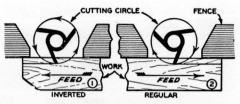

27–4. DIRECTION OF SPINDLE rotation.

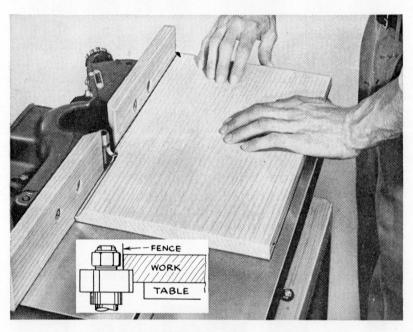

27–5. SHAPING with the use of a fence.

low the table over which a wrench can be slipped to keep the spindle from turning. Some shapers have a pin that slips in place to lock the spindle. Remove the nut that holds the cutter and replace it with the correct kind of shaper cutter. If work is to be done without a fence or jig, a depth collar must be placed above, below, or between the cutters to regulate the depth of cut. Sometimes spacers may also be needed, such as in shaping a rather complicated edge or making certain types of moldings.

ADJUSTING THE SPINDLE TO THE CORRECT HEIGHT

Loosen the spindle lock and turn the spindle up or down until the correct amount of cutter is exposed. Of course, a different-shaped edge will result with the same cutter, depending upon the position of the spindle.

CHECKING THE ROTATION OF THE SPINDLE

For most jobs, when feeding from right to left, the spindle should rotate in a counterclockwise direction as viewed from above. Fig. 27–4.

USING THE RIGHT EQUIPMENT

The correct fence, guard, or jig should always be installed to do the job in the safest possible manner.

Shaping with a fence.

1. For most jobs on straight edges, the fence should be in place. Fasten the fence to the table and hold a straightedge as a guide to make sure that both halves of the fence are aligned. If the complete edge must be shaped, the front half of the fence will have to be set back an amount equal to the depth of the cut so that the molding or edge will ride on the other half after it is completed. Lock the fence in position. Fig. 27–5.

2. Whenever possible, fasten a piece of plastic over the spindle as an added protection. When doing long moldings also use the holddowns to help to hold the work as it reaches the out-feed fence.

3. Turn on the machine and stand to the back and slightly to the left. Never stand directly back of the cutter. Hold the

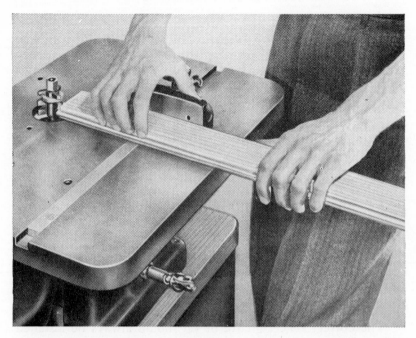

27–6. SHAPING END GRAIN with the work held against a miter gauge. See page 288.

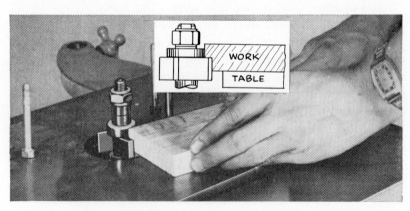

27–7. SHAPING with depth collars. See page 288.

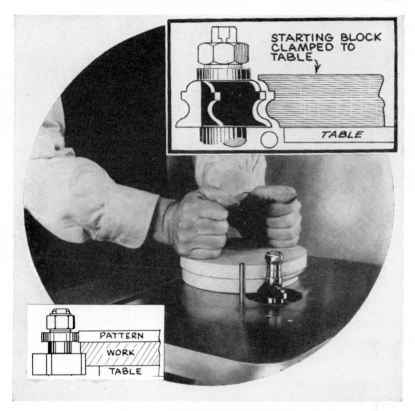

27–8. SHAPING WITH A PATTERN. See page 288.

work firmly against the fence and table with the left hand and feed the work slowly into the revolving cutter, with your right hand applying the forward pressure.

4. *Never allow your fingers to come anywhere near the cutter. Never attempt to shape a piece shorter than 8″.* If this must be done, make a temporary wood jig in which the part can be held as the edge is shaped.

5. To shape end grain, hold the work against a miter gauge.

27–9. USING THE SHAPER ATTACHMENT on the drill press.

It's a good idea to fasten a temporary wood fence to the miter gauge as added protection. Fig. 27–6.

Shaping with depth collars. If the entire edge of the stock is not to be shaped, depth collars can be fastened in the spindle to control the depth of cut. These may be above, below, or between the cutters. By this means the edges of irregular-shaped objects can be cut. Install a starting pin in the table and adjust the spindle to the correct height. Turn on the machine, hold the work against the starting pin, and, using this as a fulcrum, ease the work into the cutters. Then slowly push the stock past the cutters until the edge is shaped. Fig. 27–7.

Shaping with a pattern. If the entire edge of an irregular-shaped object must be formed, a pattern and depth collars are needed. Cut a pattern of the desired shape on a jig or band saw.

This pattern must rest against the depth collar and therefore should vary in thickness, depending on how it is to be used. The pattern should also be small enough to allow the cutting to be done to the proper depth. Place several sharp pins through the pattern. Fasten the stock to the pattern and adjust the spindle so that the pattern rides on the depth collar. Turn on the shaper and follow the same general techniques as for shaping with depth collars. Fig. 27–8.

Shaping with a jig. Some shaping jobs can be done with simple jigs. To shape the edge of round stock, cut a large V in a piece of plywood. There should be a clearance hole at the bottom of the V for the cutter. Clamp this to the table. This jig can then be adjusted forward or back until the desired edge can be cut. The stock can then be rotated as it is held against the V block.

Shaping on a drill press. All simple shaping jobs can be done by fastening an attachment to the spindle of the drill press and attaching the shaper cutters to the spindle. Fig. 27–9.

MORTISERS AND MORTISING ATTACHMENTS

The mortise-and-tenon joint is found frequently in all types of furniture construction. Since cutting mortises by hand is a long and tedious job, it is very desirable to have a mortising machine or a mortising attachment for the drill press. This latter accessory can be purchased very reasonably. The tenon can be cut easily on the circular saw, band saw, jointer, or shaper.

Mortiser. The mortising machine consists of a vertical column to which a table and motor-driven head are attached. The motor-driven head moves up and down on ways through the operation of a foot pedal. *The table can be moved in three directions: up or down* for permanent settings, *in and out* to locate the

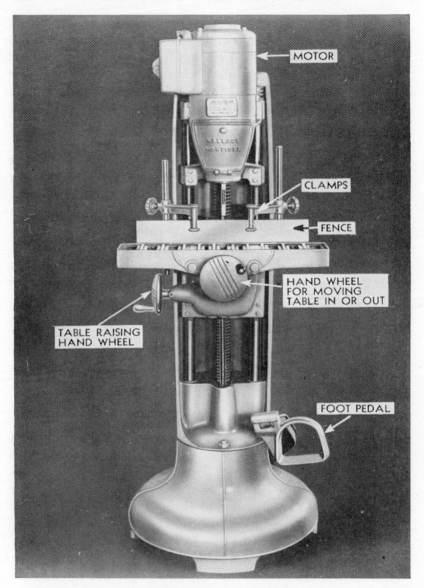

28–1. PARTS of a mortiser.

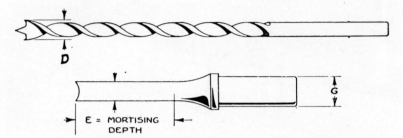

D

E = MORTISING DEPTH

G

28–2. MORTISING CHISEL AND BIT: bushing diameter (G) and bit diameter (D)

bit in the correct position over the work, and on some types to the *right and left* for cutting the mortise. Fig. 28–1.

The table has holddowns which hold the work firmly against the table. Adjustable stops limit the movement of the table, thus controlling the length of the mortise.

Mortising chisels and bits fit into the end of the motor. There is a bushing for each size of chisel to fit into the head of the mortising machine. The common sizes are ¼″, ⅜″, ½″, ⅝″, ¾″, and 1″. Fig. 28–2.

Using a mortiser.

1. Square up the stock to the desired size and lay out the location for one mortise. The mortises on the other parts will then be in the proper position when the table has been correctly set. When cutting mortises on two sides of a piece, always check the location for each.

2. Select the correct size of chisel and bit. For example, use a ½″ bit and chisel for a ½″ mortise. Also select the correct size bushing for the chisel. These split bushings are all the same diameter on the outside, with varying dimensions on the inside to hold the different sizes.

3. Insert the bushing for the chisel and then install the chisel itself. Turn the chisel with the open side to the right, or to the right and left if it is open on both sides. This opening provides an escape for the chips.

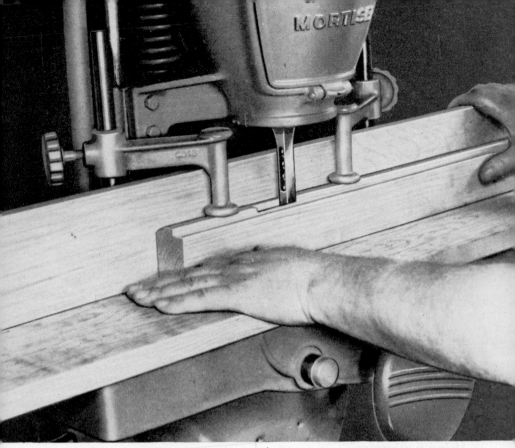

28-3. SETUP FOR MORTISING. The work must be moved on this type since the table does not move from left to right.

4. Hold a square against the side of the chisel and against the fence to align it. Then tighten the set screws that hold the chisel in place. Fig. 28-3.

5. Insert the bit until it extends about $\frac{1}{16}''$ beyond the chisel. Tighten the set screws or chuck.

6. Place the stock to be mortised on the table with a mark on the end indicating the depth of the mortise. Depress the foot pedal to its maximum amount. Turn the screw adjustment on the head until, at the end of the stroke, the chisel is in line with the bottom of the mortise. Release the foot pedal.

7. Place the end of the stock under the chisel and move the table in or out until the chisel is directly over the layout. Move

the work until the mortising chisel is under the extreme right end of the mortise. Place a stop against the end of the stock so that other identical pieces will be located automatically. Also adjust the stop on the table. Now move the table or the work to the left end of the mortise and adjust the stop. There are two holddowns to keep the work in place.

8. Move the table back to the starting position, which is the right end. Turn on the machine, depress the pedal, and cut partway to depth. Move the table to the right and cut to full depth. Fig. 28–4. Then move it back to the starting position and finish the first hole. This is done to relieve the pressure on the chisel and to provide a way for chips to escape. Continue to make full cuts until the mortise is complete.

28-4. USING ANOTHER KIND OF MORTISER. The operator can move the table from left to right on this kind by turning the handle held in his left hand.

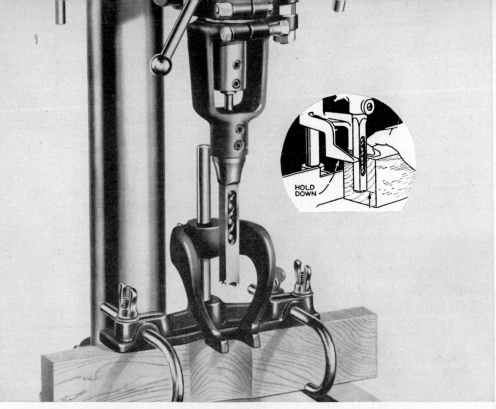

HOLD DOWN

28-5. MORTISING ATTACHMENT for the drill press. Notice that in this kind the bit is held in a special adapter.

9. Cut all identical mortises. Then reset the machine for mortises in a different location.

Mortising attachment. The mortising attachment for a drill press consists of a fence against which the work is aligned, a clamp to hold the work in position and a mortising chisel holder which is clamped to the quill. On some machines the mortising chisel bit is held in an adapter. Most often, however, it is fastened into the regular drill chuck. Fig. 28-5.

To install the mortising attachment:

1. Remove the chuck and also the feed stop bracket from the quill.

2. Replace the feed stop bracket with the mortising chisel socket and clamp it in place. Use the depth stop stud in this

chisel socket to keep the quill from turning and to regulate the depth of the chisel cut.

3. Replace the drill chuck or install an adapter.

4. Fasten the fence to the table at the approximate position. This can be moved in or out to locate the mortise.

5. Install the correct chisel in the chisel socket and square up one side with the fence. Also install the correct bit.

6. Turn the drill press over by hand to see that the bit does not scrape. Adjust the drill press to a speed of about 1000 rpm.

28–6. USING A MORTISING ATTACHMENT on the drill press. Notice that in this kind the bit is held in a Jacob's chuck.

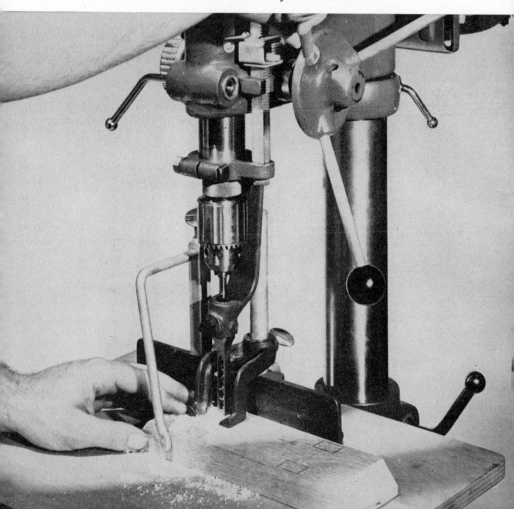

Using a mortising attachment.

1. Lay out the position of the mortise on all pieces. Place the stock on the table against the fence and move the fence in or out until the chisel is directly under the layout. Then move the stock away from under the chisel, rack the chisel down, and adjust the stop to control the depth of cut. Also place the holddowns in position to hold the work against the table.

2. Start at the right end of the mortise and proceed with the cutting as described above. The chisel movement is operated by the hand feed lever and the stock must be moved by hand. Fig. 28–6.

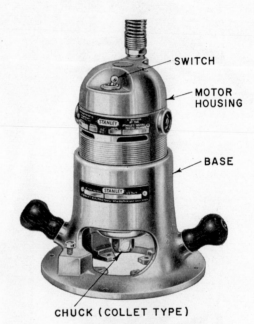

SWITCH

MOTOR HOUSING

BASE

CHUCK (COLLET TYPE)

29–1. PARTS OF THE ROUTER. The motor housing screws into the base a distance of $\frac{1}{16}''$ for each complete turn, or $\frac{1}{64}''$ for each quarter turn. STANLEY TOOLS

ROUTERS AND ROUTING ATTACHMENTS

Routing is similar to shaping except that the motor and cutters are just opposite in arrangement. While there are production routers for school and home use, the portable router is satisfactory. With a router adapter and cutters, many operations can also be done on the drill press.

Portable router. The portable router consists of a motor with a chuck attached to the spindle. Fig. 29–1. This motor screws into a base to which two handles are attached. A guide for doing straight or curved routing also can be secured. The portable router can be fastened in an attachment and used as a small shaper.

Router bits. There are many shapes of router bits that can do grooved or decorative work in the surface or edge of stock. Some of the common ones are straight bits, rounding overbits, beading bits, cove bits, and chamfer bits. Fig. 29–2 a and b. In addition, a dovetail bit is needed for cutting a dovetail joint. All router bits do the cutting on their sides rather than on the end. Fig. 29–2 c, d, e, f and g.

Using a portable router.

CUTTING GROOVES, DADOES, GAINS OR MORTISES

To make these cuts, fasten a straight router bit in the chuck

29–2a and b. A FEW OF THE HUNDREDS OF ROUTER BITS available.
STANLEY TOOLS

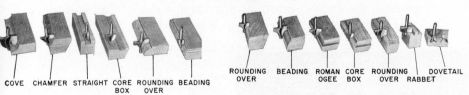

COVE   CHAMFER   STRAIGHT   CORE BOX   ROUNDING OVER   BEADING   ROUNDING OVER   BEADING   ROMAN OGEE   CORE BOX   ROUNDING OVER   RABBET   DOVETAIL

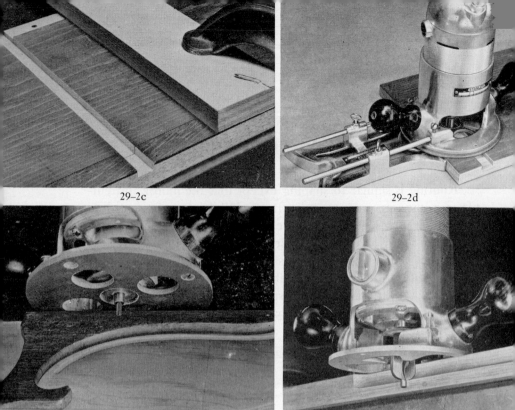

29-2c

29-2d

29-2e

29-2f

29-2c. THE AMOUNT THE ROUTER CAN MOVE SIDEWISE can be controlled in five ways: A straightedge can be clamped to the stock and the router base held in contact with it. 29-2d. A STRAIGHT OR CIRCULAR GUIDE can be attached to the base to control the lateral movement. The guide is being used here to cut a dado. 29-2e. A TEMPLATE OR PATTERN CAN BE USED. A sleeve or guide is attached to the bottom of the base and this rides against the template. 29-2f. THE PILOT EDGE of many cutters may control the amount of cut.

of the router. Screw the motor into the base until the router bit extends beyond the base the desired depth. Attach a guide to the base to control the cut. Lay out the desired cut and locate the guide in the correct position. Start at one side or end and move the router along to make the cut. Fig. 29-3 a, b, c.

29-2g. You can operate the router in a freehand manner to do the cutting such as in making this sign. STANLEY TOOLS

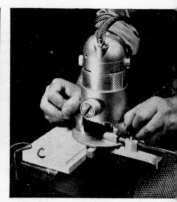

29-3. STRAIGHT ROUTING using a guide: (a) cutting an opening, (b) cutting a groove for inlaying, and (c) cutting a rabbet.

CUTTING DECORATIVE EDGES

There are many shapes of cutters for cutting decorative edges. Most of these have a pilot tip on them which does not cut but merely rides against the uncut edge of the wood. Attach the desired router bit in the machine and adjust for depth. Secure a piece of scrap the same thickness as the finished stock and clamp it to the top of a bench. Hold the router firmly against the top of the work and move the cutter into the stock. Then move it along slowly. Check to see that the desired shape is being cut. The shape can be changed by moving the motor up and down in the base.

FREEHAND ROUTING

Signs and decorations are sometimes made freehand with the router. Carefully lay out the areas to be removed. Secure a cutter bit of the desired diameter and fasten it into the machine. Clamp the work to the table top and then lower the router into the design. Move the router along to follow the outline.

PATTERN ROUTING

For irregular-shaped objects of which several duplicates are

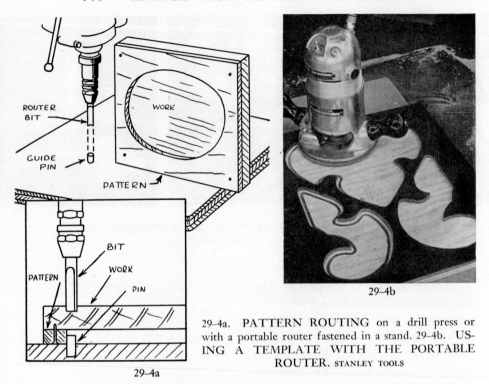

29-4a. PATTERN ROUTING on a drill press or with a portable router fastened in a stand. 29-4b. USING A TEMPLATE WITH THE PORTABLE ROUTER. STANLEY TOOLS

to be cut, it may be desirable to make a pattern. To do this, lay out on a piece of plywood the areas to be routed out. Cut these areas out on a jig saw. Then fasten this piece to another piece of plywood. Place some small pins through this template to hold the work. Select a router of the desired diameter and fasten it in a drill press or use the router that is fastened in a bench router attachment. Clamp a temporary wood board on the table and bore a hole in it with the router bit. Place a small pin in this hole. Cut the pin off so that it will be less than ¼″ above the table. Now, to do pattern routing, merely adjust the machine for the correct depth of cut, place the stock to be routed over the template, and place the template over the pin. Then move the stock and pattern around under the router. Fig. 29-4 a. Pattern or template routing can be done with the portable router by first making a template of tempered hardboard or plywood. Use a straight bit for a sharp corner or a rounding over bit for a rounded corner. Fasten the template over the work and do the routing as shown in Fig. 29–4 b.

BEADING AND FLUTING

On many traditional pieces of furniture, the rails or legs are enriched with beading or fluting. This can be done quickly with the router. Fasten the leg in a wood lathe and place a piece of plywood over the lathe bed as a support. Place the motor of the router in a beading and fluting attachment. Select a cutter of the desired shape. Adjust the cutter in the attachment in line with the center of the work. Attach a collar above or below the cutter to control the depth of cut. The indexing attachment on the head of the lathe can control the number of cuts. Hold the router firmly on the board over the bed and move it along the piece to cut.

MAKING DOVETAIL JOINTS

The most desirable joint for most drawer construction is the dovetail. This is extremely difficult to make by hand but is very simple with a router and dovetail attachment.

1. Clamp the dovetail attachment to a bench or table. Square up the stock to be used for the front and sides of the drawer or other furniture piece. Fasten a template guide to the base of the router and install a dovetail bit. Adjust the dovetail bit to extend below the base the desired amount. This amount can usually be determined by making a trial cut and readjusting the router to the exact depth.

2. Clamp board B, which will be one side of the box or drawer, inside out against the front of the base and protruding ½″ or more above the top surface of the base. Fig. 29–5 a.

3. Clamp board A, which will be the front or back of the drawer or box, inner side up. Make sure that it is in complete

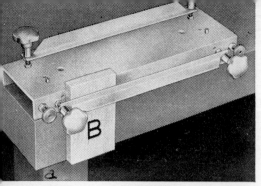
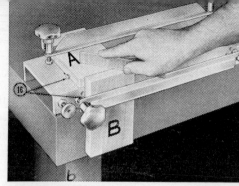
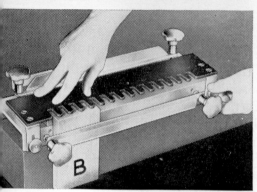

29–5. CUTTING A DOVETAIL, using a dovetailing attachment. (a) Clamp side in place. (b) Clamp front or back in place. (c) Place template over piece. 29–5d. CUTTING THE DOVETAIL.

contact with board B. It should be set flush with the top end of B. Fig. 29–5 b.

4. Place the dovetail template over the two pieces of stock and clamp in place. Fig. 29–5 c.

5. Make a trial cut, being sure that the template guide follows the template. Check the trial dovetail for fit. If it is too tight, lower the bit about $\frac{1}{16}''$. If it is too loose, raise it about $\frac{1}{16}''$. If it is too shallow, set the template guide nuts back slightly. Fig. 29–5 d.

6. The completed dovetail should appear as in Fig. 13–14. The left end of the fixture is used for cutting the right front of the drawer and the left rear corner. The left front and right rear corner are cut on the right end of the dovetail.

7. A similar type of dovetailing attachment can be secured that can be used on a drill press.

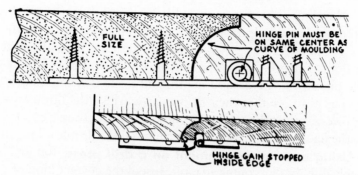

FULL SIZE

HINGE PIN MUST BE ON SAME CENTER AS CURVE OF MOULDING

HINGE GAIN STOPPED INSIDE EDGE

29–6. A DROPLEAF table joint.

29–7.   USING A ROUTING ATTACHMENT on a drill press.

MAKING A DROPLEAF TABLE JOINT

A dropleaf table joint is used frequently in furniture construction with the dropleaf hinge. Two sets of bits are needed, one a beading bit to use on the table itself and the other a cove bit to use on the table leaf. Secure some scrap stock the same thickness as the table. Fig. 29–6. Install the beading bit and adjust to the desired depth. Make the cut on the scrap piece. Install the cove bit, adjust the desired depth, and make this cut. Check the two pieces to see that they fit properly. Make the finish cuts on the pieces, using the scraps as guides. Use the router to mortise out the back of the table and leaf to install the dropleaf hinge.

Using a router attachment on a drill press. Remove the chuck and install a router adapter. Install the correct kind of cutter bit. Fasten a fence to the table. Lower the cutter bit to the desired depth and do the routing as with a portable router. Fig. 29–7.

SANDERS

In furniture construction, a most important process is finishing. To obtain a really good finish, the wood must be sanded thoroughly. There are many kinds of sanding machines, the most common of which are the floor-type belt sander, the floor-type disc sander (often these two are combined in a single machine), the drum sander, the portable belt sander and the finishing sander. With these machines, all surfaces, edges, and ends can be smoothed.

Kinds.

BELT AND DISC SANDER

Belt and disc sanders may be separate machines or, more frequently, a combination machine. Both are equipped with tables on which the work is held. The belt sander can be used in a vertical or horizontal position. Its table has herringbone slots

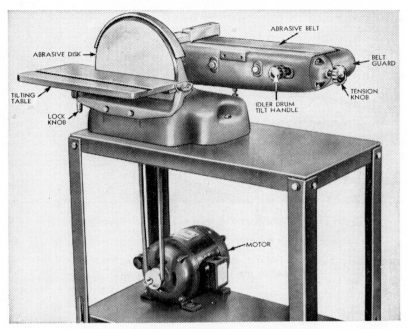

30–1. PARTS OF A BELT AND DISC sander.

cut in it to keep the underside of the belt free of dust and dirt. The belt sander often comes equipped with a fence similar to that on a jointer. Fig. 30–1. The disc sander has a rotating disc on which the abrasive paper is fastened. A table can be adjusted at any angle to the vertical surface. The machine illustrated above combines features mentioned.

DRUM OR SPINDLE SANDER

The drum sander has a revolving drum on which abrasive paper is fastened. It is used mostly for sanding the edges of stock. The drill press, lathe, or shaper can be quickly converted into drum sanders. Figs. 30–2 and 30–3.

HAND-STROKE BELT SANDER

The hand-stroke belt sander is the best machine for sanding

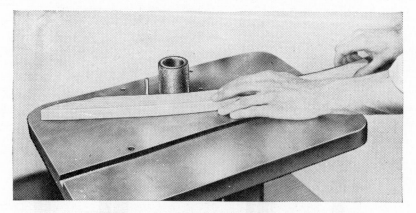

30–2. THE SHAPER can be used as a drum or spindle sander.

30–3. THE HAND-STROKE BELT SANDER. The insert shows the machine in use for sanding a table top.

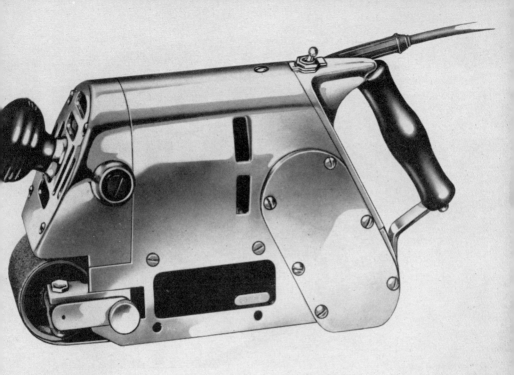

30–4. PORTABLE belt sander.

large surfaces such as the tops of desks, tables and cabinets. A large, continuous belt revolves around two drums. The work table can travel fore and aft. The operator holds a sanding block on the back of the moving belt to control the sanding. Fig. 30–3.

PORTABLE BELT SANDER

The portable belt sander operates in a manner similar to the floor machine except that the revolving belt is placed over the work instead of the work against the belt. Fig. 30–4.

FINISHING, OR PAD, SANDER

There are many kinds of finishing sanders, all of which operate on one of four basic principles. Fig. 30–5. The straight-line action leaves the least amount of cross-grain scratches. Finishing sanders are primarily used for fine finish sanding after the project is assembled.

 ROTARY ACTION   ORBITAL ACTION   STRAIGHT LINE ACTION   MULTI MOTION ACTION

30–5. FINISHING sander. See page 307.

Adjustments

BELT SANDER

To adjust the belt sander to a vertical, horizontal, or slant position, loosen the hand lock, move it to the correct position and re-lock. To adjust the belt table, loosen the two cap screws that hold it in place and raise or lower it so that it will be about $\frac{1}{32}''$ above the upper edge of the drum frame and guard. To install a new belt, first remove the drum guard. Release the tension on the belt, slip the old one off, and replace with a new one. Apply a slight amount of belt tension and turn the machine over by hand to see if the belt stays on center. To track the belt, loosen the knob which controls the tilt of the idler arm and tilt in one direction or another. Re-lock. Add additional belt tension as needed. If you start the machine without tracking the belt, it may slide off and be ruined. To remove the stop fence for sanding long or wide boards, remove the two cap screws that hold it in place.

Disc sander

Here are some of the common adjustments for the floor-type disc sander. To tilt the disc table, release the handle beneath the table and adjust it to the correct degree. When using the disc sander, it's a good idea to check the table for squareness frequently. The table is cut with a groove to permit the use of a miter gauge. To remove the disc, hold the spindle firmly and rotate the disc in a counterclockwise direction. Sometimes a small stick of wood must be inserted to keep the spindle from revolving.

To install a new sanding disc, first remove the old paper. There are several materials that can be used for fastening the disc in place, among which are glue, rubber cement, or commercial stick cement. If glue is used, the disc must be soaked in water first. If rubber cement or stick cement is used, the machine must be turned on, the end grain of a piece of hardwood held firmly

30–6. INSTALLING an abrasive sheet on a disc sander, using a commercial cement.

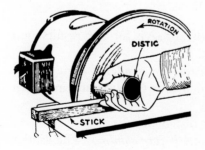

against the disc to heat it and the old disc pulled off. Cut a new sanding disc if commercial ones are not available. Apply rubber cement or glue or hold stick cement against the revolving wheel. Fig. 30–6. Put the abrasive paper in place and allow it to dry a short time. The disc sander can be made more versatile by applying a little strip of abrasive paper or cloth to the edge of the disc to change the degree of coarseness.

DRUM OR SPINDLE SANDER

To replace the abrasive paper or cloth on a drum sander, remove the worn paper. Sometimes a wedge on one side holds the paper on the drum. In other cases, the drum is made of two half segments that can be separated for replacing the new paper.

PORTABLE BELT SANDER

Replacing a belt on this machine is the same as on a floor-type belt sander.

FINISHING SANDER

Cut a sheet of abrasive paper to the required size. Usually the paper is held on the pad at either end and pressure keys lock the paper in place. To replace the paper, release the pressure keys at either end. Fasten paper in one end and lock this key. Pull the paper tightly over the pad, slip this end under the other end, and tighten this lock. The exact method of fastening the paper to the pad will vary with different sanders.

Basic procedures.

1. Always select the grade of abrasive for the results you want. See the section on abrasives.

2. Make sure that sanding on the disc sander is done on the down side or that the work is fed against the direction in which the belt sander is rotating.

3. Always sand *with the grain* of wood.

4. *Do all the cutting operations before sanding.* The sander

is designed to finish the surface of the work and not to shape it.

5. *Always sand surfaces square.* The tendency in sanding is to round all edges and surfaces. Don't spoil the accuracy of your project by careless sanding.

6. "Break" all edges *slightly* to prevent splintering. The corners should be rounded to about the diameter of the lead in a pencil.

7. Apply just enough pressure to get the job done. *The tendency of the inexperienced is to press too hard,* cutting scratches in the surface.

8. At intervals clean off the abrasive paper or cloth with a brush.

Using a belt sander.

1. To sand work in a horizontal position, first lower the

30-7. SANDING FLAT SURFACES on a belt sander.

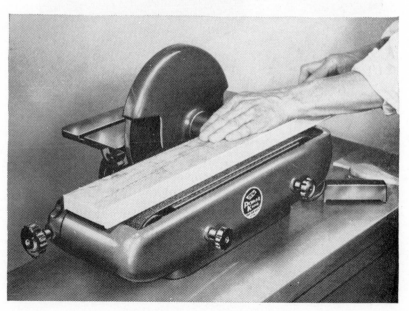

30–8. SANDING A BEVEL or chamfer on a belt sander.

belt sander into position. For smaller pieces—that is, narrower and shorter than the exposed part of the belt—hold the work lightly but firmly on the belt with one end against the stop fence. Fig. 30–7.

2. To sand edges, fasten a fence or table to the belt sander and remove the stop fence. Hold the work against the fence, moving it along slowly. Bevels and chamfers can also be sanded accurately in this manner. Fig. 30–8.

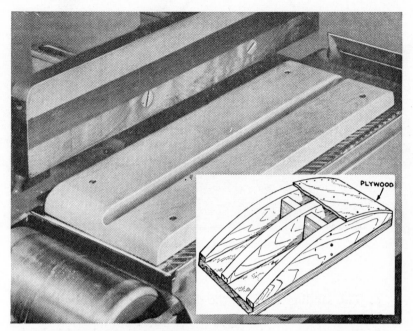

30-9. DOING FORM SANDING on a belt sander. This form is used to round
the corners of stock. The one shown in the inset may be used for sanding a large
curved part.

3. To sand the surface of larger pieces, remove the fence
and the stop fence and feed the work across the belt at a slight
angle.

4. To do form sanding, make a wood form that is exactly
opposite in shape and cover it with a piece of sheet metal. Fasten
this to the sanding table so that the belt runs over the form. Fig.
30-9.

5. To do *concave sanding*, remove the guard and use the end
of the drum. *Convex sanding* can also be done on the back of the
sander where there is no table. Loosen the tension on the belt
slightly. A slash belt, which is one cut into thin ribbons, can be
secured for this job, although a regular belt can be used.

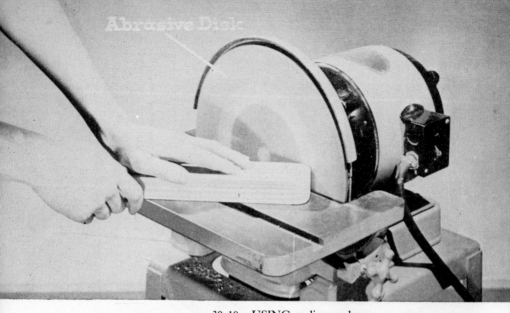

30–10. USING a disc sander.

6. The sanding table on the disc sander can also be fastened to the belt sander for smoothing ends and edges.

7. To sand an inside corner, remove the guard and hold the stock against the table.

Using a disc sander.

1. Most sanding is done freehand. The table must be square with the sanding disc and the stock held against the downward side of the rotating disc. Fig. 30–10. Remember that the closer you get to the edge of the disc, the faster the sanding action is.

2. To sand the ends of stock accurately, hold the work against a miter gauge. This is especially important when sanding mitered corners, such as for a picture frame.

3. To sand circles or arcs freehand, hold the work firmly on the table and revolve it slowly.

4. A simple jig can be made if many circles or wheels are to be sanded. Use the same kind of jig described for cutting circles on the band saw.

5. To sand shaped or bent pieces such as skiis or rail segments

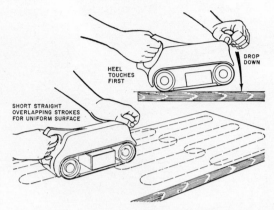

30–11. LOWER THE SANDER slowly to the surface. Move the machine in
the pattern shown.

of a round table, fasten a stop block on the table at the correct
distance from the sanding disc. Then feed the stock between the
stop block and the disc.

6. To sand the inside of a long, narrow opening, use the edge
of the disc that has abrasive fastened to it.

Using a drum sander.

1. To sand the edges of stock on the drum sander, hold the
work freehand, applying equal pressure at all times as you move
it along.

2. To do pattern sanding, turn a block of wood equal in
diameter to the drum. Fasten it to the end of the drum. Cut a
pattern of the desired size and place two small sharp screws in it.
Place the work over the pattern and adjust the drum sander so
that the pattern is held against the collar at the end of the drum
sander.

Using a portable belt sander. The proper technique is to
put the cord over your right shoulder, hold the machine with
both hands, turn on the machine, and lower the back of it slowly

30–12. USING a vibrator finishing sander.

on to the wood. Then do the sanding by moving it forward and back, moving slowly from one side to the other. Fig. 30–11.

Using a finishing sander. The finishing sander should rest evenly on the stock. Apply a moderate amount of pressure and move the sander back and forth, working from one side to the other. Fig. 30–12.

WOOD LATHE

The wood lathe combines *power operation* with *hand tool skill*. While it is not used very much commercially, it is extremely valuable to the furniture maker in turning many parts for Early American furniture and the simpler parts for some modern pieces. It can also be used for making many turned accessories, such as lamp bases, lazy Susans, and bowls.

Size. The size is indicated by the largest diameter it will turn and the length of the bed. Fig. 31–1. A typical size is the 10″ with 36″ bed.

EARLY AMERICAN PIECES that require turned parts. SPRAGUE & CARLE-TON, INC.

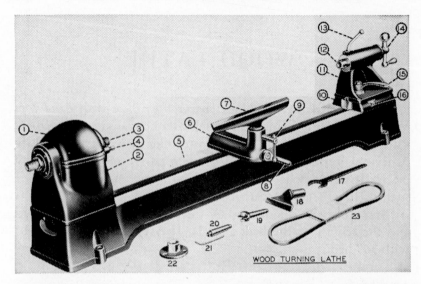

WOOD TURNING LATHE

31-1. PARTS OF A LATHE: (1) pulley guard, (2) headstock, (3) headstock spindle, (4) index pin, (5) bed, (6) tool rest base, (7) tool rest, (8) tool rest base clamp, (9) tool rest clamp, (10) tailstock base, (11) tailstock, (12) tailstock spindle, (13) tailstock spindle clamp, (14) tailstock spindle feed handle, (15) tailstock clamp handle, (16) set-over adjusting screw, (17) headstock wrench, (18) small tool rest, (19) spur center, (20) cup center, (21) wrench, (22) small faceplate, and (23) belt.

Parts. The bed is a heavy metal casting. The headstock assembly consists of a hollow spindle that is threaded on either end and a step pulley for changing the speed. There are equally spaced holes drilled around the step pulley which act as a dividing head to do many operations. Fig. 31–2. The inside end of the spindle is threaded with a righthand thread and the outside end with a lefthand thread. Faceplates can be fastened to either end for faceplate turning. The inside end has a tapered hole (No. 2 Morse taper) into which the spur center fits. On certain large machines, there is a motor in the head which can be adjusted for all spindle speeds. The tailstock assembly can be clamped to the bed at any

31–2. HEADSTOCK assembly.

31–3. ACCESSORIES.

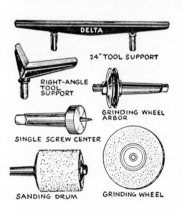

24" TOOL SUPPORT

RIGHT-ANGLE TOOL SUPPORT

GRINDING WHEEL ARBOR

SINGLE SCREW CENTER

SANDING DRUM

GRINDING WHEEL

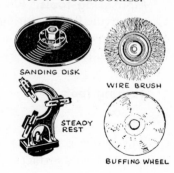

SANDING DISK

WIRE BRUSH

STEADY REST

BUFFING WHEEL

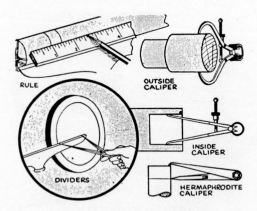

31–4. MEASURING TOOLS.

position. A hand wheel can be turned to move the tailstock spindle in or out. This spindle is also hollow, with a No. 2 Morse taper. The cup center fits into this end. The tool rest and holder clamp to the bed and can be adjusted for turning any diameter.

Accessories. There are many accessories available. The *regular faceplate* is available in several different diameters. It has a hole in the center and three or more equally spaced holes near the outside edge. It is used for all faceplate work. Fig. 31–3. The *single screw* center is used when turning small bowls and cups. A *sanding drum* or *disc* is for sanding. A *steady rest* is used when turning very thin, long stock.

Measuring tools. The wood turner needs a good one- or two-foot rule for measuring distances, inside and outside calipers for checking diameters of work, and a dividers for laying out circles, especially on faceplate work. Fig. 31–4.

Turning tools.

G OUGE

The gouge is used for straight turning and for cutting concave and convex surfaces. A bevel is ground on the convex side

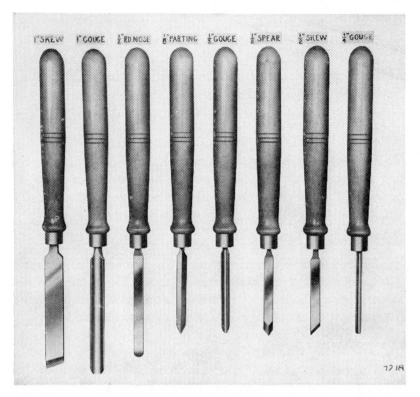

31-5. TURNING tools.

at an angle of about 30 degrees. This tool is available in several sizes. Usually a large 1″ or 1½″ gouge and a small ½″ or ¾″ gouge are needed. Fig. 31–5. See Fig. 32–8 for correct sharpening procedure.

SKEW

Skews are used for finished turning, for cutting shoulders, for trimming ends and for cutting V's and beads. They get the name from the fact that the cutting edge is askew, usually at an angle of about 70 degrees. The tool is ground from both sides. The upper end is called the toe and the lower end the heel. Usually two sizes, 1″ (large) and ½″ (small) are needed. Fig. 31–5.

PARTING TOOL

The parting tool is slightly wider at the center and narrower at either edge. The point is ground from both sides. It is used for trimming ends and for marking and turning to various diameters. When in use it is held on edge and forced into the work. Fig. 31–5.

SQUARE-NOSE

A square-nose is shaped like an ordinary wood chisel except that the blade is heavier. It is ground at an angle of about 45 degrees from one side. It is used in scraping operations for straight and taper turning. Fig. 31–5.

ROUND-NOSE

The round-nose is similar to an ordinary chisel except that it is ground with a semi-circular end. The bevel is on one side and at an angle of about 45 degrees. It is used for many scraping operations such as cutting coves or large recesses. Fig. 31–5.

DIAMOND-POINT

The diamond-point or spear is ground to a sharp point with a bevel on one side at an angle of about 45 degrees. It is used for scraping operations, such as forming sharp V's or corners. Fig. 31–5.

Safety. Follow the general safety rules for all woodworking machines. In addition, practice the following precautions:

1. Never allow any other person to stand near the lathe when it is in operation.

2. It is especially important that your sleeves be tight and that your necktie be tucked in.

3. Hold all tools firmly.

4. Make sure that the wood being turned is free of knots, checks and other defects.

5. Keep the tool rest as close to the work as possible.

6. Always maintain correct spindle speed.

Methods of turning. There are two basic methods of turning.

1. *Scraping method.* This is the simplest and easiest method for the beginner to learn. All of the tools are used as ordinary scraping tools and the wood is removed by wearing away the fibers. It does not produce as smooth a surface but, with sanding, is satisfactory. For the operator who makes only an occasional piece on the wood lathe, this method can be recommended. All faceplate work is done by the scraping method.

2. *Cutting or paring method.* With this method, the wood fibers are sheared off. This requires considerably more practice. It is the method employed by the oldtime, skilled hand wood turners. If one is to do a good deal of wood turning, it would pay to learn this method.

Basic procedures.

1. Select a piece of wood of the desired kind. Cut a piece that is slightly larger than the diameter to be turned and about 1″ longer than needed. If the stock measures more than 3″ square, cut it into an octagon shape on the band saw. This can also be done on a circular saw or jointer.

2. Draw lines across the corners of either end. Fig. 31–6. If it is round, locate the center with a hermaphrodite caliper or center head.

3. Mark the center with a prick punch or scratch awl.

4. With a driveout, remove the spur center from the lathe. Hold the stock on end over a table and place the spur center in position, striking it several times to drive it into the wood. Some operators keep an extra spur center available for this. Never place the wood against the center in the lathe and strike it, since you can ruin the headstock spindle bearings. Fig. 31–7. If the wood is extremely hard, saw a kerf about $\frac{1}{8}$″ deep across each corner and drill a small center hole, $\frac{1}{16}$″ in diameter and $\frac{1}{8}$″ deep, in either end for insertion of the centers.

5. Place the stock over the spur center of the headstock and

31–6. LOCATING THE CENTER on the end of stock.

move the tailstock so that it clears the other end of the wood about 1″. Lock in position. Then turn the tailstock handle until the cup center seats firmly in the wood. Release the pressure slightly and apply a little wax or oil. Then apply a little tension to the hand wheel and lock it in position.

6. Adjust the tool rest to clear the stock about ⅛″, while the top of the rest should be about ⅛″ above center. If the stock is quite long, adjust the tool rest with one end even with the tailstock end of the stock.

7. If the stock is between 1″ to 2″ in diameter, use the fastest speed; from 2″ to 3″, medium speed; and above 3″, slowest speed. Slower speed is needed for square stock and higher speed as it becomes a cylinder.

8. Turn the lathe over by hand once or twice to make sure that everything clears.

31–7. DRIVING THE SPUR CENTER into the end of stock.

9. Set an outside caliper to measure ⅛″ more than the diameter of the finished stock. Now you are ready to begin.

Rough turning between centers.

1. Select a large, well-sharpened gouge. If you are right-handed, hold it in your left hand, using one of the following two methods:

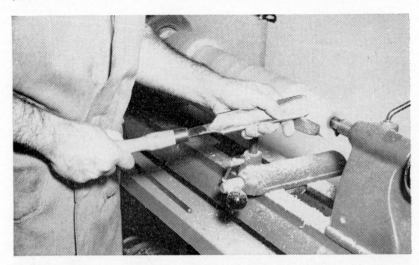

31-8. FIRST METHOD of holding a gouge.

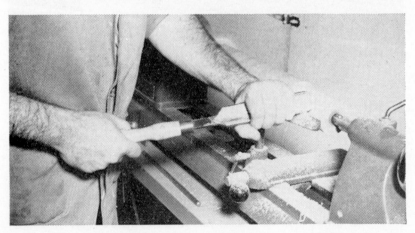

31-9. SECOND METHOD of holding a gouge.

a. Grasp the gouge about an inch from the cutting end, with the thumb on the inside and the other fingers around the outside or convex side. The index finger, then, will act as a stop against the tool rest. Fig. 31-8.

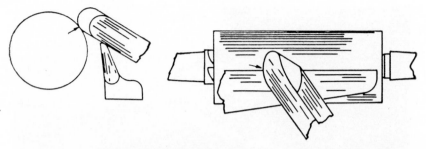

31–10. CORRECT METHOD of using the gouge for cutting.

    b. Place the hand over the concave side of the gouge, with the thumb underneath. The wrist must be bent, then, to act as a stop against the tool rest. Fig. 31–9.
    2. Hold the handle of the turning tool firmly in the right hand.
    3. Turn on the machine. Place the convex side of the gouge against the tool rest about 2″ from the right end. The index finger or your wrist should be held firmly against the rest and the cutting tool against the top.
    4. Twist the turning tool slightly to the right and force it into the revolving stock until cutting begins. The beveled edge should be tangent to the cylinder. Fig. 31–10. Then push the tool slowly toward the tailstock. After each cut, move the tool several inches more toward the headstock and repeat.
    5. When the cylinder is formed to within 2″ of the headstock, twist the tool to the left, pushing it toward the headstock. At first the cutting will be done only on the corners, but gradually on the whole cylinder. It is easy to tell if the stock is round by laying a tool lightly against the revolving surface.
    6. When the cylinder is formed, hold the outside caliper in the left hand and a small gouge in the right. Force the small gouge in slowly near (but never at) the headstock end and tailstock end until the caliper just slips over the wood.
    7. Repeat the cutting action until the stock is turned to rough size.

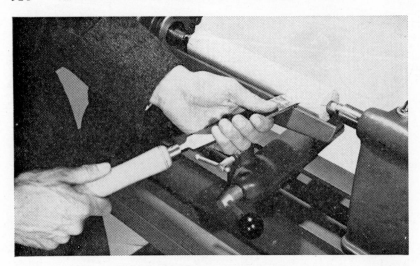

31–11. SCRAPING a plain cylinder.

Finish turning a plain cylinder.

1. Adjust an outside caliper to finished size.

2. To scrape stock to finished size, use a square-nosed tool or a large skew. Use a very high speed. Hold the cutting edge parallel to the cylinder and force it into the work until the scraping begins. Then move it from one side to the other. Always start the scraping some distance in from the ends to prevent the tool from catching and splitting the wood. Check occasionally with an outside caliper until finished size is reached. Fig. 31–11.

3. For cutting, use a large size skew. Place the skew on its side with the cutting edge slightly above and beyond the cylinder. Fig. 31–12. Start at a point 2″ to 3″ in from the end. Hold the side of the tool firmly against the tool rest. Slowly draw the skew back until the cutting edge is over the cylinder at a point about halfway between the heel and toe. Fig. 31–13. Be careful not to catch the toe of the tool in the revolving cylinder. Tip the skew slightly until the cutting edge can be forced into the wood. Then push the skew along toward the tailstock, taking a shearing

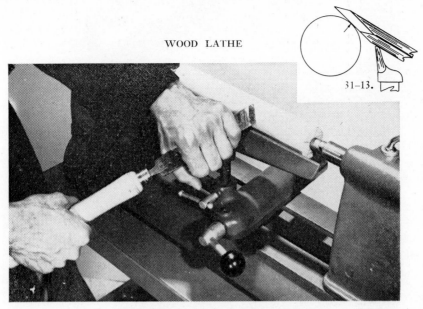

31–12. CUTTING a plain cylinder with a skew.

cut. Reverse the direction and cut toward the headstock. The major difficulty of the beginner is that he holds the tool at too great an angle to the work, thus making the tool dig in; or he holds it in one position too long, resulting in too small a diameter.

Using a parting tool. The parting tool has many uses. It can be used as a scraping tool, to cut a cylinder to length and to cut a shoulder. It is also used in cutting recesses, tapers, and complex parts (to indicate the depth of turning). Hold the parting tool on edge over the tool rest with your right hand and hold a caliper in your left. Force the parting tool into the revolving stock. At the same time hold the points of the caliper on the cylinder until they just slip over. Fig. 31–14. If the groove to be cut is fairly deep, it's a good idea to move the parting tool a little to cut a slightly wider groove than the tool itself. If further cutting is to be done, always allow about ¹⁄₁₆″ to ⅛″ beyond the layout line.

Cutting a shoulder. Turn the cylinder to the desired size and with a rule and pencil mark the position at which the shoulder is to be cut.

1. *Scraping method.* Set an outside caliper to the smaller di-

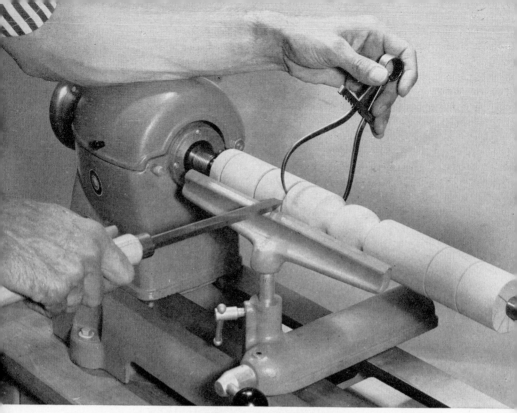

31-14. USING A PARTING TOOL and caliper.

ameter. With a parting tool cut a groove at the layout line in the waste stock. The groove should be cut to the caliper measurement. Use a square-nosed tool or skew and scrape to the smaller diameter. Fig. 31-15 a and b.

2. *Cutting method.* Hold the small skew on edge with the toe down and the heel up. Hold the skew at a slight angle so that one bevel is at right angles to the cylinder. Force the skew into the wood a little at a time; then remove it and cut a half V groove until the smaller diameter is reached. Fig. 31-16. Rough cut the smaller diameter with a small gouge. Then place the skew on its side and trim to the smaller diameter. Fig. 31-17. Use the heel of the skew to cut to the corner. Handling all tools for the wood lathe requires practice.

31–15a. SCRAPING A SHOULDER to finished size.

31–15b. A SIMPLE TURNING EXERCISE for straight turning and cutting
a shoulder.

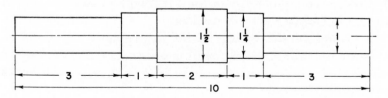

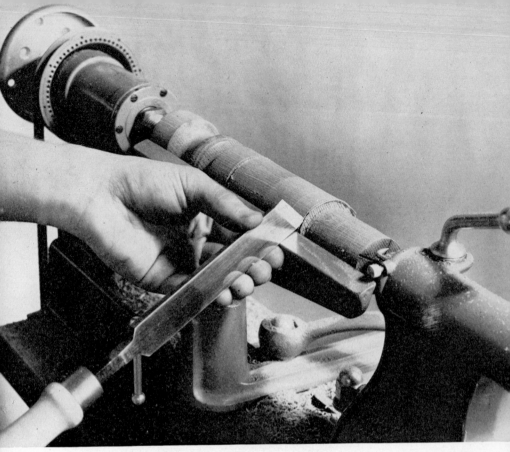

31-16. MAKING THE VERTICAL OR SIDE CUT of a shoulder with the toe of the skew.

Cutting a long taper.

1. Turn the cylinder to the largest diameter. Then place a rule against the tool rest and, with a pencil, mark the beginning and end of the taper.

2. With a parting tool cut a groove to the smallest diameter. It also may be a good idea to use a parting tool to cut a groove to several diameters at various points.

3. Rough cut the cylinder to size with a gouge.

4. Scrape to finished size with a square-nose or skew. If the taper is long, the tool rest should be set at a slight angle to make it parallel to the tapered surface.

5. Cut to finished size with the skew as in turning a cylinder. Fig. 31–18.

Cutting large rectangular recesses.

1. Turn the cylinder to the largest finished diameter. Fig. 31–19.

2. Hold a rule on the tool rest and mark the locations of the recesses.

3. With a parting tool cut a groove at the end of each recess to the desired diameter about $\frac{1}{16}''$ to $\frac{1}{8}''$ inside the layout line.

4. Scrape the recess to size, using a square-nose or skew. Trim the shoulders of the recesses with a parting tool.

5. Cut the recess to rough size with a small gouge. Finish with a skew.

31–17. MAKING THE HORIZONTAL CUT of a shoulder with the heel of the skew.

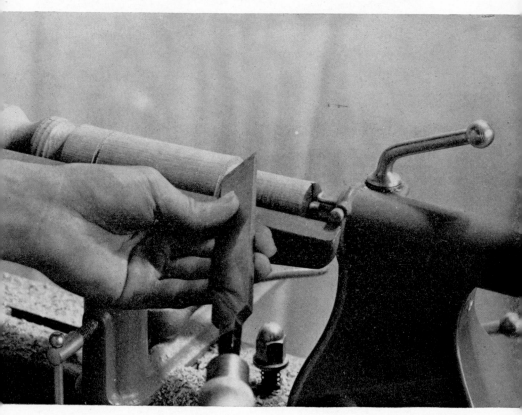

31–18. CUTTING a long taper.

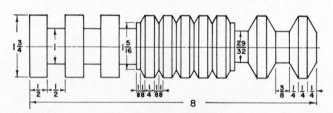

31–19. TURNING EXERCISE for V's and recesses.

Cutting stock to length. Turn the cylinder to the correct diameter and mark the length needed.

1. *Scraping method.* Force a parting tool into the stock exactly at the layout line at the tailstock end and cut to a ⅛″ diameter. Repeat at the headstock end. If you wish to cut the end off

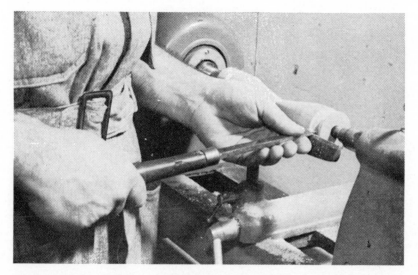

31–20. USING A SKEW for scraping stock to length.

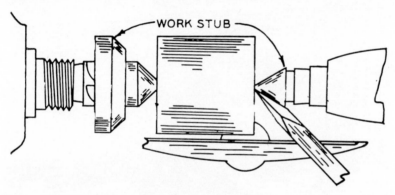

31–21. THE PROPER METHOD OF HOLDING A SKEW when cutting
stock to length.

completely, hold the parting tool in your right hand and place
the left hand loosely around the revolving stock. Continue to
force the parting tool into the wood until the cylinder drops off.
Remember to allow enough wood at the headstock end to keep

from hitting the spur center. (This procedure can also be done with a small skew held on its side as shown in Fig. 31–20.) Trim off the waste stock on the ends with a saw.

2. *Cutting method.* Hold a small skew on edge with the heel up and the toe down. Fig. 31–21. Turn it at an angle so that one bevel is parallel to the cut to be made. Force the skew in slowly; then back it out and cut a half V into the waste stock. It's extremely important to keep one cutting edge of the skew parallel to the wood, since it is easy for the tool to "hog in" and damage the stock. Do this on both ends.

Cutting V's.

1. *Scraping method.* Hold a diamond-point tool flat and force it into the wood to cut the V. Fig. 31–22.

2. *Cutting method.* Mark the center and edges of the V cut. Hold a skew on edge with the heel down; then force the skew

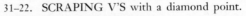

31–22. SCRAPING V'S with a diamond point.

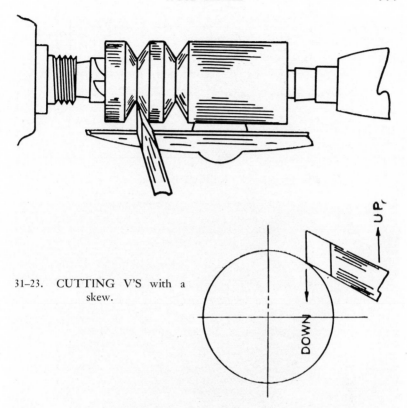

31–23. CUTTING V'S with a skew.

into the stock at the center of the V cut. Use a slight pump-handle action. Fig. 31–23. Work from one side of the V, using the heel of the skew to do the cutting. Continue to force the skew into the center of the cut and cut one side of the V to correct depth. Then cut the opposite side in a similar manner.

Cutting beads. Beads are rather difficult to cut and will require considerable practice. Fig. 31–24. Mark the position of each bead with a line indicating ends and centers of the beads. Begin the cut as you would a V cut, using the toe of the skew to start it. Fig. 31–25. Then hold the skew on its side with the heel doing most of the cutting. Fig. 31–26. Start quite high on the cylinder at the center of the bead and turn the tool in the same arc as the

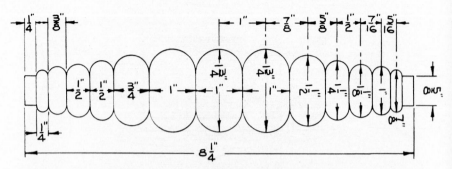

31–24. A BEAD exercise.

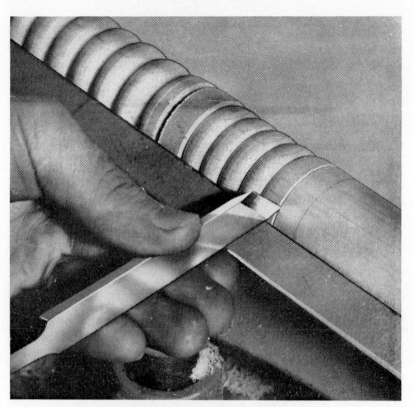

31–25. MAKING A DEEP VERTICAL CUT with the toe of the skew in preparation for cutting beads.

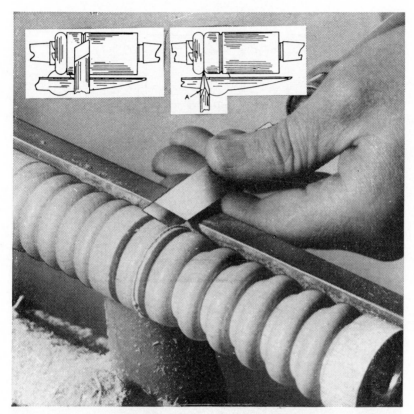

31-26. CUTTING BEADS, using the heel to do most of the cutting.

bead, at the same time drawing it backhand and moving it to a vertical position. If the tool is not turned as the cut is made, the heel will dig into the next bead.

Cutting coves. Mark the center and ends of each cove and adjust the caliper to the smaller diameter. Fig. 31–27.

1. *Scraping method.* Force a round-nosed tool into the center of the cove. Swing the tool from one side to the other using the tool rest as a fulcrum point. Continue to measure the center with a caliper until the desired depth is reached. Fig. 31–28.

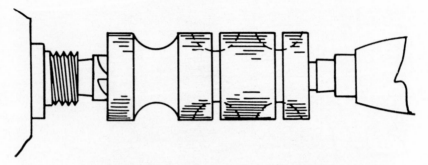

31-27. TURNING COVES or making concave cuts.

31-28. SCRAPING A COVE with a round-nosed tool.

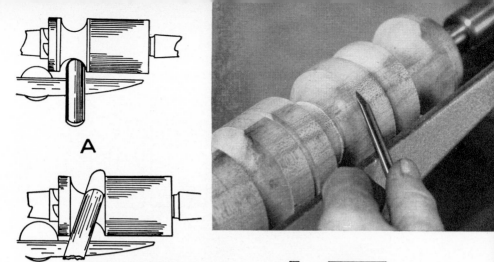

A

B

31–29. CUTTING A COVE with a small gouge. (a) REMOVE MOST OF THE SURPLUS STOCK. (b) START THE GOUGE ON EDGE. (c) TURN TO THE CENTER of the cove.

C

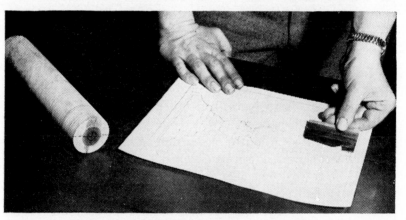

31–30. MAKING A TEMPLATE for turning a complicated part.

2. *Cutting method.* Start at one edge of the cove with a small gouge held on edge and cut toward the center. Twist the gouge as the cut is made until it lies flat on the tool rest. Cut to the center of the cove, then start on the other edge and repeat. Fig. 31–29 a, b, c.

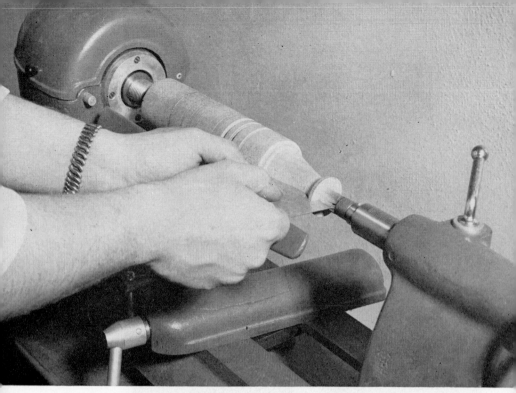

31-31. USING A TEMPLATE to check the turned part.

Turning complex parts. Many parts made on a wood lathe involve many different kinds of cuts. This is true, for example, of turned legs, lamp bases, and other similar objects. Make a drawing of the shape to full size. If several identical pieces are to be made, cut a cardboard or sheet metal template to this shape in order that the work can be checked as the turning progresses. Fig. 31–30. If it is to be a leg or lamp base, part of which is rectangular in shape, first finish the piece to size. In most cases, the piece can also be cut to correct length, since the center marks do not ruin the piece. Fig. 31–31.

Faceplate turning.

FACEPLATE

There are two common faceplates for turning. The screw

center is used for small objects no larger than 4″ in diameter. The regular faceplate usually has a hole in the center and three or more holes spaced around the outside. Available in several different sizes.

SCRAPING TOOLS

All turning done on the faceplate is with the scraping method. The common tools used are the square-nose, round-nose, skew, and diamond-point.

SIMPLE TURNING

1. Select a piece of stock slightly larger and thicker than the desired finished size. Check to see that there is no check or defect in it that will crack or split during the turning. Whenever possible on larger pieces, cut to an octagon shape or, even better, cut it round on a band saw or jig saw. Locate the center of the stock. If it is a small piece and a screw center is used, drill a small hole in the center. Apply a little wax and screw on the stock. If

31–32. FASTENING A FACEPLATE to a lathe.

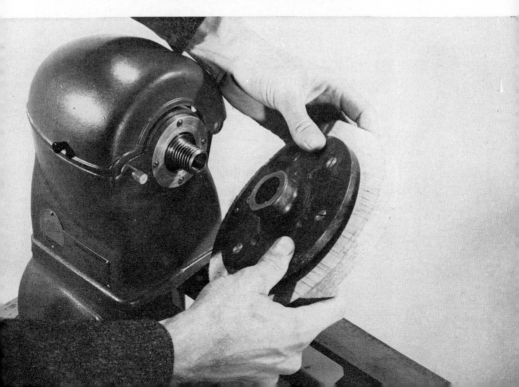

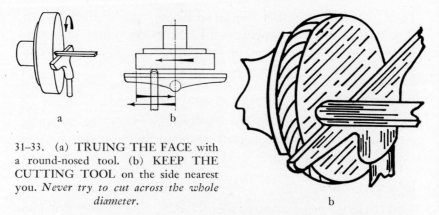

31-33. (a) TRUING THE FACE with a round-nosed tool. (b) KEEP THE CUTTING TOOL on the side nearest you. *Never try to cut across the whole diameter.*

it is a large piece, place the faceplate over the work and mark the hole location. In hardwood, drill small holes and fasten short wood screws.

2. Remove the spur center and fasten the work to the spindle. Fig. 31-32.

3. Adjust the tool rest across the face of the cylinder at slightly below center.

4. Adjust the belt so that the lathe operates at a rather slow speed.

5. Use a flat- or round-nosed tool. Hold it on its side with the cutting edge parallel to the front of the cylinder. Start at the center and take a scraping cut toward the outside nearest yourself. Fig. 31-33. Take several cuts until the stock is the correct thickness. Hold a rule or square against the face surface and make sure that it is true. Fig. 31-34.

6. Locate the center of the stock. Adjust the dividers equal to half the largest diameter that must be turned and mark a circle around the face of the work.

7. Readjust the tool rest until it is parallel to the edge of the stock. Use the same tool to turn the edge until it is the correct diameter. Fig. 31-35.

8. With the dividers mark the location of the recess or bead on the face surface of the cylinder. Readjust the tool rest across

31–34. TRUING THE FACE of stock with a square-nosed tool.

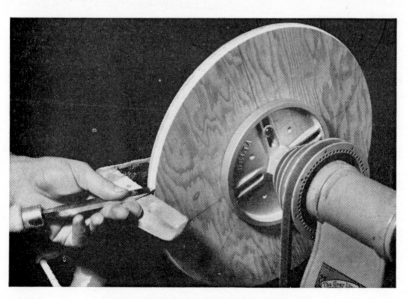

31–35. TRUING THE EDGE of stock.

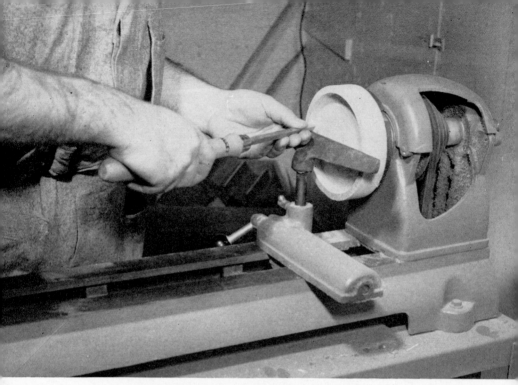

31–36. SCRAPING THE INSIDE EDGE of a recess with a spear point.

the face and turn to shape, using various kinds of tools. Fig. 31–36. For a simple recess, a round-nosed tool is usually preferred. Fig. 31–37. For cutting a bead, choose a square-nose or skew. Sometimes the tool rest must be readjusted at an angle to the work to do certain kinds of turning. Fig. 31–38 a. A diamond-point is often used to cut a sharp shoulder on the face of the work. Figs. 31–38 b and 31–39.

Turning both sides of stock

1. Many faceplate jobs require that both sides of an object be turned—for example, a simple bowl. For most of this kind of work, it is objectionable to have the screw hole in the stock. Therefore cut a piece of stock slightly larger than the finished bowl. Cut another piece of scrap stock thick enough to fasten screws into. Glue these two pieces together with a piece of paper

between for easy separation later. Fig. 31–40. Fasten the stock to the faceplate, installing the screws in the scrap piece. Fasten the work in the lathe.

2. Turn the front or top and the edge of the bowl. When this is complete, do all the sanding operations necessary to finish the top. If mineral oil is to be used as a finish, apply this now.

31–37. TURNING a simple bowl.

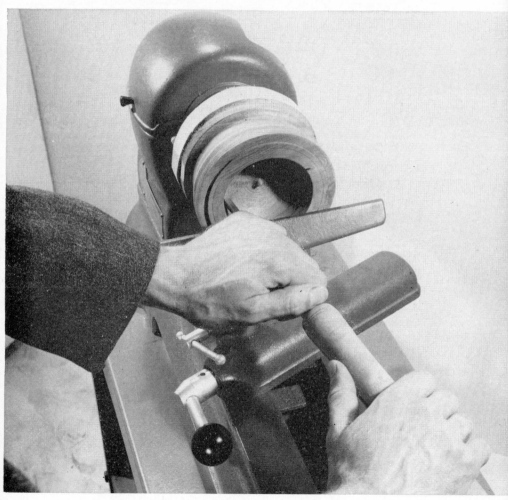

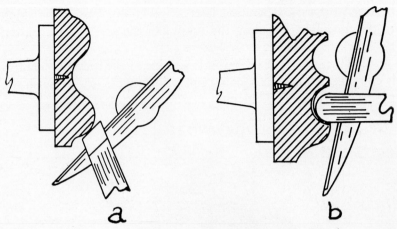

31-38. (a) Scraping convex curves with a small skew. (b) Scraping concave curves with a round-nosed tool.

3. Separate the scrap stock from the finished piece by driving a sharp chisel between them.

4. Make a simple wood chuck to hold the bowl. Fig. 31–41. Cut a piece of scrap stock slightly larger than the diameter of the bowl. Fasten this to the faceplate. Turn the cylinder and cut a recess in this scrap stock so that the bowl will just fit, with a tight, pressed fit. If the recess should be slightly large, a piece of paper can be placed between the bowl and the recess. This is called a *recessed chuck*. A chuck just opposite in shape from this is called a *spindle chuck*. Fig. 31–42. This is needed for other kinds of turning, such as in making salt and pepper shakers where the hole is bored in the stock first and this pressed over a spindle chuck to do the outside turning.

5. Press the stock into the chuck and turn the back side. The work can usually be removed by pulling it out. If necessary, the recessed edge can be cut away to release the bowl. Fig. 31–43.

Sanding. Select the correct grade of sandpaper. Usually 1/0 is used to take out the large imperfections, 2/0 to smooth the work, and 5/0 for a very fine surface.

31–39. SCRAPING A V with a spear point.

31–40(a). GLUING SCRAP STOCK to the finished piece in preparation for turning. (b) HERE YOU SEE THE FRONT OF THE BOWL TURNED. It can now be separated from the scrap stock.

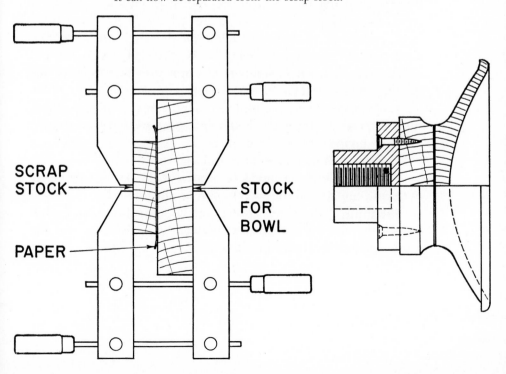

SCRAP STOCK

PAPER

STOCK FOR BOWL

31-41. USING A RECESSED WOOD CHUCK for holding a shallow tray.

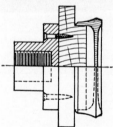

31-42. DRAWING of a spindle chuck.

1. Cut the paper into strips for sanding long cylinders and work held between centers. Fold sandpaper into squares for sanding recesses and for faceplate work.

2. Always remove the tool rest and adjust the lathe to a high spindle speed. Never wrap the paper around the work.

3. For sanding long stock between centers, hold both ends of the strip of paper and move it back and forth.

4. For sanding the inside of a bowl, hold the pad of paper over your fingers and follow the contour of the bowl.

Finishing. There are several methods of finishing turned parts. Oftentimes the parts are removed from the lathe and the finish applied as a part of the completed furniture. For small

31–43. TURNING the back of a candy dish held in a recessed chuck.

bowls and accessories used in connection with food, mineral oil is rubbed on as a finish.

31-44. APPLYING a French polish.

To apply a French polish, secure a piece of fine cotton or linen cloth and fold it into a pad. Apply a solution of about one half shellac and one half alcohol. Place a few drops of mineral oil or machine oil on the pad. Hold the pad over the work, moving it from one side to the other. Fig. 31-44. Add additional shellac and oil to keep the pad moist. Continue to apply this until the desired finish is obtained.

SHARPENING MACHINE TOOLS

To get the most out of your machine tools, it is necessary to keep them sharp. Always follow the correct working techniques, since this will make your cutting tools last longer and keep edges sharper. While it is possible for the average craftsman to sharpen the cutting edges of all his power tools, it is the accepted practice in most places to have certain sharpening done by experts. These experts, with proper equipment such as saw-filing machines, can do the job inexpenesively, while if done by hand the job is long and tedious.

Planer blades. Most large planers have a grinding attachment that can be purchased as an accessory. There are complete manufacturer's directions for using it on each particular kind of machine.

Circular saw and band saw blades. These should be sent out for sharpening at periodic intervals. Sometimes band saw blades break and can be repaired by brazing or hard soldering. This can be done in a machine brazer, or a scarf joint can be ground on either end and the ends hard-soldered together. This area must then be ground the same thickness as the rest of the blade.

Jointer blades.

SHARPENING

Jointer blades can be sent out for sharpening. It is possible for the operator to make a simple wood jig in which the blade is held for regrinding with a cup grinding wheel on the drill press as shown in Fig. 32–1. Fig. 32–2 shows another method.

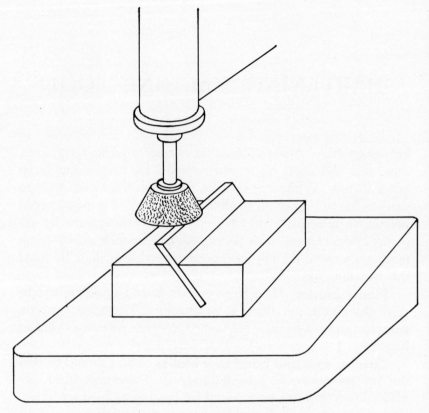

32-1. GRINDING A JOINTER BLADE on a drill press.

HONING

Honing should be done at frequent intervals or whenever the jointed surface is slightly rough or fuzzy. This is a relatively simple job.

1. Lower the front or outfeed table about ⅛″. On some machines this will mean raising the cutter head that amount.

2. Cover about two thirds of a flat oilstone with wax paper.

32-2. GRINDING A JOINTER BLADE on a grinder-hone.

Clamp scrap wood on the inner end of the infeed table so that it will not get scratched. Fig. 32–3.

3. Remove the fence and guard. Turn the cutter head so the stone is flat on the bevel of the blade. Hold the cutter head and move the stone back and forth lengthwise on the blade until it is honed.

4. Turn to the next blade and repeat.

Mortising chisel.

1. Fasten a conical-shaped grinding wheel in the chuck of the

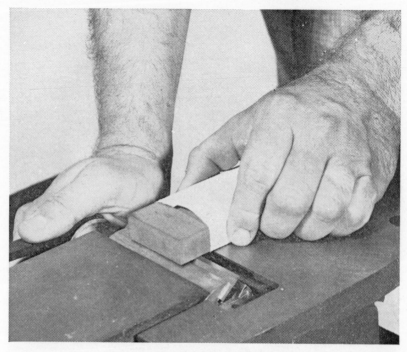

32–3. HONING a jointer blade. The protective wood piece is not shown in this picture.

drill press. Place the chisel in an inverted vertical position in a vise. Fig. 32–4.

2. Lower the revolving grinding wheel slowly and sharpen the inside cutting edge.

3. Hone the sides lightly on a fine oilstone.

Auger bits. Select a small, flat auger-bit file. File the inside of the spurs, never the outside. Fig. 32–5. This is done by holding the auger bit firmly on the table and moving the file in an arc to follow the inside shape of the spur. Also file the upper surface of the lip. Fig. 32–6. Hone the spur lightly on the outside by rotating the auger bit against a fine oilstone.

Shaper cutters. Hold the face of the shaper cutter against an

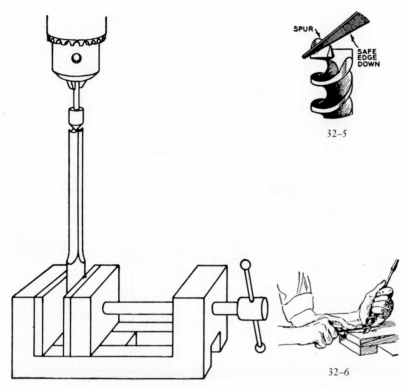

32-4. SHARPENING a mortising chisel. 32-5. SHARPENING the spurs of an auger bit. 32-6. SHARPENING the lip of an auger bit.

oilstone and work the tool back and forth. Fig. 32–7. A slipstone can be used on the beveled cutting edge, but care must be taken not to change the shape of the cutter.

Turning tools. The correct technique for sharpening turning tools is very similar to that for sharpening chisels and gouges. The proper grinding angle for each tool is shown in Fig. 32–8. You should have a good grindstone or abrasive wheel. Fig. 32–9. Dress to a clean, true edge.

To sharpen a *gouge*, hold it at an angle of about 30 degrees

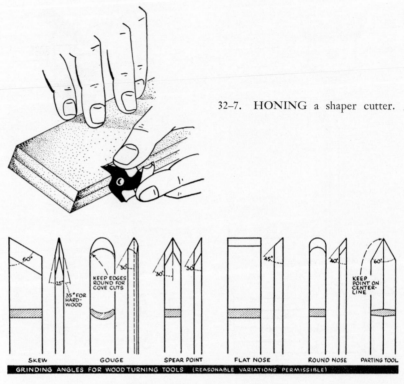

32–7. HONING a shaper cutter.

32–8. THE CORRECT ANGLE for sharpening a turning tool.

to the stone and rotate it from side to side, keeping a straight bevel on the outside. Make sure that the corners are rounded so that you can make cove cuts. Fig. 32–10. The concave surface and the beveled edge can be honed with a slipstone. Fig. 32–11.

To sharpen a *skew*, hold it at an angle of about 12½ degrees to the wheel. Turn it to one side to maintain an angle of 60 degrees. Grind each side a little at a time. Fig. 32–12. Hone the edge on a flat oilstone as you would a chisel. Fig. 32–13.

The *flat-nosed tool* is ground exactly like an ordinary chisel except that the angle of the bevel is 45 degrees.

32–9. GRINDER-HONE for sharpening tools.

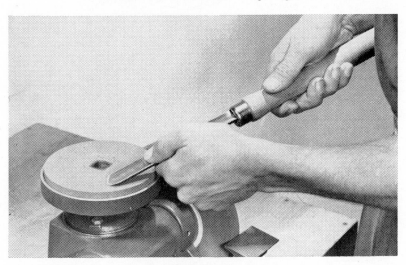

32–10. GRINDING a gouge.

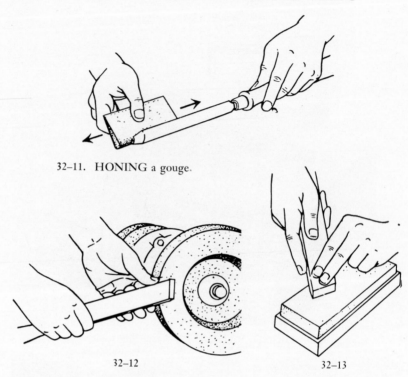

32–11. HONING a gouge.

32–12

32–13

32–12. GRINDING a skew. 32–13. HONING a skew.

The *spear-point* must be ground at two angles from one side. The bevel is 30 degrees and the included angle of the point is 60 degrees.

The *round-nosed tool* is ground in the same general manner as a gouge, with the bevel at an angle of about 40 degrees.

The *parting tool* must be ground from two edges so that the included angle is 60 degrees. The point of the parting tool should be always kept on the center line of the tool.

Section VI

Projects

COFFEE TABLE

This coffee table is typical of the type of project that can be made in advanced machine woodworking. It is similar to all standard tables and chairs that can be made and therefore will be described in some detail.

Four basic kinds of joints were used in making this table, including *edge joint* strengthened with dowels, *mortise-and-tenon joint, miter joint* strengthened with dowels, and *corner dado joint*. It also shows typical *leg and rail* construction, *frame* construction and *table leaf* construction.

Here are the steps:

1. *Select or design the project.* This was designed by the author to fit into a modern, mahogany-trimmed room. The size of the top and the height of the table are typical of modern coffee table designs.

2. *Make a sketch and a bill of materials.* The sketch of the project should show the correct dimensions and the kinds of joints to be used. In making a bill of materials, determine the amount of stock of each different thickness needed. In the case of this table, stock 1″ thick and 2″ thick is needed. If necessary, the legs can be made from 1″ stock by gluing the pieces face to face. This coffee table required 9 board feet of 1″ mahogany and 4 board feet of 2″ mahogany.

3. *Lay out and cut the rough stock to size.* Trim off the end of the stock. Then cut lengths for the rails and frame that are about ¼″ wider and ½″ longer than the finished size. In cutting the rails to length, remember that material is needed to make the tenons. Also cut the stock for the legs, shelf, and table leaves.

4. *Square up the stock.* Use the jointer and circular saw (planer also if one is available) to square up the stock for the legs, rails, and frame. Surface one face and two edges of the stock that are to be used for the shelf and the leaves. Try to use the poorer surface as the face surface. See page 68.

5. *Glue up the stock for the shelf and leaves.* It will be necessary to glue up stock to form a piece wide enough for the shelf and leaves. If the stock from which the parts are cut is over 8" wide, it is a good idea to re-cut the board again into strips not over 4" to 6" in width. Make an edge joint strengthened with dowels. Glue and clamp the boards together to make the shelf and leaves. Then square up these pieces to size.

6. *Make the mortise-and-tenon joints.* Carefully lay out the location of the mortises and the size of the tenons. Cut the mortises on a mortising machine or with a mortising attachment on the drill press, or, if necessary, by hand. Cut the tenons on the circular saw. Fit the tenons into the mortises and, as each one is finished, mark the upper edge of the rail and the top of the leg 1–1, 2–2, etc., in order to be sure these will be assembled correctly later.

7. *Cut the corner dados on the legs and shelf.* Locate the position of the corner dado and cut it as shown in Fig. 22–46. Also cut the corners on the shelf so that it fits into the corner dado.

8. *Sand all parts thoroughly.* Do not, however, sand off the marks necessary for assembly.

9. *Glue up the two ends of the table.* Use scrap blocks when clamping the legs and end rails together. Check to see that the legs are parallel and square with the rails.

10. *Make the miter frame with dowels for the table top.* Cut the mitered corners on the ends of the frame. Be very careful that the two opposite sides are exactly the same length and that the miter is exactly 45 degrees. It is a good idea to lay the frame out on the table and check these joints carefully. Locate the position for two dowels on each corner. Drill or bore the dowel holes

on a drill press or with the dowel jig attachment. Cut the dowel and point the ends. Glue up the frame.

11. *Glue the side rails and the shelf to the end assemblies to form the bottom of the table.* Be especially careful that the entire unit is square. Measure across from corner to corner and check with the square at several points. Remove any excess glue from the assembly before it gets hard.

12. *Cut the corner blocks for strengthening the corners.* Cut and install these corner blocks as described on page 106.

13. *Make the wood cleats to fasten the frame to the bottom assembly.* Method 2, in Fig. 14–7, was followed for fastening the frame to the bottom assembly.

14. *Re-sand all parts.* Fasten the frame to the base.

15. *Fasten the leaves to the table.* Two butt hinges and a single table leaf support are used at either end. The hinges are fastened flat against the bottom of the frame and leaf and the table leaf support installed from the underside of the leaf to the end rail.

16. *Cut a piece of plywood slightly smaller than the opening in the frame.* Cut two support strips that will go across the underside of the frame to support the plywood. Screw these in place.

17. *Apply the desired finish to the table.*

18. *Cover the plywood with leather and insert it in the frame.* Fasten in place from the underside.

EIGHTEEN PROJECTS

Here are a few sample projects that can be made in advanced woodworking. You will find other ideas throughout the book and reference materials for more in the Appendix.

Projects other than those indicated otherwise were built by the author for his own home.

1. *Coffee table.*

2. *Shadow box picture frame.* This can be made any size by following the suggestions in Fig. 13–11 on miter joints. All of the other wood furniture pieces shown in this illustration were made by a craftsman. Detailed drawings for each are available in the book *Industrial Arts Woodworking* by the same author, or from Source C under "Furniture Plans" in the Appendix.

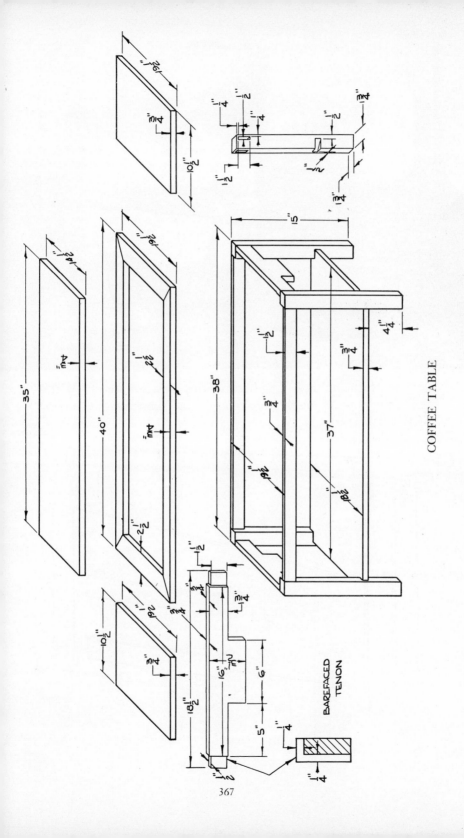

COFFEE TABLE

BAREFACED
TENON

367

3. *Magazine rack.* The back of this rack is made of "Weld-tex" plywood, although any wood can be substituted. Courtesy of *Woman's Day.*

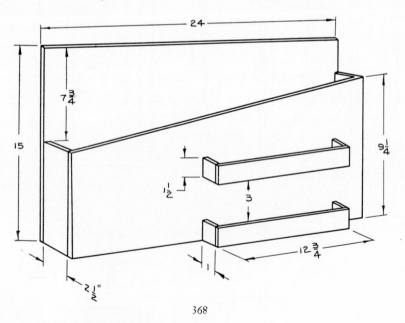

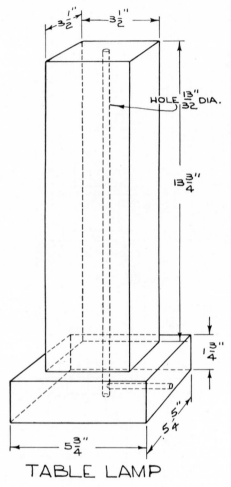

HOLE $\frac{13}{32}''$ DIA.

$3\frac{1}{2}''$ $3\frac{1}{2}''$

$13\frac{3}{4}''$

$1\frac{3}{4}''$

$5\frac{3}{4}''$

$5\frac{5}{4}''$

TABLE LAMP

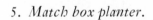

4. *Table lamp.*

5. *Match box planter.*

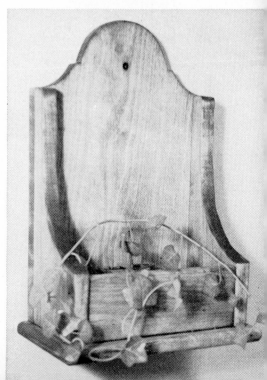

369

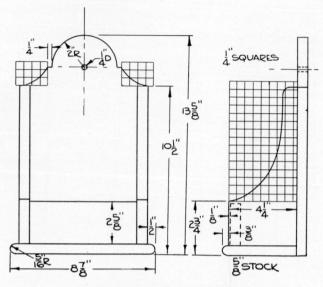

MATCH BOX PLANTER

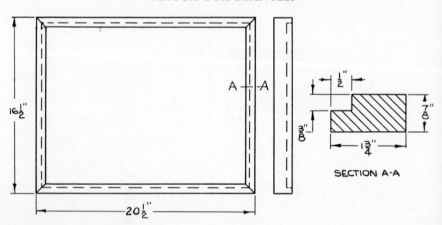

SECTION A-A

6. *Flat picture frame.*

370

7. *Clock shelf*.

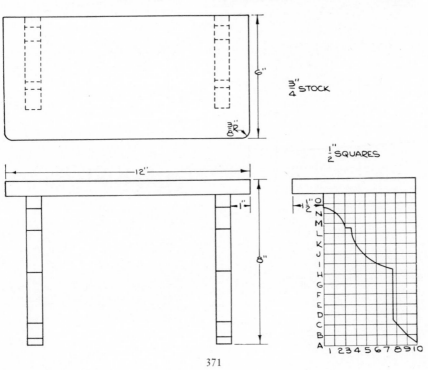

6″

¾″ STOCK

⅜″R

½″ SQUARES

12″

1″

8″

1½″

O
N
M
L
K
J
I
H
G
F
E
D
C
B
A
1 2 3 4 5 6 7 8 9 10

371

8. *Single bracket shelf.*
Courtesy of *Woman's Day.*

9. *Drawer rack.* Courtesy of *Woman's Day.*

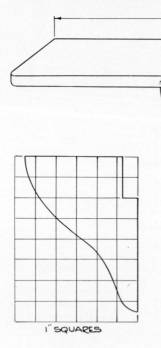

1" SQUARES

SINGLE-BRACKET
SHELF

372

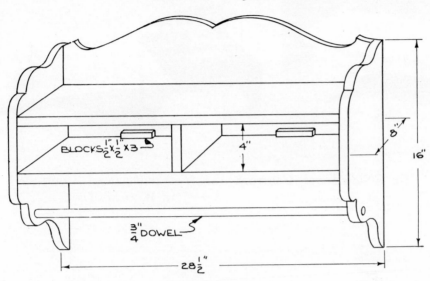

BLOCKS $\frac{1}{2}$" x $\frac{1}{2}$" X 3

4"

8"

16"

$\frac{3}{4}$" DOWEL

28 $\frac{1}{2}$"

DRAWER RACK

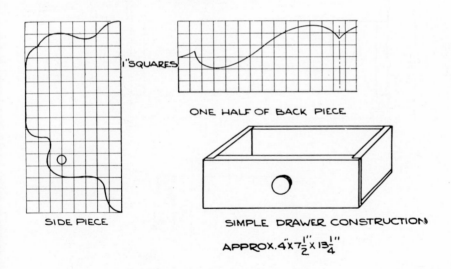

1" SQUARES

ONE HALF OF BACK PIECE

SIDE PIECE

SIMPLE DRAWER CONSTRUCTION
APPROX. 4" X 7 $\frac{1}{2}$" X 13 $\frac{1}{4}$"

10. *Child's bench*. Courtesy of *Woman's Day*. 11. *Telephone stand*. Courtesy of *Woman's Day*.

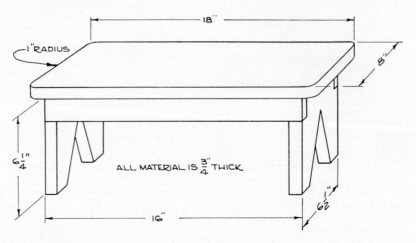

18"

1" RADIUS

8"

6 1/4"

ALL MATERIAL IS 3/4" THICK

16"

6 1/2"

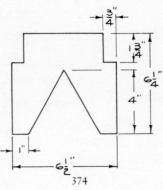

3/4"

1 3/4"

6 1/4"

4"

1"

6 1/2"

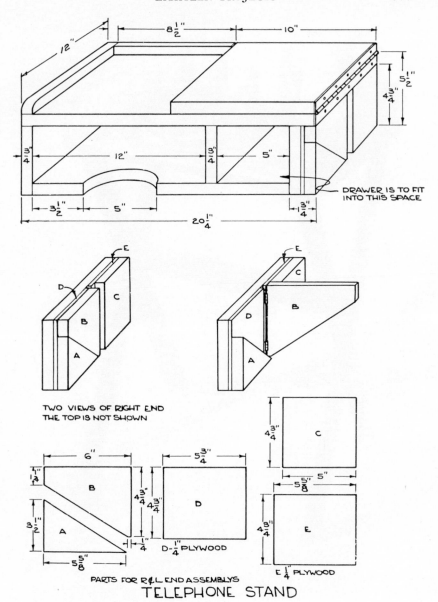

TWO VIEWS OF RIGHT END
THE TOP IS NOT SHOWN

DRAWER IS TO FIT
INTO THIS SPACE

PARTS FOR R&L END ASSEMBLYS

TELEPHONE STAND

12. *Serving table.* Courtesy of *Woman's Day*.

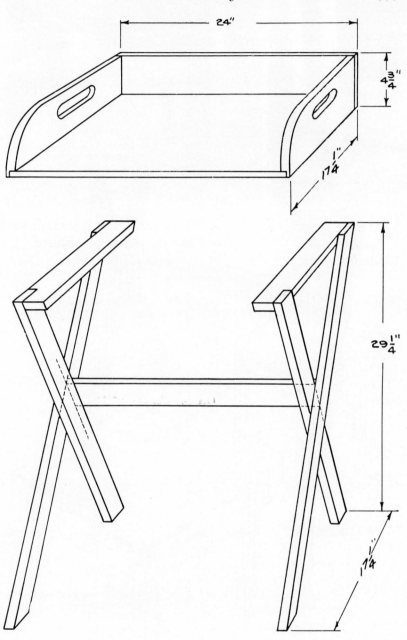

13. *Lamp table.*
Courtesy of
Lindsay Farnan.

14. *Game table.* This is made of oak
and the top is upholstered
with plastic leather.

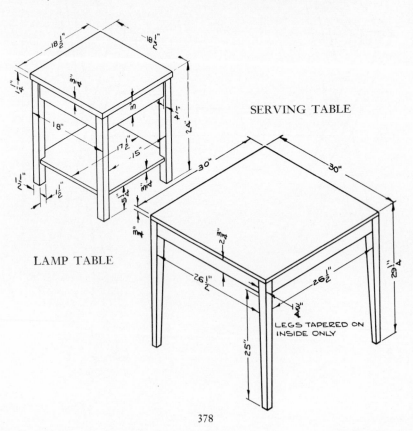

SERVING TABLE

LAMP TABLE

LEGS TAPERED ON
INSIDE ONLY

15. *Bookcase*. This case is made of 1″ x 8″, 1″ x 6″, and 1″ x 3″ stock. The frame is constructed entirely of 1″ x 8″ pieces with ends tapered towards the top and square at the base as shown. To support books, insert troughs were formed by joining two pieces of 1″ x 6″. Courtesy *Living for Young Homemakers*.

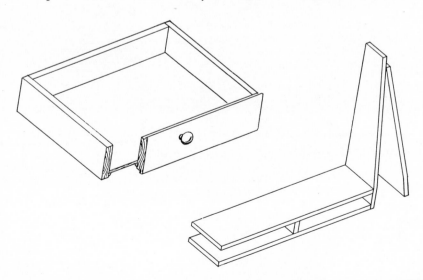

16. *Game table*. This table is made of mahogany and has a
leather insert top.

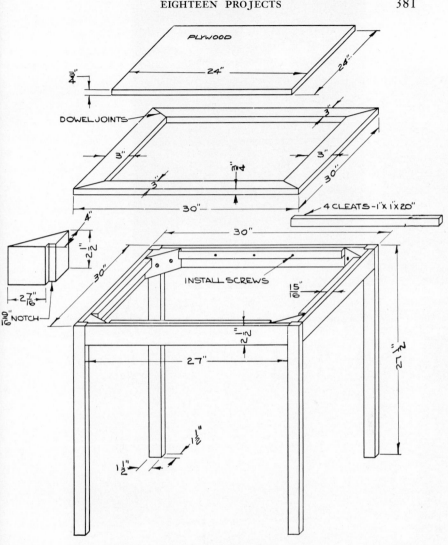

PLYWOOD

24"

24"

3/4"

DOWEL JOINTS

3"

3"

3"

3"

3"

4M

30"

30"

4 CLEATS - 1" x 1" x 20"

4"

30"

30"

2 1/2"

INSTALL SCREWS

15/16"

2 7/16"

9/16" NOTCH

2 1/2"

27"

27 1/2"

1 1/2"

1 1/2"

17. *China cabinet.*
382

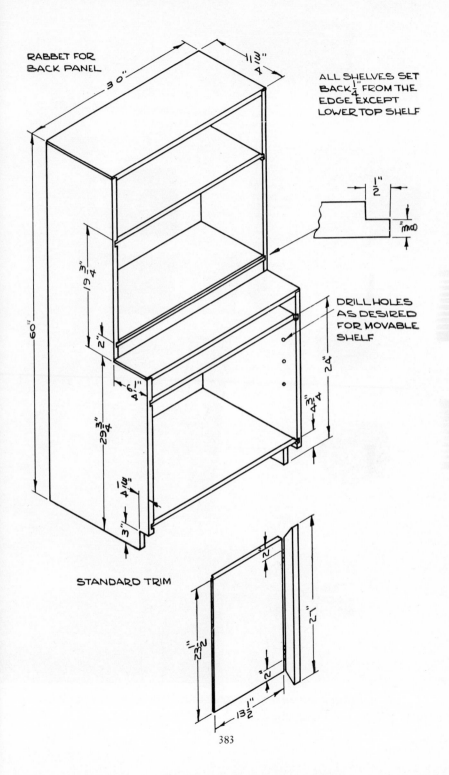

RABBET FOR
BACK PANEL

3 0"

1 3/4"

ALL SHELVES SET
BACK 1/4" FROM THE
EDGE EXCEPT
LOWER TOP SHELF

1/2"

3/8"

19 3/4"

2"

6 1/4"

29 3/4"

60"

DRILL HOLES
AS DESIRED
FOR MOVABLE
SHELF

24"

4 3/4"

4 1/8"

3"

STANDARD TRIM

2"

23 1/2"

2"

2"

13 1/2"

383

18. *Sectional furniture*. Radio cabinet, storage cabinet, bookcase, corner case, and chest.

384

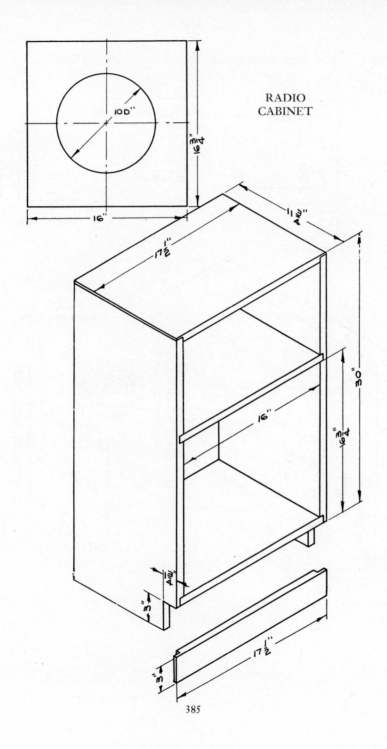

RADIO
CABINET

10D"

16¾"

16"

11¾"

17½"

30"

16"

19¾"

¼"

3"

17½"

3"

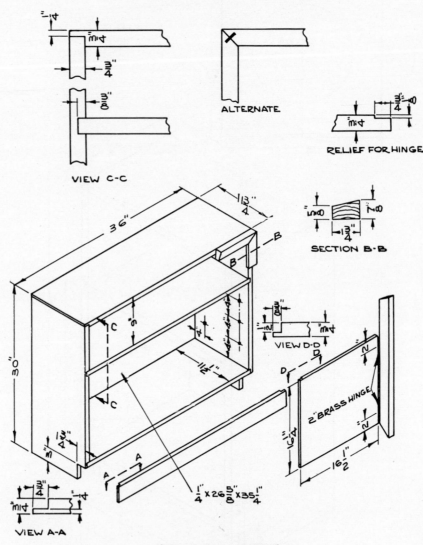

VIEW C-C

ALTERNATE

RELIEF FOR HINGE

SECTION B-B

VIEW D-D

2" BRASS HINGE

VIEW A-A

STORAGE CABINET

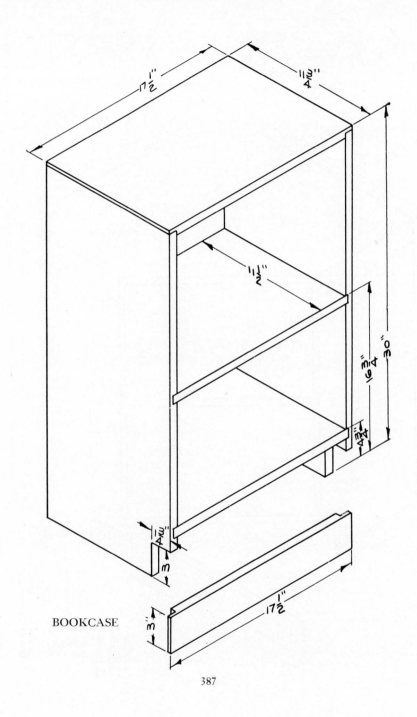

$17\frac{1}{2}''$

$11\frac{3}{4}''$

$11\frac{1}{2}''$

30"

$6\frac{3}{4}''$

$4\frac{1}{4}''$

$\frac{3}{4}''$

3

$17\frac{1}{2}''$

3"

BOOKCASE

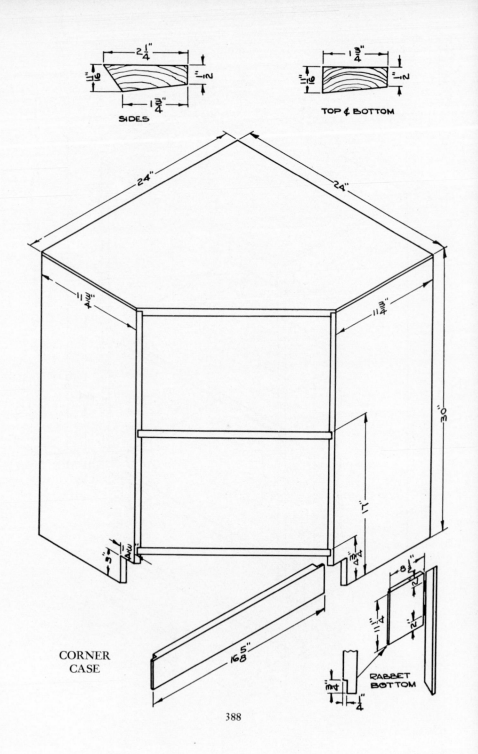

SIDES

TOP & BOTTOM

CORNER
CASE

RABBET
BOTTOM

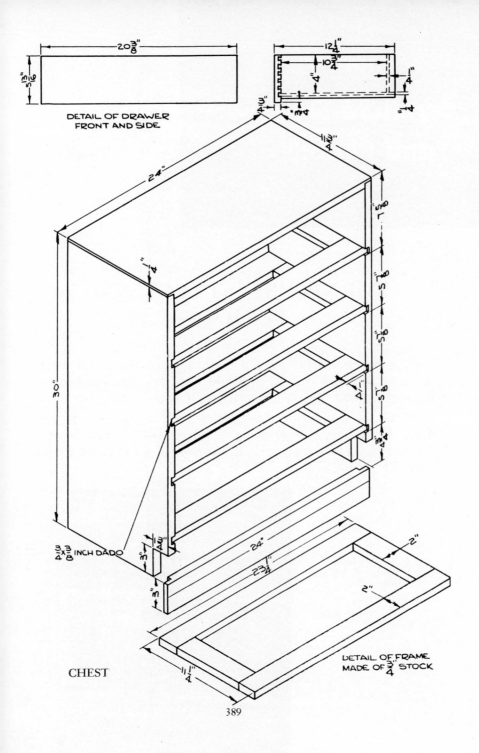

DETAIL OF DRAWER
FRONT AND SIDE

20 3/8"

5 13/16"

12 1/4"

10 3/4"

4"

4"

1"

1/4"

3/4"

3/4"

24"

1 1/4"

1 1/8"

1/4"

1/4"

30"

7 5/8"

5 5/8"

5 5/8"

5 5/8"

1"

4 1/2"

3/4 x 3/8 INCH DADO

3"

1 1/8"

3"

24"

23 3/4"

2"

2"

1 1/4"

DETAIL OF FRAME
MADE OF 3/4" STOCK

CHEST

389

FURNITURE STYLES AND PERIODS

The history of furniture is the history of the world. Each era had a different style of furniture. Study the early history of Europe and the Near East. You'll find many interesting ways in which the furniture of each period reflected the way people lived. Oftentimes, for instance, a ruler would dictate a new furniture style and then everyone throughout the country would

34-1. A BEAU-TIFUL BREAK-FRONT in 18th Century style.

imitate it. As a matter of fact, many of the furniture styles are named after kings, queens and rulers such as Louis XIV and Queen Anne.

The story of furniture fills many sets of books. In your study of history, you might be interested in looking up the style of furniture accepted in each period. Do you know, for example, what kind of furniture Napoleon liked? You should be interested in the styles of furniture that people buy today. You ought to be able to distinguish the different styles and recognize quality furniture. Various qualities of furniture are made in each style. Below this are cheaper grades, such as commercial furniture, that have no particular style.

There are four main styles of furniture.

TRADITIONAL

The "traditional" includes many styles. It was, until only a few years ago, the most popular furniture style. The most popu-

34–2. A CHAIR IN 18TH CENTURY STYLE. COURTESY OF TELL CITY CHAIR CO.

lar traditional style is called *18th Century*. Fig. 34–1. This name is given to furniture that combines the best design characteristics of the 18th century. Fig. 34–2. The work and effort of the "big four" of the 18th century designers are responsible for its greatness; Chippendale, Hepplewhite, the Adams brothers, and Sheraton. All of these gifted men lived and worked in and around London. Their designs are very superior and you should know something about their work.

Thomas Chippendale was known as a designer, wood carver, cabinet maker and manufacturer of furniture. He was extremely intelligent and made use of all the known designs of furniture, making improvements on them. He designed many different styles. Some were influenced by the French, others by the Chinese and still others by the early English designs. Fig. 34–3. He

34–3. THIS CHIPPENDALE COFFEE TABLE reflects Chinese influence. It is 18″ high and the top is 21½″ x 38½″. COURTESY OF THE BRANDT CABINET WORKS, INC.

34–5. CHIPPENDALE.

34–4. CHIPPENDALE LADDER-
BACK CHAIR.

34–6.   THE   CLAW-AND-
BALL FOOT, characteristic
of Chippendale.

34–7. A CHIPPENDALE TABLE showing the use of the claw-and-ball foot.
COURTESY OF THE IMPERIAL FURNITURE COMPANY.

was renowned as a builder of chairs. His most famous chair is the ladder back. Fig. 34–4 and Fig. 34–5. He used many different shaped feet on his chairs but his most popular was the "claw and ball" foot. Fig. 34–6. Mahogany was his favorite wood. Fig. 34–7.

George Hepplewhite was also a London cabinet maker and an original designer of furniture. In later life he established his own furniture factory. All of his furniture pieces were slender

34–8. NOTICE THE SIMPLE LINES of this Hepplewhite table. It is 29¼" high and the top is 16½" x 32". COURTESY OF THE BRANDT CABINET WORKS, INC.

and well proportioned. Fig. 34–8. He did not like the heavy, massive furniture of early England. He permitted little or no carving but used painting and inlay. Fig. 34–9. He preferred mahogany and satinwood for his furniture. His most famous design is the shield back chair. Fig. 34–10.

Robert and James Adams were architects and designers but not craftsmen as were the first two men. They designed both homes and furniture for other people to build. They developed a very classic style that was adapted from ancient Roman architecture. The legs were straight and tapered with very slender

34–9. HEPPLEWHITE.

34–10. THE SHIELD-BACK CHAIR used so frequently by Hepplewhite.

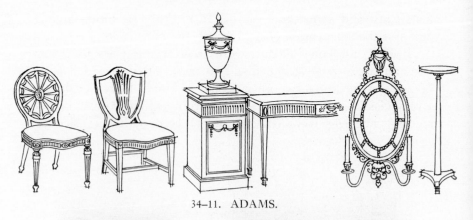

34–11. ADAMS.

34–12. THIS END TABLE SHOWS the rectangular top and drop leaf which
are characteristics of Sheraton. COURTESY OF THE BRANDT CABINET WORKS, INC.

refinements of all parts. Grooving and fluting was used on the legs and some carving was done. Fig. 34–11.

Thomas Sheraton was a designer and cabinet maker and was the last of the great men of the golden age of furniture. Besides designing and building furniture, he was a publisher, preacher, author and drawing teacher. However, he was a very poor businessman and died penniless. Sheraton used simple, straight lines, rectangular table tops with drop leaves and square-back chairs. Figs. 34–12 and 34–13.

We see in stores today modifications of the work of each of these men. For example, you might see a Sheraton desk or a Hepplewhite table. Most manufacturers have combined the features of all and called the furniture 18th Century.

Do you know who Ducan Phyfe was? You should, for he was the only American cabinet maker for whom a period or style of furniture is named. His designs were so fine that they have lived on and are still favorites with many people. Duncan Phyfe

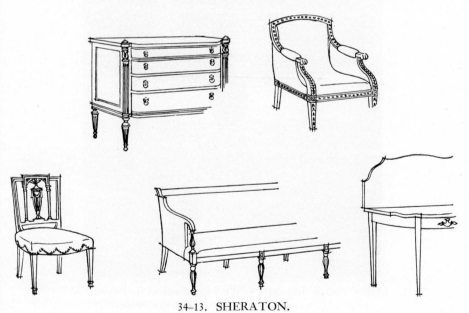

34–13. SHERATON.

34-14. DUNCAN PHYFE.

34-15. THIS DUNCAN PHYFE END TABLE shows the pedestal with four legs. COURTESY OF THE IMPERIAL FURNITURE COMPANY.

worked near the close of the 18th century in and around New York City. At one time over 100 men made furniture by hand in his factory. As a designer he was a master of the elegant style of simple graceful curves. Fig. 34–14. Some of his best known pieces are his table with the pedestal and three or four legs. Fig. 34–15. A feature of these tables is the bronze claw at the end of the leg. Another of his best known designs is the lyre back chair. Fig. 34–16. His furniture had some carving and considerable reeding. The construction of all his pieces was excellent for Phyfe was not only a designer but a master cabinet maker.

FRENCH PROVINCIAL

While this is another of the traditional designs, it is usually classified separately because it has such a distinct style.

What is French Provincial? During the reign of Louis XV and Louis XVI, great progress was made in furniture design. These kings loved rich living and commissioned the best craftsmen to develop extremely ornate furniture with heavy carving

34–16. A LYRE-BACK DINING CHAIR. COURTESY OF THE IMPERIAL FURNITURE COMPANY.

34–17. NOTICE THE BEAUTIFUL CURVED LEGS and form of the French Provincial coffee table. COURTESY OF THE IMPERIAL FURNITURE COMPANY.

and gorgeous curves. Lesser officials who lived in the countryside wanted copies of this furniture. Their local cabinet makers could make only a very simplified version, using the local fruitwoods. Since these people lived in the provinces, their furniture came to be called French Provincial. As the furniture was used, it became scratched, marked and pocked. These markings are imitated in the French Provincial of today.

The French Provincial furniture manufactured today is a modern adaptation of this furniture of France. The pieces have graceful lines with smooth, curved legs on tables and chairs. Simple ornamentation is in the form of shallow carving. Fig. 34–17. Woods used are mostly cherry and walnut. A characteristic is the presence of small black scratches called a "distressed" finish purposely put into the finish to imitate wear marks found in the original furniture. The finish applied today is called fruitwood to imitate the appearance of the original natural fruitwoods used.

HOW TO IDENTIFY PROVINCIAL FURNITURE:

One of the most distinguishing features of French Provincial is the cabriole leg—
(a) a furniture leg shaped in a double curve with the upper part swelling
out. Early, formal French Provincial can be recognized by the scroll work
(b) that adorns the cabriole leg. The heavier Provincial pieces,
such as cabinets and chests (c), have short legs which suggest either the upper
part of the cabriole leg (d), or a straight outside with a continuation
of the curve pattern adorning the bottom of the piece (e).

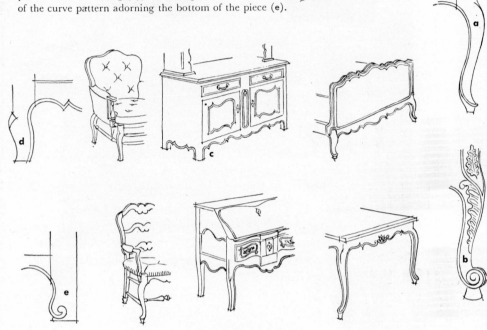

34-18. FRENCH PROVINCIAL.

French Provincial is difficult to manufacture and almost impossible to make in the ordinary shop. Fig. 34-18.

EARLY AMERICAN OR COLONIAL

The first furniture made in America was different from all others. The early settlers needed simple, useful, sturdy pieces. They used the native woods available—oak, pine, and maple. Instead of nails they assembled the parts with wooden pegs. The

34-19. AN EARLY AMERICAN DESK. COURTESY OF THE WILLETT FURNITURE
COMPANY.

earliest pieces had hand whittled legs instead of turned legs. They
also had flat, sturdy surfaces instead of ornamental carvings.
Fig. 34–19. Early American was such a functional, useful style
that it is still very popular today. Characteristics of the style are
the many turned parts and simple curves. Fig. 34–20.

Later, the colonists began to be interested in making a furniture that was a little more decorative. This, then, became known

34–20. TWO COLONIAL STYLE CHAIRS. COURTESY OF TELL CITY CHAIR CO.

HOW TO IDENTIFY COLONIAL FURNITURE:

One of the quickest ways to identify Colonial pieces is by the presence of turned
elements, almost always in the legs (**a**). Simple balusters and the vase
turnings found in Windsor chairs (**b**) are also good identification keys.
Heavier pieces, such as the Goddard-type chest, (**c**) used short, thick legs
with the curve on both the inside and outside. However, earlier pieces
of this weight (**d**) had a simple variation of this leg with a curve on the inside
only (**e**). Four-poster beds (**f**) are still popular in Colonial reproductions.

Also see page 404.

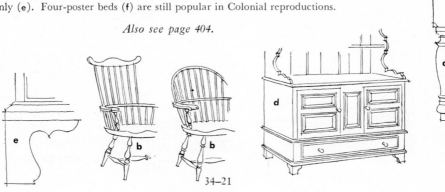

34–21

34–21. COLONIAL.

as Colonial. The colonial furniture was somewhat more ornate and was influenced by the French designers. Colonial furniture was made from maple, pine, oak, and walnut. Characteristic pieces are the hutch cabinet, cobbler's bench and Windsor chair and desk. Fig. 34–21.

34–22. A MODERN TABLE with simple, clean lines. COURTESY OF JENS RISOM DESIGN, INC.

34–23. A DOUBLE CHEST FINISHED in natural, light brown. It is made of walnut with sterling silver tips on the handles. COURTESY OF THE WIDDICOMB FURNITURE COMPANY.

MODERN OR CONTEMPORARY

Modern began about the middle of the 1920's in the United States. The earliest form of modern furniture was geometric in shape. There were many harsh, square lines and sharp angles. There were also round inserted corners. The fronts of chests and beds often featured the "waterfall" design. This is the furniture we have come to think of as "modernistic."

Since then, modern has grown and developed to be the most widely accepted style of furniture in America. It is easy to see why it fits our way of life. It is functional, simplified, and informal. Fig. 34–22. Pieces can be adapted to many different uses. For instance, a chest might be used in the living room, dining room, bedroom or den. Heights, depths, and other measurements have been standardized so that many different arrangements can be made using the same pieces. Most good modern is not sold in sets. Pieces can therefore be purchased as needed. It is most important to recognize good modern because, unfortunately, there is a great deal of poor modern. Fig. 34–23.

Some of the characteristics of good modern are simple lines, excellent construction, good wood and fine finish. Little or no ornamentation is to be found. Modern furniture is made from walnut, cherry, oak, and mahogany with some use of almost every other wood. The woods are finished natural or with a soft hue or tone. There is little bleaching.

34–24. MODERN.

HOW TO IDENTIFY MODERN FURNITURE:

Clean, unadorned legs are one of the most distinguishing characteristics of modern furniture. The tapered, round leg (a) is found quite often on sofas, chests and larger pieces. Tubular steel legs and supports (b) are used on occasional chairs and various forms of angle steel have been employed for pieces that are available in sections (c). Preformed wood and plastic seats and backs (d) are symbols of modern, as are heavy, plate glass (e) table tops that reveal underside construction. Sculptured lines (f) are becoming more evident in modern, too.

This furniture was designed to be mass produced and therefore its construction can be duplicated. Good modern, though, requires the finest craftsmanship as well as excellent design. There are many good modern designs that can be made in the shop. Fig. 34–24.

APPENDIX A

The following is a selected list of companies from which equipment, tools, and supplies can be secured. Most of these listed have helped with the illustrations for the book. Special thanks should be given the Atlas Press Company and Delta Power Tool Division for the many fine photographs contributed.

Woodworking Power Tools

A. Atlas Press Company, 2036 N. Pitcher Street, Kalamazoo.

B. Delta Power Tool Division, Rockwell Manufacturing Company, 40 N. Lexington Avenue, Pittsburgh, Pennsylvania.

C. Walker-Turner Division, Kearney & Trecker Corporation, South Avenue, Plainfield, New Jersey.

D. J. D. Wallace & Company, 170 S. California Avenue, Chicago, Illinois.

E. The Porter-Cable Machine Company, Syracuse 8, N. Y.

F. Stanley Electric Tools, New Britain, Connecticut.

G. Boice Crane Company, 930 W. Central Avenue, Toledo.

H. DeWalt Division American Machine and Foundry Company, Lancaster, Pennsylvania.

Woodworking Hand and Portable Electric Tools

A. Adjustable Clamp Company, 405 N. Ashland Avenue, Chicago, Illinois.

B. Greenlee Tool Company, 2136–12th St., Rockford, Ill.

C. The Cincinnati Tool Company, 1966 Waverly Avenue, Cincinnati, Ohio.

D. Henry Disston & Sons, Inc., Philadelphia 35, Penn.

E. Stanley Tools, New Britain, Connecticut.

F. The Black & Decker Mfg. Co., Towson 4, Maryland.

Furniture Hardware

A. The Stanley Works, New Britain, Connecticut.

B. Ball & Ball, Inc., Whitford, Pennsylvania.

Finishing Supplies

A. General Finishes Sales and Service Co., 1548 W. Bruce Street, Milwaukee 46, Wisconsin. (Sealacell Penetrating Process. Wood finishing manual free upon request.)

B. Brodhead-Garrett Co., Cleveland, Ohio.

C. Albert Constantine & Sons, Inc., New York 64, N. Y.

D. The DeVilbiss Company, Toledo 1, Ohio.

Lumber and Plywood

A. Frank Paxton Lumber Co., Chicago, Illinois.

B. Brodhead-Garrett Co., Cleveland, Ohio.

C. Hardwood Corporation of America, Asheville, N. C.

D. Douglas Fir Plywood Association, Tacoma, Washington.

E. Craftsman Wood Service, Chicago, Illinois.

F. Gordon-MacBeath Hardwood Co., Oakland, California.

Furniture Plans

A. U-Bild Enterprises, 15155 Saticoy Street, Van Nuys, California.

B. Easi-Bild Pattern Company, Pleasantville, New York.

C. Atlas Press Company, 2036 N. Pitcher Street, Kalamazoo, Michigan.

D. Douglas Fir Plywood Association, Tacoma, Washington.

E. Canadian Forest Products Limited, New Westminster, British Columbia, Canada.

F. Delta Power Tool Division, Rockwell Manufacturing Company, 40 N. Lexington Avenue, Pittsburgh, Pennsylvania.

G. *Woman's Day* Workshop, 19 West 44th Street, New York 36, New York.

H. *Living for Young Homemakers*, 575 Madison Avenue, New York 22, N. Y.

INDEX

APPENDIX B———

TABLE FOR COMPOUND MITER CUTS

Tilt of Work	4-Side Butt		4-Side Miter	
	Blade Tilt	Miter Gauge	Blade Tile	Miter Gauge
5 degrees	½	85	44¾	85
10 degrees	1½	80¼	44¼	80¼
15 degrees	3¾	75½	43¼	75½
20 degrees	6¼	71¼	41¾	71¼
25 degrees	10	67	40	67
30 degrees	14½	63½	37¾	63½
35 degrees	19½	60¼	35¼	60¼
40 degrees	24½	57¼	32½	57¼
45 degrees	30	54¾	30	54¾
50 degrees	36	52½	27	52½
55 degrees	42	50¾	24	50¾
60 degrees	48	49	21	49